Jerusalem and Athens

Jerusalem and Athens

Reason and Revelation in the Work of Leo Strauss

Susan Orr

Rowman & Littlefield Publishers, Inc.

ROWMAN & LITTLEFIELD PUBLISHERS, INC.

Published in the United States of America
by Rowman & Littlefield Publishers, Inc.
4720 Boston Way, Lanham, Maryland 20706

3 Henrietta Street
London, WC2E 8LU, England

Copyright © 1995 by Rowman & Littlefield Publishers, Inc.

"Progress or Return? The Contemporary Crisis in Western Civilization," by Leo Strauss was originally published in *Modern Judaism*, vol. 1, 1981. Excerpts reprinted by permission of the Johns Hopkins University Press, Baltimore/London.

"Jerusalem and Athens: Some Preliminary Reflections," by Leo Strauss (The Frank Cohen Public Lecture in Judaic Affairs), The City College Papers, no. 6, 1968, is reprinted here by permission of the City University of New York.

"On the Interpretation of Genesis," by Leo Strauss from *L'Homme: Revue Française d'anthropologie*, vol. 1, 1981, reprinted here by permission of the publisher.

All rights reserved. No part of this publication may be reproduced, stored in a retrieval system, or transmitted in any form or by any means, electronic, mechanical, photocopying, recording, or otherwise, without the prior permission of the publisher.

British Cataloging in Publication Information Available

Library of Congress Cataloging-in-Publication Data

Orr, Susan, 1960–
Jerusalem and Athens : reason and revelation in the work of
Leo Strauss / Susan Orr.
p.   cm. —
Originally presented as the author's thesis (doctoral—Claremont
Graduate School, 1994) under the title: Jerusalem and Athens, a
study of Leo Strauss.
Includes bibliographical references (p.   ) and index.
1. Strauss, Leo. Jerusalem and Athens. 2. Bible. O.T. Genesis—Criticism, interpretation, etc.—History—20th century. 3. Philosophy, Ancient.
4. Faith and reason. 5. Judaism—Doctrines. 6. Judaism and philosophy. I. Title.
BS1236.S783077   1995   181'.06—dc20   94-24302   CIP

ISBN 0–8476–8010–X (cloth : alk. paper)
ISBN 0–8476–8011–8 (pbk. : alk. paper)

Printed in the United States of America

 ™ The paper used in this publication meets the minimum requirements of American National Standard for Information Sciences—Permanence of Paper for Printed Library Materials, ANSI Z39.48–1984.

To my mother and father

Contents

Acknowledgments		ix
Chapter One	An Introduction to the Question	3
Chapter Two	"Preliminary Reflections"	21
Chapter Three	The Beginning of "The Beginning of the Bible and Its Greek Counterparts"	35
Chapter Four	The Biblical Account of the Beginning	59
Chapter Five	The Greek Counterparts	97
Chapter Six	"On Socrates and the Prophets"	121
Chapter Seven	Conclusion	147
Notes		159
Appendix: Two works by Leo Strauss		
"Jerusalem and Athens: Some Preliminary Reflections"		179
"On the Interpretation of Genesis"		209
Bibliography		227
Index		237
About the Author		247

Acknowledgments

I would like to thank my family for seeing me through this endeavor. In particular, I would like to express my appreciation to my father for helping me through graduate school and especially the dissertation process, my mother for reading every version and always encouraging me, and my sister Sarah and brother Sherman for proofing the various drafts. I will always be grateful to my friend, Mary Parker Lewis, for many things, not the least of which was her willingness to read this book so meticulously and her excellent judgment in helping me to refine my thoughts.

I would be a most ungrateful student if I didn't express my indebtedness to my professors at Claremont Graduate School: to Harry V. Jaffa for his unflagging support and inspiration, to William B. Allen for reading my dissertation so carefully and asking such insightful questions, and to Charles Kesler for his support. A special thanks to Joseph Cropsey for giving me permission to reprint "Jerusalem and Athens: Some Preliminary Reflections" and "On the Interpretation of Genesis."

Jon Sisk, Jennifer Ruark, and Julie Kirsch at Rowman & Littlefield deserve praise for their patience and advice. My thanks also go to Kersti Payton and Sara McCray for proofing "On Genesis." This is not an exhaustive list. I could not have done it without these people and numerous others that I have failed to mention. For everyone's help, I owe a debt of gratitude. It goes without saying that all of the errors are of my own making.

I know all your ways; you are neither hot nor cold.
How I wish you were either hot or cold!
But because you are lukewarm, neither hot nor cold,
I will spit you out of my mouth.

> Revelation 3: 15–16

Chapter One

An Introduction to the Question

Leo Strauss dedicated his life to the rejuvenation of the serious study of political philosophy and because of this dedication, there has been a renewed interest in the serious study of political things. Prior to Strauss's work, political philosophy was given quarter in places few and far between. Academics deluded themselves into believing that political science had progressed beyond the need for philosophy's guidance and political philosophy in most universities was supplanted, as Strauss notes, by "the history of political philosophy," which "replaces doctrine which claims to be true by a survey of more or less brilliant errors."[1] Science was enthroned in its stead. Political science had undergone a revolution similar to that found within the natural sciences, and political scientists blindly translated the ideas found in Darwin and Einstein to political science without accounting for any difference between atoms and human beings or human beings and animals. Departments of political science, enthralled by the fact-value distinction that eliminated any notion of a transcendent good, had become frivolous. As Strauss noted trenchantly:

> Only a great fool would call the new political science diabolic: it has no attributes peculiar to fallen angels. It is not even Machiavellian, for Machiavelli's teaching was graceful, subtle, and colorful. Nor is it Neronian. Nevertheless one may say of it that it fiddles while Rome burns. It is excused by two facts: It does not know that it fiddles, and it does not know that Rome burns.[2]

For Strauss, there was nothing noble in this new political science; indeed, he held that it was, in fact, dying even if it remained unaware of its decrepitude: "modern philosophy, [is] a phenomenon which we know through seeing, as distinguished from reading, only in its decay, its state of deprivation and dotage."³ Unlike Aristotle, whom Strauss credited with the founding of political science, the new political scientist, informed by the understanding that all is relative, could not make even the most basic distinctions between tyrannical and just rule; instead, the preference for democracy over despotic rule was understood as simple prejudice. The world was seen in Hobbesian terms as simply matter in motion. Nothing was permanent; all was changeable. Embracing this relativistic science and translating it to politics, the new political science rejected any hierarchical understanding of man. Human life held no intrinsic meaning and, therefore, was not superior to anything else. In refusing to recognize any limits inherent in man or elsewhere, political scientists blindly placed their faith in progress. It was left to Strauss to show his colleagues that, while they mistakenly thought themselves free, they had indeed bound themselves more completely than the medievals they despised to chains of superstition: for they had replaced the belief in God with the belief in the inevitable march of history toward progress.

Thus devastated by the effects of historicism and positivism, academia had become unable to say anything coherent about anything. And this malaise in the academy only mirrored that felt throughout Western Civilization, where Verdun, Auschwitz, and the Gulag had betrayed the vision of the infinite progress of man as a vain hope. With this realization came the true end of the Enlightenment. It was amidst the intellectual wreckage of modernity that Leo Strauss made his contribution to the field of political science by uncovering the roots of modern political science and the intellectual barrenness of the remains of the modern project. He did this by bringing our focus back to an ancient understanding of man and his place in the universe. In his essay "What is Political Philosophy?," Strauss points to the vacancy of the marriage of modern science and political thought:

> To understand man in the light of the whole means for modern natural science to understand man in the light of the subhuman. But in that light man as man is wholly unintelligible. Classical political philosophy viewed man in a different light. It was originated by Socrates. And Socrates was so far from being committed to a specific cosmology that his knowledge was knowledge of ignorance. Knowledge of ignorance is not ignorance. It is knowledge of the elusive character of the truth, of the whole. Socrates, then, viewed man in the light of the mysterious character of the whole. He held therefore that we are more familiar with the situation of man as man than with the ultimate causes of that situation. We may also say he viewed man in light of unchangeable ideas, i.e., of the fundamental and permanent problems.⁴

Because of his persistent questioning of the conventional wisdom of his day and the intriguing manner in which he examined political philosophy, Leo Strauss caused a resurgence of interest in exploring the thought of both ancients and moderns. He brought his students to see political philosophy, not as a history of brilliant errors, but as a pursuit intrinsically worthwhile. Political philosophy, in Strauss's view, asked the important and permanent questions that man as man must always face. Moreover, he insisted that great men's ideas were not bound by the time in which they lived, i.e., that historicism was false. As he states, "All philosophers of the past claimed to have found *the* truth, not merely the truth for their time."[5] To understand a philosopher one must attempt to understand him as he understood himself. This means that texts should be taken seriously and studied with great care. And it was his intention to take all those worthy of the name philosopher seriously.

By battling the plagues of both historicism and positivism, Strauss made it possible for political philosophy to become a subject of renewed interest within academia once again. Although not yet held as the queen of the social sciences in all universities, it is certainly taken more seriously than in the recent past. Leo Strauss and the school that he founded have been instrumental in resuscitating the reputation of this ancient and venerable study. Because of Leo Strauss, students may once again read the works of Plato and Aristotle as if they had something true to say, and once again look at such texts with the wonder that, as Aristotle himself notes, is the beginning of philosophy. Yet Strauss did more than merely resuscitate a genuine interest in political philosophy, an accomplishment in itself.

Before proceeding further, however, we must lay some preliminary groundwork. Let us begin by defining what are the most basic terms for Strauss. First, the study of political philosophy is the study of regimes and, above all, of the best regime. To study the best regime, one must have an idea about man's purpose, that is, about what is the good for man. It is also important to note that political philosophy depends upon philosophy but is not itself philosophy because its end is not being, but the good regime. Although political philosophy is not the highest science, it is important because it asks the question of what is best for man and, in asking that question, also points to higher things by asking what is man's end. As Strauss states in his essay "What is Political Philosophy?," political philosophy is "the attempt to replace opinion about the nature of political things by knowledge of the nature of political things."[6] Thus, much of political philosophy's work consists of distinguishing between that which is by convention and that which is by nature, i.e., the trappings of civilization and the things that are truly good. It goes without saying, of course, that the study of political things is intimately bound up with the study of morality and particularly with the question of justice. Of crucial importance to students of political philosophy is whether morality exists by nature or convention. Thus, a perennial theme in political philosophy revolves around the distinction between the good man and the good citizen: can they be one and the same, and if not, how do they differ? *The* question for political philosophy is what is the difference between man and citizen, in other words, whether there is a distinction between the noble and the good. As Strauss writes, "The theme of political philosophy is the City and Man."[7] These distinctions, in turn, lead to focusing on the fundamental tension between philosophy and the city. For if wisdom is the highest pursuit, what is its fate when it disagrees with the city, i.e., with those things that the city holds dear? This theme was of paramount importance to Strauss and is illustrated by his constant return to Socrates and his fate.

The possibility of political philosophy, however, presupposes the possibility of philosophy. Indeed, the two are often commingled because the highest part of political philosophy points to philosophy. In *Natural Right and History*, Strauss defines philosophy as the "knowledge of what one does not know, or awareness of the problems and, therewith, of the fundamental alternatives regarding their solution that are coeval with human thought."[8] That philosophy, which is conventionally understood as wisdom, i.e., a knowledge of something, is defined by Strauss first as an awareness of a lack of knowledge appears strange only to those who have not studied him. For this, in a nutshell, is what makes studying Leo Strauss at times both fruitful and frustrating. He often writes in a manner that leaves passages deliberately ambiguous, indeed that suggests two vastly different interpretations. This, of course, is also his charm. For example, his definition of philosophy as the knowledge of what one does not know is daunting at first but it goes to the heart of the philosophical question: Can man know anything? Is there anything to know? In other words, is there such a thing as being? By taking seriously the Socratic dictum that, unlike others who think they know something and do not, Socrates' wisdom consists in knowing that he does not know, Strauss reopens the question and thereby makes it possible to consider both the ancient and modern answers freshly. By making philosophy a quest and not a possession, he reopens the possibility of philosophy itself. Yet it is important not to forget that in his definition of philosophy, he points to the need to be aware of the fundamental alternatives. But what are those alternatives for Strauss?

At first glance, the answer appears to be the choice between ancient and modern philosophy. Indeed, Strauss spent a great part of his time drawing our attention to their differences. Strauss always understood that, despite their differences, the things that Plato and Aristotle held in common were much more telling than those on which they disagreed, and the same could be said of modern philosophers.[9] His constant questioning of all conventional wisdom, coupled with a persistent skepticism toward modernity, was instrumental in bringing the ideas of political philosophers, particularly the Greeks, alive again. The ability to ask questions about the ultimate end for man and to define philosophy as a search allowed him to reconsider the question of whether the ancients or the moderns had a truer understanding of philosophy. But of even greater significance for Strauss were the divergent claims of philosophy and theology, for to question the foundations of modernity means to question the denigration of the sacred, to question whether man is truly only what he makes himself. Thus, it is not surprising to find that the study of the relationship of faith and reason to politics was of crucial importance to Strauss. It began with his early studies of Maimonides in *Philosophy and Law* (1930) and Spinoza in *Spinoza's Critique of Religion* (1935) and continued to his death. Shlomo Pines, who translated Maimonides' *The Guide for the Perplexed* (for which Strauss wrote an introduction), and who first met Strauss in the late twenties, makes this claim: "Many of the views which he upheld to the end of his life were crystallized during that period, and I remember things which he said then and which one can find in his books written thirty years later."[10] It is on Strauss's understanding of the relationship of philosophy and theology, or as he would phrase it, reason and revelation, that we focus our attention in this book.

That Strauss's work should be taken seriously is something that few would now deny. From critics as diverse as Shadia Drury, Frederick Wilhelmsen, and M. B. Burnyeat to students of Strauss such as Harry Jaffa, Allan Bloom, and Thomas Pangle, all are forced to confront him. Indeed, anyone who takes the study of political philosophy seriously has to examine his work. Whether or not we appreciate his ideas, we must confront them, and refute them or agree with them.[11]

Yet this is not an easy task. As we have already suggested, there is a problem in trying to find out what Leo Strauss himself thought. The problem is twofold. First, his writing is usually in the form of a commentary on a given text, written to bring the ideas within that text to life. It is, therefore, difficult at times to distinguish between his elucidation of any given text and his own thought, to separate the philosopher being analyzed from the analyzing philosopher. The second problem is the one for which Strauss and his school have been most excoriated: his teaching on esotericism, or reading between the lines.

Strauss thought that modern men had lost the ability to read books, that all subtlety was lost to them. Living in an age of unparalleled freedom, moderns had become unable to comprehend why anyone would not speak clearly and openly on any subject. Strauss, however, insisted that all great writers write for all generations, but in order to do so, they must cloak certain thoughts: ones that might be or might one day become dangerous.[12] Only in this way could they guarantee the survival of their work and make it accessible to serious thinkers throughout the ages. Thus, to get at the meat of a great book, one must take the structure seriously and note any apparent contradictions within the text because great thinkers do not make obvious mistakes. One must also take note of the author's silences, for they too reveal something of value. Strauss states, "If a wise man is silent about a fact that is commonly held to be important for the subject he discusses, he gives us to understand that that fact is unimportant. The silence of a wise man is always meaningful. It cannot be explained by forgetfulness. . . . This is, in fact, the most effective way of showing one's disapproval."[13] To put it simply, Strauss thought that great thinkers do not always reveal their teachings as openly as we would wish or think. Because great writers write carefully, words are important and distinctions between words are important as well.

The dangerous nature of truth in the political realm is thus also a persistent theme in Strauss. Truth can be dangerous, in part, because of the necessary particularity of each regime, which is intimately bound up with equating the fatherland, or one's own, with the good. Philosophy, in contrast, may show that the good and one's own, or what we hold dear, are distinct. The realization that "the good is of higher dignity than one's own, or that the best regime is of a higher consideration than the fatherland" can be dangerous knowledge; for, among many possibilities, it can lead to a desire for political change.[14] Wishing to avoid a tyrant's ire is only one obvious example of why it is necessary to write with caution, especially when writing on political philosophy.

That his esotericism has been his most unpopular teaching is understandable: no one wishes to be told that he has missed the point. And Strauss did just that. Strauss consistently showed his contemporaries that in their failure to read texts carefully they had, in fact, misunderstood many philosophers.[15] Yet, his teaching on reading between the lines is also fundamental to his appeal. Part of Strauss's ineluctable charm is in his challenging those students who are eager to prove themselves potential philosophers to unravel the mysteries within a given text.

Strauss himself followed his predecessors, for he too is a subtle writer. Fundamental to Strauss's teaching on reading between the lines is that only a few will be sufficiently intelligent and diligent enough to discover any hidden meaning in a text. As he states in *Thoughts on Machiavelli*, "to speak the truth is sensible only when one speaks to wise men."[16] By its very nature, of course, the written word cannot control who its readers will be, so esoteric writing is necessary. It is a good rule of thumb when reading Strauss, therefore, to read him as if he wrote as he says Plato did:

> the proper work of a writing is truly to talk, or to reveal the truth, to some while leading others to salutary opinions; the proper work of a writing is to arouse to thinking those who are by nature fit for it; the good writing achieves its end if the reader considers carefully the "logographic necessity" of every part, however small or seemingly insignificant, of the writing.[17]

Upon reflection, it is easy to see that there are different types of speech, i.e., that one speaks differently to different people. Hence, one would speak more openly to a friend than to a stranger. According to Strauss, good writing should be like good conversation.[18] When considering his work, therefore, it is best to proceed with caution and to assume that there are different levels of meaning to be found: some meant for friends, others for strangers.

As if understanding Strauss's writing were not challenging enough, the difficulty is compounded by dissension among his students, all claiming to be carrying on the tradition begun by Strauss and each carrying out a decidedly different tradition. The split between the West Coast and the East Coast Straussians is much more than a geographical division. It is a dispute over ideas, over the legacy of Leo Strauss. His East Coast students, such as Allan Bloom and Thomas Pangle, have collapsed the distinction between ancient and modern philosophy, claiming that the real dispute is between philosophy and poetry, poetry being simply the code word for the spiritual realm or revelation. Thus, Thomas Pangle could write in his introduction to *Studies in Platonic Political Philosophy*:

> Strauss did not overlook, he rather brought out and stressed, the enormous differences between biblical thought and the thought of the Greek poets;

but he regarded those differences as, in the final analysis, secondary. What is most essential in the quarrel between Plato and the Bible is already present in the quarrel between Plato and the poets. . . .[19]

In the section entitled "The Quarrel between Philosophy and Poetry," Pangle makes it clear that philosophy, for Strauss and for any thinking man, triumphs over revelation:

> Belief in the gods is seen to veil from man the evidence whose reasonable interpretation would lead toward knowledge of the true causes of things. In particular, it seems plausible to suppose that the gods are needed as supporters of nobility and justice because nobility and justice lack intrinsic support in the hearts of men—in their natural and not simply imagined needs and inclinations.[20]

According to Pangle's version of Strauss, gods are needed but they are not real; they only serve to hide reality.

Against this claim, Harry V. Jaffa, leading the West Coast Straussians, explicitly denies that this is Strauss's teaching: "Pangle's account of the quarrel between poetry and philosophy has nothing whatever in common with anything that might be attributed to Leo Strauss. For Pangle, it is the quarrel of one or another species of Epicureanism with *both* Jerusalem and Athens, with the morality of *both* the Bible and classical political philosophy."[21] Jaffa understands Strauss's contribution to political philosophy in this way: "Strauss's distinctiveness—indeed, his uniqueness, I had thought—lay above all else in the fact that he was the first great critic of modernity whose diagnosis of the ills of modernity did not end by seeking a solution of those ills through a radicalization of the principles of modernity."[22] Jaffa also writes:

> Because his detachment from modernity was so much greater than all previous critics of modernity, Strauss alone could supply us with a theoretical foundation for a moderate politics within modernity. For Strauss *did* have a practical teaching, and it took the form of a celebration of the virtues, above all, of Anglo-American constitutionalism at its best. The preoccupation among his students, with the American Founders, with Lincoln, and with Churchill, is a direct reflection of this teaching.[23]

For Jaffa and his students, following Strauss consists in reflecting upon good citizenship and the question of the best regime and applying these considerations to the here and now. Such ideals are of crucial and practical interest specifically in relation to the American regime as it is based on principles of natural law. Using Strauss's esotericism as a shield, the East Coast Straussians claim that Jaffa has missed the point, i.e., that he succeeds in getting only the political and therefore exoteric teaching of Strauss, but misses the inner core which reveals the hidden emptiness of the political realm.[24]

Allan Bloom, in *Giants and Dwarfs: Essays 1960–1990*, makes this claim for philosophy: "there are two threats to reason, the opinion that one knows the truth about the most important things and the opinion that there is no truth about them. Both of these opinions are fatal to philosophy; the first asserts that the quest for truth is unnecessary, while the second asserts that it is impossible."[25] Thus, what should be a starting point for philosophy becomes an end in itself. Of course, for Bloom, it is understood that religion falls into the category of those mistaken attempts to know the truth. Bloom is equal to Pangle in his disdain for religion. For example, in "Western Civ," his essay on the current academic controversy over the canon of great books, Bloom makes the following remark: "The Canon is the list of books of the Bible accepted by the Catholic Christian church as genuine and inspired. These books are supposed to compel our faith without reason or evidence."[26] And later in the essay he adds, "Science is somehow transcultural. Religion seems pretty much limited to cultures, even to define them. Is philosophy like science or is it like religion? What we are witnessing is an attempt to drag it away definitively to the camp of religion."[27] Of course, if religion is simply a product of culture, then philosophy alone would be true everywhere and always and thus transcendent of culture. In fact, there are passages in Strauss that sound remarkably similar even if they are much more subtle.

Strauss was fond of pointing out, for example, that Plato's most political work was also the only dialogue that begins with the word "God," thus leaving the reader to wonder just how political the concept of God is.[28] Again, we find Strauss saying in the essay "The Law of Reason in the *Kuzari*" that the author, Judah Halevi, "knew too well that a genuine philosopher can never become a genuine convert to Judaism or to any other revealed religion. For, according to him, a genuine philosopher is a man such as Socrates who possesses 'human wisdom' and is invincibly ignorant of 'Divine Wisdom.'"[29] In both examples, Strauss seems to suggest that the gap between philosophy and revelation is unbridgeable and the wiser man stands on the side of philosophy; that, similar to the tension between philosophy and the city, there must be an antagonism between philosophy and revelation. Moreover, Strauss's definition of philosophy bears some resemblance to Bloom's discussion on the threats to reason. But there is a difference. Strauss says of philosophy that it "is essentially not possession of the truth, but quest for the truth. The distinctive trait of the philosopher is that 'he knows that he knows nothing' and that his insight into our ignorance concerning the most important things induces him to strive with all his power for knowledge."[30] This formulation of the problem, unlike Bloom's, leaves open the possibility that revelation is true, just not knowable philosophically. As Strauss says, "every one of us can be and ought to be one or the other, the philosopher open to the challenge of theology or the theologian open to the challenge of philosophy."[31]

There are also many passages in the Straussian corpus that suggest that he was more than open to the call of revelation and, hence, more in accord with Jaffa's interpretation that "the skepticism that is the core of philosophy, the honest skepticism that must always be distinguished from dogmatic skepticism, always leaves philosophy open to the challenge of revelation. It always leaves philosophers open to the undeniable fact that the claims of autonomous human reason cannot be fully vindicated by that reason."[32] For Jaffa, Strauss may have been a skeptic, but he was anything but a dogmatic skeptic. Again, there are passages in Strauss's work that suggest that Jaffa's interpretation is correct. For example, in his 1962 preface to the English translation of his early work, *Spinoza's Critique of Religion*, Strauss states that:

> The genuine refutation of orthodoxy would require the proof that the world and human life are perfectly intelligible without the assumption of a mysterious God; it would require at least the success of the philosophic system: man has to show himself theoretically and practically as the master of his human life; the merely given world must be replaced by the world created by man theoretically and practically.[33]

To suggest that Strauss remained skeptical regarding man's ability to accomplish this task would not be putting it too strongly. One is, therefore, forced to ask which of these two schools is following Strauss? Who are his true disciples? Why did his teaching cause such a divergent reaction? And, most important, which of these accounts of Strauss is the correct one? It is certainly ironic that, although named for their geographic locations, the West Coast and East Coast Straussians also represent what the West and the East stand for in philosophy: the West, outward-looking and life-affirming; the East, inward-looking and filled with despair. But it is obvious that we cannot turn to Strauss's students—at least immediately—to obtain an accurate understanding of him. Whatever the answer may be, we can assert that Strauss seems to have imitated Plato successfully by writing ironically, which he says means "to speak differently to different people."[34] And this, of course, is the root of the controversy surrounding his work.

The most interesting critics of Strauss and his school charge that the East Coast Straussians are correct, that underneath Strauss's analyses of philosophic texts there is a hidden contempt, an aversion, to traditional morality and especially to Christianity.[35] Shadia Drury, in *The Political Ideas of Leo Strauss*, the most comprehensive attack on him to date, lodges this complaint against Strauss: "Strauss is a philosopher with a unique and disturbing set of ideas that he is reluctant to state clearly and unambiguously."[36] As she puts it, Strauss thought that "religion and morality are two of the biggest but most pious swindles ever perpetrated on the human race. But paradoxically, there would be no human race were it not for these swindles."[37] In Drury's analysis, Strauss held that man as a political animal needs myth to keep him within the bonds of society; those myths, however, whether they are called civil religion or morality, are little more than Plato's shadows on the cave, serving only to keep most men civilized. They are, therefore, necessary shackles. Those fortunate few who free themselves and see that the restraints of civil society are simply myths or pious untruths are the philosophers who stare unflinchingly into the light of truth: a light that reveals that most human endeavor is built upon a sham. According to Drury, Strauss deliberately cloaked this doctrine so that this truth would be known only to those few students who took the time to read him carefully because it was, after all, a dangerous truth. But is this a correct assessment of Strauss's deliberate esotericism?

Drury's solution is a tempting one, in part, because Strauss himself constantly harkens to Socrates' fate, which he understood as the direct result of an inevitable clash between philosophy and the city, and thereby the city's gods. Strauss's constant focus on this inevitable tension makes the reader wonder about the current fate of philosophy in the city. The reader is tempted to equate the ancient gods with the Judeo-Christian God or to equate poetry and revelation. At the same time, the reader begins to wonder whether there are any dangerous truths, in this age of unbelief, that the city would still do best to silence? Strauss seems to suggest that the answer must always be yes. In his lecture "The Problem of Socrates," Strauss states that "philosophy is primarily political philosophy because political philosophy is required for protecting the inner sanctum of philosophy."[38] Citations such as these are numerous in Strauss's writing. What is not immediately evident, however, is what exactly he means by this cryptic statement, i.e., what is it that needs protecting? Is Drury's assessment correct that for Strauss philosophy is nihilistic at its core? If Socrates was put to death because he corrupted the Athenian youth and turned them away from the city's gods, what would happen to a persistent gadfly now? More important, what gods would he turn the youth away from today? The problem is one to which we have already alluded: who exactly are the gods of modernity? Strauss would be the first to point out that religious piety, much less civic piety, appears moribund at best. The altars where it is fashionable to sacrifice are not to be found in churches but in those temples of progress, laboratories, and the god that modern man worships is none other than himself.

Critics such as Drury do not attack Strauss openly on these grounds but insist that it was traditional morality that he eschewed. These are indeed harsh charges. To make them stick, however, one must make several assumptions. The first and most important is that Strauss saw no distinction between Zeus and Yahweh, not to mention between Zeus and Christ. But as we have seen, albeit briefly, it is very difficult to say exactly what Strauss himself thinks. To assume that he saw a moral equivalence between the Greek pantheon and the Judeo-Christian conception of divinity would, I think, be an injustice. Moreover, it is important to note that just because philosophy shows that a city worships false gods, it does not answer the larger question of whether or not there is a true God. A deeper examination of Strauss is necessary. To reach the answer to these questions it is necessary to turn to Leo Strauss himself, to take him seriously, and to try to understand what he considered his philosophic project to be.

There are persistent themes in Strauss's work: first, as already mentioned, his continued fascination with Socrates; and second, his interest in the medievals, particularly the Islamic and Jewish philosophers. Strauss looked to Socrates not only because he was the founder of political philosophy but also because his life and death show the place of philosophy in the city, a relationship that must by its very nature be tenuous at best. Strauss credits Socrates accordingly: "We have learned from Socrates that the political things, or the human things, are the key to the understanding of all things."[39] Strauss learned from Socrates that the nature of political life is one of limits. Although political philosophy looks to the universal and best regime, political life itself is one of particulars. It is important to remember the distinction between the good man and the good citizen. The two meet only in the best regime, a regime that for Socrates is at best a remote possibility. Because not all human beings are capable of philosophy, the governments they erect are imperfect as well. These are the perennial problems that political philosophers must face. But human beings also have something in them that pushes toward the infinite, toward the divine. That desire is satisfied only by the contemplative life, which, as Aristotle states in his discussion of the best life in Book X of the *Nicomachean Ethics*, is partly divine:

> However, such a life would be more than human. A man who would live it would do so not insofar as he is human, but because there is a divine element within him. This divine element is as far above our composite nature as its activity is above the active exercise of the other kind of virtue. So if it is true that intelligence is divine in comparison with man, then a life guided by intelligence is divine in comparison with human life. We must not follow those who advise us to have human thoughts, since we are men, and mortal thoughts, as mortals should; on the contrary, we should try to become immortal as far as that is possible and do our utmost to live in accordance with what is highest in us. For though this is a small portion, it far surpasses everything else in power and value. One might even regard it as each man's true self, since it is the controlling and therefore better part.[40]

Following this classical understanding of man, Strauss rightly perceived that man's pursuit of the transcendent leads to either philosophy or theology.

This insight was also the reason why Strauss was drawn to the medieval thinkers. They not only understood the natural limits of politics, but they were keenly interested in the relationship of philosophy and theology as well. Strauss saw that the medievals he most admired had learned from Plato how to avoid Socrates' fate; they had learned to avoid the temptation to be edifying.[41] The medievals, particularly the Jewish and Islamic philosophers, understood the threat that philosophy could present to the city and vice versa. In the introduction to *Persecution and the Art of Writing*, Strauss states, "The precarious position of philosophy in the Islamic-Jewish world guaranteed its private character and therewith its inner freedom from supervision."[42] It is not a coincidence, then, that Strauss understood the Middle Ages as the beginning of the crystallization of the conflict between reason and revelation. In "How to Begin to Study Medieval Philosophy," he writes, "One may say that the Middle Ages witnessed the first, and certainly the most adequate, discussion between these two most important forces of the Western world: the religion of the Bible and the science or philosophy of the Greeks."[43] Perhaps one reason Strauss remained interested in the medievals was precisely because, unlike the poetry of the Greeks, medieval theology offered revelation at its highest point, in other words, a worthy rival of philosophy.

This interest in the serious consideration of the claims of revelation was one that, with few exceptions, modern political scientists and philosophers alike scorned. As Strauss noted, "The new science uses sociological or psychological theories regarding religion which exclude, without considering it, the possibility that religion rests ultimately on God's revealing Himself to man."[44] The Enlightenment had tossed aside religion as monkish superstition, the only purpose of which was to enslave others; religion had retained that tarnish within academia. But Strauss would not let revelation go at that. He understood only too well what we had lost by giving up the notion of the divine, or even of considering its possibility. For he understood that the highest questions that political philosophy asks—e.g., what is justice?—point to questions about God. As he states in the final sentence of *The City and Man*, "Only by beginning at this point will we be open to the full impact of the all important question which is coeval with philosophy although the philosophers do not frequently pronounce it—the question *quid sit deus*."[45]

Whatever his final understanding of the relationship of reason and faith, it can be said at the outset that Strauss took the question of that relationship seriously. This study will focus on Strauss's understanding of the relation of reason to faith and the differing claims of philosophy and theology by examining his essay "Jerusalem and Athens: Some Preliminary Reflections." For in "Jerusalem and Athens," he tackles this important philosophic question most directly: is it to reason or to revelation that one should look for answers about the highest things? By looking closely at this essay, we can judge more adequately whether Strauss, as Drury and ultimately the East Coast Straussians contend, sees a moral equivalence between the Greek pantheon and the Judeo-Christian God.

The essay is a debate or dialogue between the two rival claimants, revelation and reason, in their own words, as it were,—in the words of the author of Genesis and the prophets on the one side and the Greek poets and philosophers, particularly Hesiod and Socrates, on the other. Many matters of great import for political philosophy—for example, the place of man in the universe, his need for politics, his yearning for justice, and his simultaneous dread and courting of evil—hinge upon whether reason or revelation is the final guide for man. Both philosophy and theology speak to these important notions, and they sometimes say very different things. The decision as to which has the final authority will have a profound impact on the political realm. Even those who remain unconvinced by Pangle's equating of poetry and religion do not deny the close bond between religion and politics. To show their close correspondence, Strauss puts it starkly, "Political thought is as old as the human race; the first man who uttered a word like 'father' or an expression like 'thou shalt not . . .' was the first political thinker."[46] Although this statement sounds as if Strauss makes religion simply political, the jarring manner in which he states the issue entices the modern reader to think about the nature of laws and the manner in which regimes compel obedience. He often reminds us that, for the ancients, what the law does not command, it forbids. The question remains, however, whether Strauss thought that religion was only political.

As any perusal of his writings will make abundantly clear, Strauss never forgot his own roots. As a German Jew forced to flee his native land in the wake of Hitler, the perennial Jewish problem and the imminent possibility of persecution were not abstract considerations for him. As he understood it, Jewish thinkers before him had mistakenly thought that the modern solutions of either assimilation or Zionism would resolve the Jewish problem. The events of the twentieth century, however, had made it painfully clear that neither solution was permanent. As Strauss somberly notes in "Progress or Return," "the attempts to solve the Jewish problem by purely human means ended in failure. The knot which was not tied by man could not be untied by man."[47]

It is possible to assume that his interest in the Jewish question was motivated solely by a concern for the Jewish people and that all references to revelation are simply rhetorical. But to assume that Strauss thought the Jewish question was not a serious intellectual problem means not taking Strauss at his word. He himself tells us, in *Persecution and the Art of Writing*, "The issue of traditional Judaism versus philosophy is identical with the issue of Jerusalem and Athens."[48] The two fundamental alternatives that cause him to focus on the Jewish problem are, in turn, a paradigm of the human problem; the human problem, moreover, is eminently a political problem. As Strauss states in the "Introductory Essay" of *Spinoza's Critique of Religion*:

> Finite, relative problems can be solved; infinite, absolute problems cannot be solved. In other words, human beings will never create a society which is free of contradictions. From every point of view it looks as if the Jewish problem is the manifest symbol of the human problem as a social or political problem.[49]

The study of this question of the relationship between reason and faith and a reconsideration of whether the moderns were correct in their denigration of the sacred can be found nowhere so clearly laid out as in his lecture on Jerusalem and Athens given at the City College in New York in 1967, and published later that year in an abbreviated version in *Commentary*. That Strauss published it in *Commentary* indicates that he considered what he had to say on the topic to be important to more than just the academic world. It is also interesting to note that the book that Strauss was working on at the time of his death was to have the essay on Jerusalem and Athens as its central chapter—yet another indication of the importance he placed on this work in particular and the subject as a whole.[50]

As we have said, the essay focuses on the Jewish, and ultimately the human, problem of reconciling reason and faith. Strauss concentrated a great deal of his writing on the relationship of reason and faith. Indeed, Seth Benardete characterizes his teacher's work as an "articulation of the theological-political problem."[51] Because of the immensity of the task, we will confine ourselves to an analysis of "Jerusalem and Athens," referring when necessary to Strauss's other writings to illuminate obscure passages. Limiting the discussion to one essay will serve two purposes: economy and clarity. First, it would be too great an undertaking to cover Strauss's understanding of reason and faith in all his work, and the attempt could lead us to incorrect assumptions. The subject matter is too complex to cover in its entirety here. We must consider this as only a first step in elucidating his thoughts on the subject as a whole. Second, by only looking at one essay, we will be proceeding as Strauss did in his analysis of great texts and thereby, we hope, learning all that he wishes to teach us in this essay.

By examining "Jerusalem and Athens" carefully, we are going to read this essay as Strauss says that we should any carefully written work. We will assume that the essay was written properly, i.e., that it will be like a good conversation that reveals things to those who approach it with care. This means, among other things, that we will always consider what Strauss calls the "logographic necessity" of the essay. Thus, what he writes, the order in which he considers items, and what he fails to mention will all be deemed important and illuminating. Only then can we hope to understand what Strauss himself can teach us.

The essay is beautifully written. It would not be unjust to say that it is a most revealing work for it contains what appear at times to be very personal reflections, a rarity in the Straussian corpus.[52] Obviously, the subject of the essay was dear to his heart. It has been said that the two things that absorbed Strauss throughout his lifetime were questions concerning God and politics.[53] In this essay on the two rival claims to man's allegiance, these two subjects meet. Our study of it should provide a preliminary understanding of the thought of Leo Strauss on the relationship of reason and faith. By examining the essay carefully, we hope to come to an understanding of this central theme of the crisis of Western civilization and to understand Strauss's contribution to the debate. For it would appear that Bloom is correct, at least in his assessment of the importance of Strauss, when he suggests, "Echoing the *Apology* with what will seem a threat to some, a blessing to others, I believe our generation may well be judged by the next generation according to how we judged Leo Strauss."[54] In considering "Jerusalem and Athens: Some Preliminary Reflections," we hope to come to some preliminary judgment as to who this man was who inflamed so many of his students with a yearning for truth no matter how harsh that truth might be. After careful consideration of "Jerusalem and Athens," we hope to be able to suggest, at least tentatively, which account of Leo Strauss is the more accurate: the cautious nihilist or the reluctant believer? Perhaps the answer to that question lies in this particular essay.

ens." First, he gave a series of three lectures in 1952 to the B'nai B'rith Hillel Foundation at the University of Chicago that have come down to us as "Progress or Return? The Contemporary Crisis in Western Civilization" (the first two lectures) and "The Mutual Influence of Theology and Philosophy" (the final lecture). These three lectures are an articulation of the same themes found in "Jerusalem and Athens" and prove invaluable when we confront difficult or unclear passages in the essay. One important distinction, however, is that these lectures specifically address the Jewish problem, whereas "Jerusalem and Athens" does not. In short, these three lectures are a consideration of the Jewish problem in its modern form. Strauss tells us that his Jewish audience, for the most part, is not orthodox; modern Jews are, therefore, confronted with two alternatives: either to return to Judaism, and thereby repent, or to transcend the past and turn completely away from their tradition by choosing progress.

The question of progress or return is yet another formulation of the struggle between reason and revelation. Both begin with a reconsideration of the past, of the beginnings. If the past is understood as better than the present, as more perfect, as having divine beginnings, then a return to the past is a turning toward revelation, a turning toward God. If the past is understood as imperfect, as less than noble, then progress and indeed philosophy are chosen; because if we admit that man at the beginning was imperfect, we are saying that man betters himself through knowledge that he acquires on his own. This series of lectures culminates with an elucidation of the common ground between theology and philosophy. Both theology and philosophy understand the importance of morality, especially regarding man's concern with justice. At the same time both also understand morality's incompleteness. The disagreement, Strauss shows us, is in where each turns to supply the completeness that is lacking in morality itself. For Strauss, reason points to contemplation, revelation to obedience. Reason is autonomous; faith implies surrender. For philosophy is the attempt to imitate the divine; theology, in contrast, must inevitably bow before the divine, accepting that what it knows about God, it knows because God has chosen to reveal it. At least on the surface of this series of lectures, neither reason nor revelation wins the debate. Indeed, Strauss ends the last lecture with the oft-quoted phrase: "But every one of us can be and ought to be one or the other, the philosopher open to the challenge of theology or the theologian open to the challenge of philosophy."[10] At least in this lecture series, Strauss suggests that neither side can be supremely self-confident.

In January of 1957 Strauss gave another lecture at the University of Chicago, for its series "Works of the Mind." The lecture was entitled "On the Interpretation of Genesis."[11] "Jerusalem and Athens" draws much from this essay. "On the Interpretation of Genesis" is a detailed consideration of the first few chapters of Genesis, i.e., the two creation accounts and the fall. In this lecture Strauss says he will try to understand "something of the Bible without relying entirely on what the authorities both contemporary and traditional tell me."[12] This is very much the way he proceeds in "Jerusalem and Athens." Although he does draw some of his insights from biblical commentator Umberto Cassuto, he does not analyze Genesis in a traditional manner, nor does he take his cues from modern biblical critics. Because Strauss covers the first three chapters of Genesis more thoroughly here, this essay will prove helpful when a passage in "Jerusalem and Athens" seems obscure.

Another place to turn within the works of Strauss for guidance on the relationship between reason and revelation is his "Introductory Essay" to the English translation of *Spinoza's Critique of Religion*. This beautiful essay is an account of Strauss's own understanding of the theological-political question and how that understanding had changed since he first wrote the book in 1930. It is the most personal, and therefore the most revealing, of all his writings. In this introduction, he distances himself from his original work, saying that "the author was a young Jew born and raised in Germany who found himself in the grip of the theologico-political predicament."[13] In the course of his essay he tells what he has learned in the intervening years about that "theologico-political predicament." The essay is an examination of the mistaken turns that various Jewish thinkers have taken in trying to overcome "the Jewish problem," a problem that Strauss considered permanent.

I would add another work that will not appear immediately obvious: *Natural Right and History*, which is based on the Walgreen lectures of 1949. This book is an answer to the historicist critique of natural right as well as a study of the classical and modern understanding of natural right. But it can be said to have the question of reason and revelation as one of its underlying themes. Natural right is intimately bound up with the question of justice. Justice, the queen of the virtues, concerns itself, more than any other virtue, with questions of the divine, perhaps because it is also the rarest of virtues, the most difficult to attain. Strauss writes, "But when speaking of natural right, one implies that justice is of vital importance to man or that man cannot live or live well without justice; and life in accordance with justice requires knowledge of the principles of justice."[14] Strauss traces the origin of the idea of natural right to the account of the beginning of things, which is intimately bound up with questions about the divine. Here again we are reminded of the contrast between reason and revelation and what that contrast implies:

> The idea of natural right must be unknown as long as the idea of nature is unknown. The discovery of nature is the work of philosophy. Where there is no philosophy, there is no knowledge of natural right as such. The Old Testament, whose basic premise may be said to be the implicit rejection of philosophy, does not know "nature": The Hebrew term for "nature" is unknown to the Hebrew Bible. It goes without saying that "heaven and earth," for example, is not the same thing as "nature." There is, then, no knowledge of natural right as such in the Old Testament.[15]

Here Strauss is explicit about the antagonism between philosophy and the Bible, calling the Old Testament an "implicit rejection of philosophy." We have already learned from Strauss that philosophy begins, at least in Athens, with a rejection of the traditional account of the divine. Each, therefore, rejects the other; both, of course, cannot be right. Yet this leaves unanswered the question of why we should look to *Natural Right and History* to illuminate "Jerusalem and Athens" in particular.

I think Strauss himself refers us to it because he uses two biblical quotations for the frontispiece of *Natural Right and History*. The first quotation is the same one he uses in the last section of "Jerusalem and Athens." Indeed, it is the last biblical quotation in the essay. The passage is from 2 Samuel 12:1–7, where the prophet Nathan rebukes King David for the tyrannical and unscrupulous manner in which he has acquired Bathsheba. Nathan tells him a parable about two men, one rich, the other poor; the rich man, although he has plenty of his own, takes the poor man's only sheep to entertain a traveler. On hearing this tale, David becomes incensed and swears to exact justice upon the offending man. At this point, Nathan informs David that the rich man is none other than King David himself. It is not accidental that Strauss closes one essay with the same biblical passage with which he opens another work. We will consider this passage more closely when we examine "On Socrates and the Prophets" in detail.

Each of these works speaks to the same themes as "Jerusalem and Athens: Some Preliminary Reflections." Of course, a thorough examination of the subject would also have to include Strauss's work on Maimonides and Spinoza.[16] But our primary task is to determine what this particular essay has to teach us about the subject.

At this point, we should note what Strauss does not mention in this essay. For example, there is only one reference to Christianity in the essay. His allusion to Christianity's place in this great debate appears in the second part of the essay and is mentioned only as if to remind us that he has not mentioned it. The reference occurs when Strauss, in discussing Hermann Cohen's essay on Plato and the prophets, makes the following remark: "Being concerned with 'the social ideal,' [Cohen] does not say a single word on Christianity in the whole lecture."[17] With the exception just noted, Strauss mimics Cohen's silence about Christianity's contribution to the debate over reason and revelation.

The failure to mention Christianity and its influence is not unusual for Strauss. Many critics of Strauss and the school that he founded have noted this failure. Frederick Wilhelmsen, in *Christianity and Political Philosophy*, notes that, despite Strauss's aid in rejuvenating political philosophy, "very little is taught us about the contribution, if any, of Christian thought to politics."[18] Wilhelmsen attributes this "principled suppression" to the fact that Strauss was a Hellenized Jew convinced by the argument of Averroes that religion is necessary only in so far as it allows a regime to have good citizens.[19] As we have begun to see, it is possible to understand Strauss in that light. He certainly leaves himself open to that interpretation.

There are other reasons that could account for his reticence on Christianity, but at this point, it is unclear which is probable. What immediately springs to mind is that his silence regarding Christianity and its influence could be a Machiavellian silence, i.e., a silence that reveals that Strauss considers the subject intrinsically unimportant. This possibility suggests two alternatives. The first is that his silence is a rebuke. One could argue that Strauss saw the influence of Christianity waning; as a dying religion, its effect upon politics, although dangerous when it held sway, no longer merited attention. Certainly, many of his students hold Christianity in contempt. Another possibility is that this omission is a necessary result of his denial that any synthesis between reason and revelation is possible. Because he holds this position, he avoids discussing Christianity. Christianity, specifically Catholicism in the person of Thomas Aquinas, holds that since truth is one, no contradictions can be found between reason and revelation. Strauss points to this possibility in *Natural Right and History* in his brief discussion of Thomas's contribution to natural right. Calling Thomas's version of natural right a "doctrine," Strauss states that it is "free from the hesitations and ambiguities which are characteristic" of the classical understanding. He continues:

It is reasonable to assume that these profound changes were due to the influence of the belief in biblical revelation. If this assumption should prove to be correct, one would be forced to wonder, however, whether the natural law as Thomas Aquinas understands it is natural law strictly speaking, i.e., a law knowable to the unassisted human mind, to the mind which is not illuminated by divine revelation.[20]

For Strauss, Thomas blurs the distinction between reason and revelation too much. Strauss wants to stress that there must be a choice, a clear-cut choice between reason and revelation; Christianity, in contrast, says that the answer is both; it even has, in Rome, a city that answers to that name.

Strauss's treatment of Christianity is a delicate topic. As a Jew, no one expects him to accept Christian doctrine. Indeed, it is obvious that Strauss is most concerned with the problems of Judaism. At the same time, it would be a failure not to note the absence of Christianity's contribution to the debate of reason and revelation in "Jerusalem and Athens." This absence goes unnoticed partly because of Strauss's own terminology, and his terminology leads us to yet another possible reason why Christianity is not mentioned.

As noted earlier, Strauss uses the Christian term "Bible" when speaking of the Scriptures throughout the essay. Although in this particular essay he limits himself to the Old Testament, he does not use the term "Hebrew Bible" as he does elsewhere to qualify the term.[21] Perhaps he is using the inclusive term because the account of the beginning is something both Christian and Jew share and must come to terms with. Although it is unclear what this means at the present time, it should nonetheless be noted. What is clear is that what Strauss wishes to impart regarding Jerusalem and Athens is not something of importance only to Jews.

Another interesting omission in "Jerusalem and Athens" is very surprising. One would expect to find, in an essay dealing with reason and revelation, some reference to Maimonides, especially given Strauss's indebtedness to Maimonides' understanding of the relationship of philosophy and theology. It is strange not to find even one reference to *The Guide for the Perplexed*, especially as Strauss says,

> Its first purpose is to explain terms, and its second purpose is to explain biblical similes. The *Guide* is then devoted above all to biblical exegesis, although to biblical exegesis of a particular kind. That kind of exegesis is required because many biblical terms and all biblical similes have an apparent or outer and a hidden or inner meaning; the gravest errors as well as the most tormenting perplexities arise from men's understanding

the Bible always according to its apparent or literal meaning. The *Guide* is then devoted to "the difficulties of the Law" or to "the secrets of the Law." The most important of these secrets are the Account of the Beginning (the beginning of the Bible) and the Account of the Chariot (Ezek. 1 and 10). The *Guide* is then devoted primarily and chiefly to the explanation of the Account of the Beginning and the Account of the Chariot.[22]

Strauss does not, or does not openly, take his understanding of the beginning from Maimonides. Thus, Maimonides is also conspicuous by his absence. This is most startling given the subject matter. Strauss does cite Spinoza, but his failure to even mention Maimonides is interesting.

All of these observations must be kept in mind when considering Strauss's purpose in writing "Jerusalem and Athens: Some Preliminary Reflections." It is hoped that these remarks will be a sufficient gloss on some details that should be kept in mind before proceeding to the work as a whole. Next we turn to the structure of the essay.

The Structure of "Jerusalem and Athens"

Strauss divides the essay into two parts: "The Beginning of the Bible and Its Greek Counterparts" and "On Socrates and the Prophets." The first part contains the same theme he employs in *Natural Right and History* as well as in "Progress or Return." He begins "Jerusalem and Athens" with a consideration of what theology and philosophy think about the beginnings of things or the first things. "The Beginning of the Bible and Its Greek Counterparts" is also the longest part. The bulk of this section consists of an examination of the first book of the Old Testament as well as a comparison of it to the Greek understanding of the beginnings of things as reflected in the poetry of Hesiod. Strauss does turn briefly to Exodus as well as to Parmenides, Empedocles, Plato, and Aristotle; however, the majority of the first section is devoted to Genesis. The next largest segment in the first part of the essay is his treatment of Hesiod's *Theogony*.

The second part, "On Socrates and the Prophets," is much shorter. This part of the essay is dedicated to a comparison of the different missions of the prophets and Socrates. The difference in length between the two parts could be because the first part, the account of the beginnings of things, whether in Genesis or in Greek poetry and philosophy, is more important. For the account of the beginning lays the groundwork upon which morality rests, which is of tantamount importance to both Socrates and the prophets. Both Socrates and the prophets are concerned with morality: the prophets, with getting the Israelites to remain true to their covenant with the God of Abraham, Isaac, and Jacob; Socrates, with teaching his fellow citizens to remain true to knowledge and, thereby, to attain virtue.

The essay can be subdivided even further, and although the division is not arbitrary, it is also not obvious at first glance.[23] Strauss does not tell us how to break it down. The entire essay is forty-one paragraphs long. The first part, "The Beginning of the Bible and Its Greek Counterparts," is composed of thirty paragraphs and can be divided into five sections: an introduction consisting of one paragraph, a critique of culture, four paragraphs; a section on biblical criticism, four paragraphs; the biblical account, fifteen paragraphs; and, finally, its Greek counterparts, six paragraphs. Thus, Strauss devotes the major portion of "The Beginning of the Bible and Its Greek Counterparts" to the biblical account. In contrast, only six paragraphs are dedicated to the Greek understanding of the beginning of things.

The Bible, despite being considered a collection of memories, is presented as a coherent whole, or at least Genesis is—an idea shored up by Strauss's reliance on the biblical scholar Umberto Cassuto. The Greek accounts, in contrast, are varied and numerous; each Greek presents a different understanding of the beginning of things. Indeed, some are poets and some are philosophers, and poetry and philosophy do not agree. Yet neither poetry nor philosophy agrees with the account presented by the author of Genesis. This leads us to wonder how Strauss wants us to think about the author of the Biblical account: is he a poet, a philosopher, or something completely different? The answer is not readily apparent. We are thus confronted with the leading problem that revelation presents: how does revelation come to us? The immediate answer is: through a book or a collection of books that are held to be inspired by God. We trust that they are from God, first of all, because we trust the man who wrote it; we must trust the prophet. Revelation thus comes to us through intermediaries, through men who we believe are telling the truth. This difficulty will be in the background of "The Beginning of the Bible and Its Greek Counterparts," and indeed of the entire essay.

Part Two of "Jerusalem and Athens," as previously noted, is much shorter, having only eleven paragraphs. It is also much more difficult to break down into subsections. Strauss begins the second part with an analysis of Hermann Cohen and his understanding of Plato and the prophets, which takes up four paragraphs; the next section on the prophets is covered in a mere two paragraphs. Thus, Strauss dedicates much more time to Genesis than to the prophets, although the reasons for this are not immediately apparent. Perhaps he is simply imitating the difference in status between the Torah and the prophets within Judaism, i.e., the difference in status between Moses and those prophets who come later: only Moses saw God face to face. The subsequent two paragraphs are spent considering Socrates' mission according to Plato. The final three paragraphs compare Socrates and the prophets. Hence, the second half can be broken down roughly into four subsections.

For a clearer picture of the structure of "Jerusalem and Athens," I have drawn up the following outline:

I. "The Beginning of the Bible and Its Greek Counterparts" (paragraphs 1–30)
   A. The introduction (paragraph 1)
   B. The critique of culture (paragraphs 2–5)
   C. Biblical criticism (paragraphs 6–9)
   D. The biblical account (paragraphs 10–24)
   E. The Greek counterparts (paragraphs 25–30)
      1. The introduction (paragraph 25)
      2. Hesiod (paragraphs 26–27)
      3. The philosophers (paragraphs 28–30)
II. "On Socrates and the Prophets" (paragraphs 31–41)
   A. Hermann Cohen (paragraphs 31–34)
   B. The prophets (paragraphs 35–36)
   C. Socrates (paragraphs 37–38)
   D. The comparison of the two missions (paragraphs 39–41)

If one looks at the essay as a whole, and if our subdivision is correct, then the central section of the essay is that dedicated to the Greeks. The middle section of "The Beginning of the Bible and Its Greek Counterparts" is toward the beginning of the essay and is devoted to biblical criticism. (As we shall see, Strauss's critique of biblical criticism is crucial to his entire argument.) "On Socrates and the Prophets," in contrast, has no middle section. It should also be noted that although the first section has no middle paragraph, if you consider the essay as a whole, the middle paragraph of the entire essay (paragraph 21) falls within the first section on the beginnings. This paragraph deals with the curse of Canaan, the excellence of Nimrod, and the Tower of Babel. This paragraph, according to Strauss, contains the biblical understanding of the beginning of man as a political animal. Although the first section has no middle paragraph, there is one in "On Socrates and the Prophets" (paragraph 46), the subject of which is the problem of distinguishing between true and false prophets. Again Strauss reminds us of the difficulty that revelation presents to us, i.e., what is its source: does it really come from God and how do we know this?

We can now proceed to an in-depth analysis of "The Beginning of the Bible and Its Greek Counterparts," the first part of "Jerusalem and Athens." In this analysis, we will study Strauss as he says we should study other authors; we will attempt to analyze this essay, taking it quite seriously, noting omissions, indeed following all the rules that Strauss himself said were necessary to understand a difficult and important text.

Chapter Three

The Beginning of "The Beginning of the Bible and Its Greek Counterparts"

**The Introduction
(paragraph 1)**

The first section of "Jerusalem and Athens" begins in a stirring manner. And, in a fashion typical of Strauss, the middle sentence of the opening paragraph goes to the heart of the question: "In order to understand ourselves and to illuminate our trackless way into the future, we must understand Jerusalem and Athens."[1] This brief paragraph—only seven sentences—is filled with impassioned rhetoric. It is Strauss at his most compelling and therefore his most accessible; for he opens "The Beginning of the Bible and Its Greek Counterparts" beautifully. He is self-effacing, almost humble, about his ability to accomplish his purpose as he tells us that his task may be beyond his powers. Not only is the scope of the subject matter immensely difficult, but the fact that he must limit himself to the confines of two public lectures is equally daunting. In pushing himself to the limits, he stirs in his audience a desire to strive nobly as well because "it is better to fail nobly than to succeed basely."[2] He then reminds us that the task before him is something he was asked to do, not one of his own choosing.

We are reminded of the passage in the *Republic* where Socrates is taken against his will by Polemarchus and friends to speak about justice. In the subsequent discussion on the cave, Plato makes it clear that the philosopher is compelled to go back in the cave, in other words, to return to the political realm. The philosopher returns from his contemplation of the highest things out of a sense of duty, not desire. He is, in a sense, coerced. I don't think it is improbable that we are meant to think in these terms given the poetic character of Strauss's words as well as his reminder that he did not set about this task on his own, but at the urging of others. This is not to suggest that Strauss is not being ironic, but that his irony has a purpose behind it. We are thus left to wonder whether, if given the chance, he would have written in a different manner, i.e., if the essay would have taken the same form, or if he would have written it at all. We suspect that Strauss found it necessary to speak about the two great elements that ought to struggle for the allegiance of man's soul.

The opening sentence uniquely summarizes the results of the modern project: "All the hopes that we entertain in the midst of the confusions and dangers of the present are founded positively or negatively, directly or indirectly on the experiences of the past."[3] We are thus confronted with "confusions and dangers" and a "trackless way to the future." We are lost; we have wandered off the path. Modern man attempted to break with the past. In so doing, he has forgotten his foundations or his beginnings; he has forgotten that he was not his own first cause. In terms with which we are already familiar, modernity's aim was progress, not return. Therefore we, as modernity's heirs, are confronted with confusions and dangers that are due to modern man's efforts to transcend and even eradicate the past. As a result, we have forgotten our roots, and it is a self-forgetting. It is immediately understood that this self-forgetting is a loss. Because we do not know where we have been, we do not know where we are going. As Strauss tells us, the deepest roots of Western civilization are in Jerusalem and Athens. But there is a problem: we no longer understand our past; Jerusalem and Athens are a crucial part of that past; therefore, we no longer understand what it means to speak of Jerusalem and Athens. Although we may have forgotten our roots and what they mean, nonetheless, they are a part of us. Strauss insists, "Western man became what he is and is what he is through the coming together of biblical faith and Greek thought."[4] The opening paragraph shows us just what a loss our lack of self-understanding is.

Strauss's break with modernity is immediate: he asserts that we can no longer afford to be ignorant of Jerusalem and Athens. We must turn back in order to illuminate our way into the future. We are what we are most of all because of these two elements. Modernity may have caused confusion, but Strauss does not suggest that it has left an indelible mark upon us in the way that Jerusalem and Athens have. We are what we are more because of these two elements in our soul than because of modernity. Strauss thus immediately rejects modernity by helping us to rediscover our past and, thereby, ourselves. Perhaps we are meant to think of the Socratic dictum, "know thyself." In "Progress or Return," Strauss defines it in the following manner: "'Know thyself' means for the Greeks, know what it means to be a human being, know what is the place of man in the universe, examine your opinions and prejudices, rather than 'Search your heart.'"[5] But self-knowledge is impossible for Western man without knowledge of the past. The end of this rediscovery is twofold: self-understanding and, through that illumination, finding a path to the future. We are at a crisis point, a time for action, and Strauss sets for himself the task of recovery.

The melancholy that begins the essay is a reflection of the destruction brought on by modernity. Philosophers such as Spinoza (who figures predominantly in the paragraphs ahead) had attempted to avoid disputes and destruction, war and death, over questions of theology by making freedom the end of civil society. This lowering of the ends of politics from the classical understanding of forming the citizen's soul ended in bitter failure. Thinking that they were overcoming what they considered to be the irrational character of politics, the moderns developed a purely rational politics based on the principle of self-preservation. By making theology a private concern, the new science of politics could secure man's most basic needs and leave each to his own to consider the highest questions. As a result of this lowering of the ends of politics, there was a correspondent lowering in what was understood as the best regime. Since all men share this basic desire for self-preservation, men were seen as equals. There was, quite naturally, a rise in the republican form of government. In *The Theologico-Political Treatise*, Spinoza defines a republic thus:

> where everyone's judgment is free and unshackled, where each may worship God as his conscience dictates, and where freedom is esteemed before all things dear and precious, I have believed that I should be undertaking no ungrateful or unprofitable task, in demonstrating that not only can such freedom be granted without prejudice to the public peace, but also, that without such freedom, piety cannot flourish nor the public peace be secure.[6]

Although Spinoza thought that lowering the ends of politics would result in a dampening of the cruel tendency within man, events proved otherwise. For freedom cannot be an end in itself without cost, that cost being the destruction brought on by modern attempts to overcome the past. The French Revolution, the rise of Communism, and the Third Reich are but three examples. Modern regimes seem able to survive only if they are tied to a higher end such as natural law. Without that higher purpose, modern regimes remain uncorrupted only as long as the memory of traditional morality lasts. Once that memory fades, corruption inevitably sets in, leading eventually to the excesses of a Weimar Germany. As Strauss knew only too well, the unfettered freedom of the Weimar Republic did not lead, as Spinoza's heir, Hermann Cohen, had suspected, to a new age of toleration and peace, but instead to destruction on a scale hitherto unknown. It was left to Spinoza's and Cohen's successor to pick up the pieces of what remained of the modern project. This was a task Strauss was willing to undertake, and in his analysis of "Jerusalem and Athens," we will see where he suggests modern man should go. Whichever way we are to turn, it will be a turn based on a better understanding. To borrow Strauss's phrase, the question is whether it will be a progress or a return.

The Critique of Culture
(paragraphs 2–5)

Strauss begins his study of reason and revelation with an examination of Genesis. But before he proceeds to the heart of the question, he begins with an indictment of the study of culture. The next four paragraphs are a distillation of his argument against modern social science.[7] He wastes little time debunking social science; yet despite its brevity, his critique is devastating. That Strauss begins in this manner may appear puzzling. It may appear odd that someone whose ostensible purpose is a consideration of the two great claims of reason and revelation would begin his essay with an indictment of sociology. However, strange beginnings are not atypical for Strauss. And, it is not really an unreasonable beginning; for it is the so-called science of sociology that looks at all philosophies, all faiths, all cultures and treats them as all equally valuable. Strauss summarily demonstrates the emptiness of this position.

Strauss begins with an indictment of the study of culture because the study of culture has replaced the study of regimes, a profound lowering of the position of politics. Sociology claims to be a science and understands itself as superior to the ancient study of political things, as an improvement upon classical political philosophy. In imitation of Strauss's subject, this section loses all its beauty immediately, even as soon as the first sentence. These are paragraphs filled with the words of science—"object," "culture," "science," "subjectivity," "concept." They are dry and unmoving and are meant to be. At one point Strauss even makes reference to the poetry of the Arabian Nights as if to remind us of how lacking in beauty this section is, in other words, of how scientific he is being. At the same time, the author's presence becomes removed and remote. With one brief exception, everything is written in the third person.

This rhetorical device is itself a subtle critique of the modern project. Elsewhere Strauss has made it clear that, although the modern project was supposed to be dedicated to the relief of man's estate, the age of science instead heralded a cruelty hitherto unfathomable in its devastation.[8] We are, therefore, confronted with the inhumanity of science, which views human beings and atoms in the same light. Thus, in this section on cultural relativism the prose, in imitation of the modern project itself, becomes sterile. In that sense, this whole section is highly ironic.

The second paragraph begins by turning the two cities into objects; they become, as sociology would have it, "cultures." As "cultures," Jerusalem and Athens appear as only two among many choices. Even more important, as Alan Udoff explains, "Culture proclaims the union of faith and philosophy, Jerusalem and Athens; indeed, it claims to be that union."[9] The study of cultures, in turn, must be done by someone outside those cultures, one who has no preference or bias for any culture, one who thinks objectively, that is, one who thinks that all cultures are equal. This objectivity stands in marked contrast to how these cultures view themselves. Social science's bias is that he who studies a culture understands it better than it understands itself. But this is a mistake. To support this belief, social science must see the high in light of the low. But, as Strauss tells us in his "Introductory Essay" to *Spinoza's Critique of Religion*, "It is safer to try to understand the low in the light of the high than the high in the light of the low. In doing the latter one necessarily distorts the high, whereas in doing the former, one does not deprive the low of the freedom to reveal itself fully as what it is."[10] Fittingly, the paragraph ends with a comparison of electrons, dogs, and cultures. We are reminded again of the inhumanity of modern science. To the social scientist, electrons, dogs, and cultures are equally worthy objects of observation, equally interesting. More important, all of them lack self-knowledge. Just as dogs do not know that they are dogs, cultures do not know that they are cultures. We are, therefore, led to wonder, if these things lack self-knowledge, what of the scientist himself? How can his status be any higher?

Strauss seems to suggest an answer, if only subtly. He opens the paragraph by speaking of "the scientist" who looks at cultures; by the end of the paragraph the scientist has changed to "the scientific student." Assuming that this demotion in rank is intentional, what are we to make of it? The turn is from someone who has knowledge to someone who is attempting to learn, i.e., someone who lacks knowledge. We must also wonder about two other things. First, where does Strauss's audience fall? Are we in the same league as the social scientists? And more important, what of the author himself? Is he also simply a student of cultures? Does he stand above both objects, superior to both Athens and Jerusalem? This question, in particular, will be one that occurs again in "Jerusalem and Athens." One tentative suggestion is that by demoting the scientist to a student Strauss suggests that Jerusalem and Athens may be superior to the student, i.e., capable of teaching him something.

In the third paragraph, Strauss begins his attack on cultural relativism with Zarathustra's "Of 1,000 Goals and One." Here, according to Strauss, Nietzsche speaks of "our subject." This paragraph is quite lengthy—the longest of the section, having twenty-one sentences. The middle sentence, as in the first paragraph, goes to the heart of the problem: it focuses on Nietzsche's inability to belong to any culture, no matter how noble. Nietzsche must remain outside, an unattached yet not detached beholder, because Nietzsche knows that both Jerusalem and Athens are simply prejudices. Nietzsche is different from the social scientist in that he maintains his fierce prejudice, which distinguishes Athens and Jerusalem from dogs and electrons. Yet he knows that it is simply prejudice on his part, for truth is like a woman: each man has his own.

It is interesting that in this section on the Bible and its Greek counterparts the first philosopher cited is Nietzsche. Nietzsche, the man noted for his laughter at the claims of both reason and revelation, is the first one called to speak to the current crisis. Nietzsche is the philosopher who makes it possible to look at the question freshly. Nietzsche, as Strauss says, "started the questioning."[11] After Nietzsche, if philosophy is to be possible at all, it must begin again. Moreover, Nietzsche is the philosopher to show that science, far from being an objective pursuit, had simply replaced one belief system for another that was equally empty. For Nietzsche showed that by its own account of itself, there was no intrinsic superiority of science to any other pursuit.

Nietzsche remained intensely interested in faith despite his pronouncement of the death of God. As Strauss tells us, Nietzsche did not mock Athens and Jerusalem but rather had a "deeper reverence than any other beholder for the sacred tables of the Hebrews as well as of the other nations in question."[12] In "An Introduction to Heideggerian Existentialism," Strauss gives us a hint as to why Nietzsche cannot remain disinterested in religion, indeed why he cannot simply return to classical paganism:

> But there is one decisive difference between Nietzsche's philosophy of the future and Plato's philosophy. Nietzsche's philosopher of the future is an heir to the Bible. He is an heir to that deepening of the soul which has been effected by the Biblical belief in a God that is holy. The philosopher of the future, as distinct from the classical philosopher, will be concerned with the holy. His philosophizing will be intrinsically religious.[13]

Nietzsche's awareness of the necessity of religion, therefore, gives us an indication of why Strauss first turns to Nietzsche. Also, the deepening of the soul that Strauss notes is a further indication of the inherent superiority of Jerusalem to classical mythology. There *is* a distinction between the Judeo-Christian God and Zeus. Whatever we will learn from Hesiod, we will not learn that Zeus is holy. It should be pointed out that Strauss, too, not unlike the philosopher of the future, is very much interested in faith. Indeed, this passage may well suggest how Strauss understood his own efforts. In *Beyond Good and Evil*, Nietzsche calls for a "new species of philosophers." He describes them as the philosophers of the dangerous maybe: "But who will concern himself with such dangerous maybes? For that, one really has to wait for the advent of a new species of philosophers, such as have somehow another and converse taste and propensity from those we have known so far—philosophers of the dangerous 'maybe' in every sense."[14] Perhaps we should consider Strauss a "philosopher of the dangerous maybe" who, as an heir to the Bible himself, is willing to consider the two claimants of reason and revelation. In doing so, sometimes he will ask or at least appear to ask dangerous, even impious, questions. But asking these sorts of dangerous questions may be necessary if there is to be a recovery.

In keeping with his understanding of Nietzschean philosophy, Strauss cites Nietzsche's most "theological" book In *Thus Spoke Zarathustra*, Nietzsche presents his prophet, Zarathustra, who comes down from his mountain with a new message to inspire the last men. Nietzsche describes the last men who now inhabit the world:

> Hourly, they are becoming smaller, poorer, more sterile—poor herbs! poor soil! and soon they shall stand there like dry grass and prairie and verily, weary of themselves and languishing even more than for water—for fire.[15]

To these last men, Zarathustra brings down a new tablet that is beyond good and evil; he foretells the coming of the superman. Zarathustra, combining Moses and John the Baptist, brings a new morality and heralds the coming of a new man. In this sense, then, *Thus Spoke Zarathustra* cannot be understood as an entirely philosophic work, at least as philosophy is conventionally understood.

Only when Strauss mentions Nietzsche does the playfulness that began the lecture return: we move from "*n*" cultures to "1,001 cultures." In keeping with this change, the use of the first person returns here at the transition from science to Nietzsche. Prefiguring this move to Nietzsche, poetry is mentioned. Strauss compares the study of different cultures to a series of exciting tales, Arabian tales. What are we to make of his allusion to the Arabian Nights? Perhaps it is a reminder that the Islamic thinkers, whom Strauss regarded so highly elsewhere, will be absent from the discussion.[16] His reference to the Arabian Nights, in turn, leads to Zarathustra's "Of One Thousand Goals and One." In this speech, Zarathustra mentions many different people and "the tablet of the good which hangs over them" that "is their will to power."[17] Strauss notes that although Nietzsche says that there are a vast number of cultures, he only addresses four and their particular "tables of the good." Strauss, in turn, only mentions two of the four that Nietzsche singles out. Appropriately, Strauss cites the Greeks and the Hebrews. Thus, the first glimpse we have of Jerusalem and Athens is a general one, through the people of the Greeks and the Hebrews.

It is worth comparing Strauss and Nietzsche here. Strauss states: "The peculiarity of the Greeks is the full dedication of the individual to the contest for excellence, distinction, supremacy. The peculiarity of the Hebrews is the utmost honoring of father and mother."[18] In contrast, Nietzsche speaks of them in this manner:

> "You shall always be the first and excel all others: your jealous souls shall love no one, unless it be the friend"—that made the soul of the Greek quiver: thus he walked the path of his greatness. . . . "To honor father and mother and to follow their will to the root of one's soul"—this was the tablet of overcoming that another people hung up over themselves and became powerful and eternal thereby.[19]

Strauss does not, as Nietzsche does, mention the Greek's regard of friendship; he is, however, faithful in his account of Nietzsche's understanding of Hebrew greatness. It is interesting that neither refers to the Greeks as lovers of wisdom. Perhaps that is only an Athenian virtue. We do not think of Spartans as being particularly concerned with philosophy. It is also of interest that the singular thing that most think of as the Jewish contribution to civilization is not mentioned by either Nietzsche or Strauss, i.e., their insistence that their God is one and absolute. The polytheistic nature of other ancient religions is not an unimportant distinction. Yet Strauss does not refer to this. Our first view of Jerusalem and Athens, therefore, fails to mention either reason or revelation and instead refers to what appear to be secondary considerations of friendship and family.

Strauss does makes a parenthetical reference to religion by mentioning the unqualified prohibition against incest in the Jewish religion, which he says is the underpinning of the honoring of mother and father. We should not forget this when we proceed to the analysis of Genesis and consider the children of Adam and Eve. Strauss will not remind us of this prohibition then.

The entire paragraph should be compared to the discussion in *Natural Right and History* regarding the beginning of philosophy.[20] There Strauss speaks of the intelligent man, perhaps a traveler, who discovers through his wanderings that not all people hold the same things dear. Indeed, what one people holds sacred, others do not. The divine origin of these codes is called into question. Nature then becomes the standard. But instead of discovering nature, Nietzsche remains simply a beholder, albeit an admiring one, of the great tables, of the differing wills to power. The middle sentence reminds us: "Yet since he is only a beholder of these tables, since what one table commends or commands is incompatible with what the others command, he is not subject to the commandments of any."[21] Nietzsche cannot rely on nature; a teleological understanding of nature is only a sham for him, another will to power that has no separate existence of its own. In *Beyond Good and Evil*, Nietzsche says of nature:

> Imagine a being like nature, wasteful beyond measure, indifferent beyond measure, without purposes and consideration, without mercy and justice, fertile and desolate and uncertain at the same time; imagine indifference itself as a power—how *could* you live according to this indifference?[22]

Since he cannot refer to nature as a standard, Nietzsche demands a universal, even a superhuman, culture that will overcome the lack of unity in cultures so that truth will no longer be particular, but universal; that is, truth will no longer contradict itself. In the last sentence of this paragraph, Strauss gives us a hint about what that culture would need to be when he speaks of the superman: "The super-man is meant to unite in himself Jerusalem and Athens on the highest level."[23]

The question of where Strauss stands becomes more emphatic in this paragraph; it is the difficulty already mentioned in the introduction, that of separating Strauss from his subject. Except for the transition to Nietzsche, everything is written in the third person. It therefore becomes difficult to separate Nietzsche and Strauss. This problem becomes even more apparent in this paragraph as Strauss makes it clear that Nietzsche's critique of culture is compelling. We are thus led to suspect that he is a disciple of Nietzsche's. However, Strauss does set himself apart from Nietzsche, in a decisive respect, by stating forcefully: "Truth is not a woman so that each man can have his own truth as he can have his own wife."[24] Strauss may agree with Nietzsche's critique of culture, but he does not ally himself with Nietzsche's philosophy. If, as the East Coast Straussians insist, Strauss sides with Nietzsche in the end, we would expect to find this to be the alternative that Strauss eventually embraces.

The problem with social science or the science of cultures, as Nietzsche illustrates so accurately, is that it is culture-bound, an act of "spiritual imperialism" of "19th century Western culture." Far from being truly objective, it is "radically subjective." Strauss asserts that "one cannot behold, i.e., truly understand, any culture unless one is firmly rooted in one's own culture or unless one belongs in one's capacity as a beholder to some culture."[25] This is a peculiar and complex statement, which Strauss does not explain. It is unclear what a beholder is. The only person whom Strauss calls a beholder is Nietzsche. Thus we are left with a puzzle. Again, we wonder about Strauss: does he consider himself a beholder as well?

In the fourth paragraph, Nietzsche disappears and we return to the pedantic tone of the opening of the section. The entire paragraph is only two sentences long—the shortest paragraph of the entire work. The preceding one exposed the science of cultures as fraudulent: social science's first premise cannot withstand logic. In this brief paragraph, Strauss exposes another problem: the moral bankruptcy of the science of cultures. Because the science of cultures remains neutral regarding the goodness or badness of any culture, much less of any philosophy or morality, it must posit pluralism as the goal, as its table of the good. However, its very assertion that pluralism is the right way lends itself to the criticism that "pluralism is a monism," the very thing that it wishes to avoid.[26] The problem of cultural relativism is that it is self-contradictory. It is not able to maintain its own relativism. It wants a universal culture of tolerance, a universal culture of last men. Through Nietzsche, Strauss has let us see what a contemptible goal this is.

In the fifth paragraph, Strauss posits his own method of proceeding. He rescues social science by showing the true manner in which one should proceed to study cultures objectively, i.e., by attempting to understand peoples as they understood themselves. Of course, this is also how he always maintained that great books should be read and, therefore, it comes as no surprise. Here we learn of social science's derivative character because the study of cultures is the study of a by-product. The final sentence of this paragraph aptly summarizes his position that "culture is the accidental result" of a concern "with the Truth."[27] We sense that we will soon be leaving the world of the scientist, the world of "*n*" cultures, in order to come to grips with grander questions. Indeed, that is exactly what happens. The ascent has begun. Having sufficiently destroyed the notion of the science of cultures, the conversation is immediately elevated. We are no longer interested in culture but in wisdom.

Biblical Criticism
(paragraphs 6–9)

The next four paragraphs are dedicated to exposing biblical criticism, the bastard child of the Enlightenment. Modernity's rejection not only of natural teleology but also of an omnipotent God required the destruction of the belief in God's providence. With the rise of Protestantism, the Bible became the chief instrument that espoused a providential understanding of God. Hence, in order to root out the belief in providence, it was necessary to destroy man's faith in the Bible. The attack was begun in earnest by Spinoza. In "Progress or Return," Strauss reveals that Spinoza was the first to abandon Judaism for progress:

> That break was effected in a classic manner by a solitary man—Spinoza. Spinoza denied the truth of Judaism—Judaism, which includes, of course, the Bible, is a set of prejudices and superstitious practices of the ancient tribes. Spinoza found in this mass of heterogeneous lore some elements of truth, but he did not consider this as peculiar to Judaism.[28]

Once again, the Jewish problem is a paradigm for the human problem; for the rejection of the Torah leads to the rejection of the entire Bible.

This section is a preparation for turning to the Bible itself. In a sense, it will tell us how to turn to the Bible because in this section Strauss will have to begin to answer the question of what the Bible is. The section on the Bible that follows will be the lengthiest section not only of the first part, but of the entire lecture. Its prelude, although short in comparison, is dense and at times difficult.

Jerusalem and Athens, once they were turned into objects, faded into the background during Strauss's critique of culture. In the opening paragraph of this section, however, they return. At the same time, the audience is reminded once again of the author as the use of the first person becomes omnipresent. Strauss makes his presence felt with such phrases as "our intention," "compel us," "we must," "we see," "we are," etc. In all, there are fourteen uses of the first person in this paragraph—the same as the number of sentences. It is a paragraph filled with short, easily read, rapid-fire sentences: Strauss has once again become compelling.

Strauss insists that because he is to speak of Jerusalem and Athens, he is forced "to go beyond the self-understanding of either."[29] We recall his peculiar statement regarding the beholder. Here again, there is an allusion to the element of force as Strauss is compelled. Of more interest, however, is Strauss's decision to go beyond either Jerusalem or Athens. How is it possible to go beyond either? Did we not just discover that the scientific ideal of complete objectivity was impossible unless we are rooted somewhere? Is there a higher ground than reason and revelation? As we have seen, Strauss has insisted rather emphatically elsewhere that the answer is no.[30] In "Jerusalem and Athens," however, Strauss evades the question by pointing to something that both the Bible and the greatest works of the Greeks claim is the highest thing, and that is wisdom.

Of course, Jerusalem and Athens each say wisdom is something different. The distinction between the two is immediate. Strauss mentions Greek philosophers, Greek poets, and the Torah; all three are said to be wise. The first two, obviously, are groups of men; they were held to be wise by others. The Torah, a work (for we still have not been told whether or not it is a book) and not a person, asserts it is "'your wisdom in the eyes of the nations.'"[31] The Greeks, both poets and philosophers, at least at this point make no claim for themselves; the Torah, on the other hand, literally speaks for itself and for God.

The first quotation from the Bible, it should be noted, has no citation except that Strauss tells us it is from the Torah. It is taken from the fourth chapter of Deuteronomy. According to Robert Sacks, who has done an exhaustive commentary of Genesis by following Strauss's lead, this passage and the verses that follow "declare that the greatness of the Torah is visible to all men."[32] Thus, Strauss lets our first encounter with the Bible leave the impression that it is knowable to everyone who approaches it with care. But it is not as simple as he would have it seem.

In "How To Begin To Study *The Guide of the Perplexed*," Strauss refers to the same biblical passage in his consideration of Maimonides' discussion on God's incorporeality. In this essay, he states the problem forthrightly:

> But both [Maimonides and the addressee] know that the literal meaning of the Law is not always its true meaning and that the literal meaning is certainly not the true meaning when it contradicts reason, for otherwise the Law could not be "your wisdom and your understanding in the sight of the nations."[33]

Interestingly, in "Jerusalem and Athens," Strauss never makes the distinction between the literal and true meaning of any given passage in Genesis. Instead, we are to rely on Strauss's own exegesis to make these distinctions silently or to avoid such problems entirely.

Keeping in mind that the essay is like a dialogue or a conversation between reason and revelation, it is important to note that Nietzsche speaks first, and the Torah second. It is also worth mentioning that Strauss uses the term "Torah" and not "Bible" here. Thus, the first to speak for Jerusalem is the sacred text of the Jews.

Since both Jerusalem and Athens claim to have wisdom and both define it differently, we are forced to understand both of them to see which truly has wisdom. Both cannot be correct; and more important, each deny the other's claim to wisdom. We, therefore, begin to wonder whether Strauss really thinks it is possible to go beyond the self-understanding of either Jerusalem or Athens.

To begin, the Bible says that the beginning of wisdom is fear of the Lord. Again, the citation is unattributed and this time, it is not even a direct quotation. Moreover, we are back to the more general term of "Bible." There are several possibilities for the origin of this citation: it could be taken from Proverbs 1:7, "The fear of the Lord is the beginning of knowledge, but fools scorn wisdom and discipline"; Job 28:28, "The fear of the Lord is wisdom, and to turn from evil is understanding"; or Ecclesiasticus 1:14, "The essence of wisdom is fear of the Lord."[34] It is interesting that the most likely candidate is Proverbs, which tradition attributes to King Solomon, the wisest of men. The other possibility is the Gentile Job. The book of Job is the only book in the Old Testament that is not written by or about a Jew.[35] Ecclesiasticus or Sirach is yet another book from the wisdom literature. Although Strauss does not tell us which text he is referring to, it is not necessary. Each of the possibilities declares the same thing: wisdom begins in fear of the Lord. It should be noted, however, that none of these possibilities is from the Torah.

Strauss contrasts this account of wisdom with the Greek understanding that wisdom begins with wonder. On their face, these two notions of how to attain wisdom appear decidedly different. Moreover, fear of the Lord and wonder, Strauss insists, are mutually incompatible. It is worth quoting Strauss at length here:

> We are thus compelled from the very beginning to make a choice, to take a stand. Where then do we stand? We are confronted with the incompatible claims of Jerusalem and Athens to our allegiance. We are open to both and willing to listen to each. We ourselves are not wise but we wish to become wise. We are seekers for wisdom, "philo-sophoi." By saying that we wish to hear first and then to act to decide, we have already decided in favor of Athens against Jerusalem.[36]

We must listen to each claim because we are not wise. This is completely in accord with the Straussian definition of a philosopher as one who desires but does not have wisdom. Strauss even speaks of "philo-sophoi." Still, his statement that he has already decided in favor of Athens by even considering the question comes as somewhat of a surprise. In asserting this, Strauss must insist that this openness or willingness to consider either claim is somehow contrary to Jerusalem. It is easy to see that philosophy, if it is understood as a search for wisdom, must remain open; but, apparently, faith cannot remain open.

This decision in advance for philosophy is contrary to what we had thought from simply looking at the inclusive nature of the title "Jerusalem *and* Athens." It would seem that we need proceed no further, that philosophy has won. If even considering the two claims violates the principles of Jerusalem, then thoughtful human beings must side with Athens. For if, in order to be faithful to Jerusalem, we must somehow deny our ability to reason, then it seems almost inhuman to side with Jerusalem. But Strauss does not stop here. Indeed, he proceeds at great length. Is this not a contradiction? Could it be that he does not think it as simple as he presents it here?

Part of the problem seems to stem from the use of the word "fear." We sense immediately that fear is somehow ignoble, but wonder is an attitude worthy of men. But perhaps this notion of ours is a modern one. Perhaps because we are ignorant of the past, we do not understand what fear of the Lord means. Traditionally, fear of the Lord, which is a virtue for Christians and Jews alike, is not understood simply as fear but as something more akin to awe, a synonym for wonder.[37] It is unclear what Strauss is up to at this point. One thing is certain, however: he can count on the fact that the majority of his audience will miss this problem.

No matter what fear of the Lord is, the first thing that should be said about it is that it must be learned; the prerequisite for this Judeo-Christian virtue is faith. Although faith may be understood as a gift, we are not born with it, nor is it something simply intuited. Similar to philosophy, we must learn about it if we are to use the gift properly. Unlike philosophy, it is not something that we can learn through studying nature. Revelation is necessary precisely because human beings by their very nature are limited in what they can know about God on their own. He must reveal Himself: one has to hear about revelation whether it be from the prophet directly, from the writings he leaves behind, or from tradition. In other words, we have "to hear first" and then decide. It therefore seems that we are confronted with an assertion that isn't meant to be taken seriously, although many take this as Strauss's final word on the subject.[38] It should also be noted that, rather than denying man his use of reason, Scripture asserts that man is made in the image of God.[39] Traditionally, this has been understood to refer to the rational element in man's soul.[40] Although man is not God, he is a reflection of Him. Indeed, as we will soon find out, the Bible itself has a reasonable beginning. Jerusalem therefore cannot be completely irrational. Strauss is constantly telling his readers that first-rate minds do not make obvious mistakes. This seems to be one; therefore, it must be intentional. If it is, what does it mean to cloak the compelling rationality of Jerusalem? Could it be that he is lulling the atheists to sleep?

The next paragraph, consisting of eighteen sentences, is the longest one in this section. It is also the most difficult paragraph of the essay so far. Here Strauss attacks the historical-critical method of studying the Bible begun by Spinoza, who, in turn, learned it from Machiavelli. Although present-day biblical criticism and that begun by Spinoza are different in focus, they have the same first principle: the denial of the possibility of miracles. The main difference between Spinoza and the biblical critics who followed him in the 19th and 20th centuries, Strauss maintains, is the raising of imagination from the subrational status it held in Spinoza.

Strauss begins this discussion with the comment that the preemptive decision in favor of Athens over Jerusalem is a necessary one for anyone who cannot be orthodox. Those who cannot be orthodox must agree with the "historical-critical study of the Bible."[41] We are led to assume that Strauss includes himself in this group because he says "all of us who cannot be orthodox."[42] This is an interesting revelation. We had not expected Strauss to side so openly with Spinoza and his successors on how to study the Bible. Strauss next considers what tradition says about the Bible: "The Bible was traditionally understood as the true and authentic account of the deeds of God and men from the beginning till the restoration after the Babylonian exile."[43] Thus, although Strauss uses the inclusive word "Bible," he limits the term to the Torah and the prophets. The deeds of God, Strauss explains, are both His law and His inspiration of the prophets. Men's deeds consist of praise of God, prayers to God, and spreading God's warnings against iniquity to others. The Bible is, thus, a recording of God's deeds for man and man's deeds before God. As Strauss notes in "The Mutual Influence of Theology and Philosophy," "The book, the *Bible*, is the account of what God has done and what he has promised. It is not speculation about God."[44] We already know from the title that Strauss is limiting his discussion to the beginning of the Bible only. In keeping with this, he will only look at Genesis except during his discussion of the Lord's name, in which he turns to Exodus.

As has been suggested, the historical-critical method is derivative. Its foundation was laid by Machiavelli, who spoke in terms of "memories of ancient histories." Strauss gives a citation for this in his first footnote, *Discourses*, I.16. But when we turn to this chapter in the *Discourses* for a further clarification of what Machiavelli meant by "memories of ancient histories," we find something entirely different. Instead of being about the Bible, this chapter is about what happens to a people who, accustomed to living under a prince, find themselves accidentally free. This is odd and therefore requires further investigation.

In I.16, Machiavelli maintains that a newly free people will have a difficult time maintaining their liberty for two reasons. First, being used to a tyrant's rule, they willingly change masters; although the people clamor for freedom, what they truly prefer is security. Second, even if they truly desire liberty, they will have many enemies, namely the nobility. Machiavelli thus urges them to kill the sons of Brutus. The second brutal act that he mentions in this chapter is the one perpetrated by the tyrant Clearchus, whom Machiavelli applauds for chopping the entire nobility to pieces. Through this dreadful act, Clearchus eliminated the problem of the nobility and gained the populace's trust as well. Machiavelli next speaks of how a prince must gain the trust of the people if he wishes to maintain his rule: "He then who sets out to govern the masses, whether in a free state or in a principality, and does not secure himself against those who are hostile to the new order, is setting up a form of government which will be but short-lived."[45] The key to everything is the condition of the multitude, i.e., whether or not they are corrupt. Thus, Machiavelli concludes his chapter with praise of the Roman people, who due to their lack of corruption were able to regain their freedom upon the death of the sons of Brutus.

To find the passage that Strauss actually quotes, it is necessary to turn to Book III.5, entitled "Changes of Religion and of Language, together with such Misfortunes as Floods and Pestilences, obliterate the Records of the Past."[46] This passage is crucial to understanding Machiavelli's and Spinoza's critique of the Bible, because in III.5 Machiavelli lays out the arguments that Strauss presents in encapsulated form here. In this chapter, Machiavelli attacks the doctrine of creation. Machiavelli argues that people believe in creation because our memories of events go only to a certain point and no further. Machiavelli argues that this misunderstanding is due to periodic universal floods in which the only ones who survive are

> rude mountain-dwellers who have no knowledge of antiquity and so cannot hand it down to posterity; and should there be among the survivors anyone who has such knowledge he will conceal it or distort it in his own fashion so as to establish his own reputation and that of his family, with the result that there will remain to his successors just so much as he has chosen to record and nothing more.[47]

Although he does not mention Noah specifically, it takes little imagination to guess that Machiavelli is hinting that Noah invented the tales in Genesis to bring glory on himself and his family. And he argues further in this chapter that any given religion can last no longer than a few millennia, with each new religion wiping out all traces of the preceding one.

Why should Strauss reference one chapter while quoting from another? There are several possibilities. First, Strauss could be drawing our attention to man's current status. Modernity, having freed man from the bondage of not only nature but religion as well, has succeeded only in destroying that which is noble. Man, having been cut off from the noblest things, has become little more than a slave to his own tyrannical desires. He has, therefore, become easy prey for tyrants himself. On the other hand, Strauss could also be showing us that, after he has decimated the arguments of social science, he has given us the status of a newly freed people. With that new-found freedom comes danger. Does Strauss want us to compare him to the tyrant Clearchus? Is his task the beheading of Spinoza and Machiavelli? If so, we must watch who or what Strauss puts in their place. Of course, Strauss may want us to think of both alternatives; they are not mutually exclusive. More important, by referring the reader indirectly to Machiavelli's critique of the Bible, Strauss keeps the impious nature of such questions hidden.

It is worthwhile to take a brief look at Strauss on Machiavelli. In *Thoughts on Machiavelli*, Strauss describes the *Discourses* in the following manner: "If it is true, as I believe it is, that the Bible sets forth the demands of morality and religion in their purest and most intransigent form, the central theme of the *Discourses* must be the analyses of the Bible." [48] Strauss later clarifies Machiavelli's position, saying that it is a "criticism of Biblical theology."[49] Furthermore, he writes that according to Machiavelli:

> the Biblical writers present themselves as historians, as human beings who report what God said and did, while in fact they make God say and do what in their opinion a most perfect being would say and do; the ground of what presents itself as the experience of the Biblical writers is their notion of a most perfect being; that notion is so compelling that the "Ought" comes to sight as the "Is"; this connection is articulated by the ontological proof; there is no way which leads from "the things of the world" to the Biblical God; the only proof which commands respect, although it is not a genuine proof, is the ontological proof.[50]

Notice that Strauss, through Machiavelli, is much more explicit than he is in "Jerusalem and Athens" about what is at stake in the problem of the Bible and its authorship.

The criticism of biblical theology found in Machiavelli was made more explicit by Spinoza in his *Theological-Political Treatise*, which, as Strauss explains in "Jerusalem and Athens," "is frankly anti-theological; Spinoza read the Bible as he read the Talmud and the Koran."[51] Machiavelli, although anti-theological, was not frankly so. Spinoza was much bolder than his predecessor.

Standing against tradition, Spinoza and those who follow him are quite frank in their assessment that the Bible is not an account of the deeds of God and men, but only a compilation of ancient stories that are a mixture of legend, superstition, and prejudice. Strauss insists that the only way in which Spinoza and the biblical critics can come to this conclusion is by presuming the impossibility of miracles. The ar-

The Beginning of the "Beginning" 53

gument against miracles is a powerful one, for he says in the "Introductory Essay" that a return to orthodoxy is possible "only if Spinoza was wrong in every respect."[52] In "Jerusalem and Athens," Strauss summarizes Spinoza's critique of the Bible: "the Bible consists to a considerable extent of self-contradictory assertions, of remnants of ancient prejudices or superstitions, and of the outpourings of an uncontrolled imagination; in addition it is poorly compiled and poorly preserved."[53] In order to defend the Bible, and thereby Jerusalem, Strauss must address Spinoza's charges. What is at stake is the possibility of the recovery of Jerusalem as an alternative to philosophy. As we will see, Strauss will show that the Bible, or at least Genesis, presents itself as a coherent whole.

What is the historical-critical study of the Bible, which those who cannot be orthodox must accept? Strauss tells us that it is the "attempt to understand the various layers of the Bible as they were understood by their immediate addressees."[54] Because the Bible is from the remote past, because it may simply be "memories of ancient histories," it is a difficult task to understand it as it was understood then. Although there is much in the Bible that is historical, there is also, Strauss allows, much that is considered mythical today. But this distinction between history and myth is Greek in origin and, therefore, alien to the Bible. The distinction must be discarded as the Bible treats the mythical and historical parts as equally true: "what Israel 'in fact' did or suffered cannot be understood except in the light of the 'facts' of Creation and Election."[55] The distinction between myth and history has arisen simply because unbelievers have declared only certain parts of the Bible to be historical or true. Thus, Strauss presents us with the first failure of biblical criticism: it fails to understand the Bible as it was understood by the immediate addressees of the Bible.

It should be noted that a not so subtle distinction is made between how Strauss says the Bible ought to be read and how he has said other great books must be read. Strauss, as we have seen, contends that the proper way to read a great book is to read it as it was understood by the author himself, but here he focuses our attention on the addressees of the Bible. Why the change from author to audience? One unstated yet plausible reason for this change is that it would be impious to suggest the possibility of understanding the author of the Bible if that author is God Himself.[56]

To reinforce the failure of biblical criticism, Strauss ends the paragraph with the declaration that the Bible considers unbelievers fools. This is yet another unattributed reference from the Bible. Psalm 14 declares, "The impious fool says in his heart, 'There is no God.'" From the point of view of the Bible, everything in the Bible is believable to those who fear the Lord. For those who believe, there is no distinction between myth and history because miracles are possible. Strauss tells us that the miracles recorded in the Bible are not there to convince atheists but rather to help those who have little faith or who worship false gods. He reminds us that there is no biblical word for doubt.[57]

This leads us to question the Bible's ability to convince those who cannot be orthodox. We must also wonder how this relates to the passage in Deuteronomy 4 that Strauss pointed to previously, which suggested that the Torah is accessible to all. It is beginning to appear as if those who wish to study the Bible will need someone to guide them.

Strauss ends this complex paragraph with a restatement of Psalm 14. This time, however, he refers the reader to Francis Bacon's essay, "Of Atheism." Unlike his use of the *Discourses*, the reference to Bacon does include the use of the Psalm. Strauss's use of Bacon is peculiar because Bacon is not known for his piety, but in this particular essay Bacon cites the Psalm in order to argue that "atheism is rather in the lip than the heart of man."[58]

Bacon begins by siding rather forcefully with the belief in divine order and providence. He acknowledges that "It is true that a little philosophy inclineth man's mind to atheism, but depth in philosophy bringeth men's minds about to religion. . . ."[59] The entire essay is an attempt to persuade the reader that philosophy is harmless, that it leads man to a belief in God and even to a providential God. He also contends that history has incorrectly accused past philosophers of atheism. Bacon argues that Democritus and Epicurus, although notorious for their disbelief, were far from atheism. He further insists that problems in religion, such as the division of sects and the scandalous behavior of some priests, not philosophy, lead men to atheism. He ends the essay by noting that Cicero was correct that the belief in God's providence results in virtue among the citizenry.

At first glance, Bacon appears as a champion of religion in this essay but closer examination shows that all he really applauds is religion's utility. Belief in a deity is useful because it encourages man to strive beyond himself. This reading is confirmed by an examination of his other works, such as *The New Atlantis*, in which science becomes the new religion and good citizens sacrifice themselves readily for the advancement of knowledge. Interestingly, though, in "Of Superstition," the essay that follows "Of Atheism," Bacon contradicts his argument that atheism is harmful by stating that atheists do no harm. He writes, "Atheism leaves a man to sense, to philosophy, to natural piety, to

The Beginning of the "Beginning" 55

laws, to reputation; all which may be guides to an outward moral virtue. . . ."[60]

It is interesting to note that Strauss mentions this same essay of Bacon's in "Mutual Influence." There, in conjunction with Bacon, he also refers to Elijah's defeat of the priests of Baal on Carmel (1 Kings 18): the Israelites return to the worship of the God of Israel and the worshippers of Baal are convinced that the Israelites' God is the true one because they do not question that the God of Israel could send fire from heaven. Idolaters are capable of believing in miracles because they believe in the possibility of a god or gods intervening in human affairs. As Strauss notes, the Bible does not record whether there were any impartial witnesses to the event, in other words, any unbelievers. He uses Bacon's essay to buttress his argument that "unassisted human reason is invincibly ignorant of divine revelation."[61] Strauss is quick to state that this does not prove the impossibility of miracles but rather that man must choose: "For if there were certain knowledge, there would be no need for faith, for trust, for true obedience, for free surrender to God."[62] Again, Strauss confronts us with a choice—although he argues revelation's case more forcefully in "Mutual Influence" than he does in paragraph seven.

With this paragraph, the scope of "Jerusalem and Athens" has widened immeasurably. It is not simply Nietzsche and Strauss against current-day social scientists. Strauss has now set himself against the founders of modernity: Machiavelli, Spinoza, and Bacon. There is an echo from the opening paragraphs of "Jerusalem and Athens," in which Strauss set himself against modernity so forcefully.

In paragraph eight, Strauss makes a series of assertions. He has now become *the* authority on the Bible. He begins by making an interesting distinction between the Bible and theology. Remember that Strauss has yet to address the question of what exactly the Bible is. At this point, he is content to assert that theology, as distinct from the Bible simply, has a concept of miracles because it has a concept of nature. Nature is something foreign to the Bible. Remember that Strauss has argued elsewhere that there is in fact no word for nature in the Hebrew Bible.[63] The temptation, then, is to assume that a "poetic concept of miracles" is at work, but this, too, is foreign to the Bible. Poetry cannot be ascribed to the Bible either, although song may be. We learn that the concept of song is distinct from poetry, although we are not told in what way. As an example of what might be considered a poetic concept of miracles, Strauss calls our attention to Psalm 114, in which nature behaves "unnaturally": in the presence of God, the mountains skip and the sea flees.[64] Strauss says that it is unclear whether the author meant the Psalm to be taken literally.[65] But Strauss does allow that the presence of God evokes extraordinary behavior from His creatures; they behave other than is their "way."[66] It is interesting that he uses a psalm as an example of what might appear to be a poetical miracle. Strauss does not use any example that tradition holds to be miraculous, such as the parting of the Red Sea. In other words, he does not refer to any miracles found within the Torah itself.

Rather than developing these distinctions between poetry, song, nature, and miracle, Strauss states that it is simpler to assert that the impossibility of miracles has now been relegated to the standing of an undemonstrable hypothesis. As he argues in "Mutual Influence," philosophy "suffers a defeat as soon as it starts an offensive of its own, as soon as it tries to refute, not the necessarily inadequate proofs of revelation but revelation itself."[67] This demotion, he insists, is due to the victory of science over natural theology. Thus, the ability to deny miracles disappears when nature is unknowable. The hypothetical character of the impossibility of miracles fits in with the rest of biblical criticism, which is based on undemonstrable hypotheses as well.

As we approach paragraph nine, we are in a quandary. With the foundations of biblical criticism destroyed, there seems to be no place to turn for those who cannot be orthodox. How is it possible for them to look at the Bible objectively? Strauss surprises us yet again. Even though he has just asserted that biblical criticism is based on unfounded premises, he grants it the upper hand, albeit qualifiedly:

> Let us grant that the Bible and in particular the Torah consists to a considerable extent of "memories of ancient histories," even of memories of memories; but memories of memories are not necessarily distorting or pale reflections of the original; they may be re-collections of re-collections, deepenings through meditation of the primary experiences.[68]

With this passage, Strauss has found a neutral ground that will allow all of us to consider the Bible seriously. Because memories have deepened through meditation, it is unimportant to find the original author. This understanding of the Bible will be discussed again in the second part, "On Socrates and the Prophets." Thus, at the close of the section on biblical criticism, he rescinds his determination to make an advance decision in favor of Athens. We have come full circle. It is now possible to consider Jerusalem reasonably. This marks the essay's transition to the biblical account of the beginning.

The last thing we learn in this section is that although the Bible presents us with what theology would call miraculous events, the Bible does not present itself as miraculous. What is written about may be miraculous, but it does not say that the writing and the compiling of the speeches of God and the deeds of man are miraculous. Thus, we are allowed to consider the Bible as a rational document. The Bible may record supernatural events, but it does not claim to be supernatural itself. It does claim to be God's wisdom before the nations.

Paragraph nine closes with an abrupt change. Strauss announces that he will look at the beginning of the Bible, which rather coincidentally deals with the beginning of things. As Strauss says playfully, "The Bible begins reasonably."[69]

Chapter Four

The Biblical Account of the Beginning

Strauss and the Bible

We are now ready to proceed to Strauss's consideration of the Bible. "The Biblical Account of the Beginning" is the longest section not only of the first part, but of the entire essay.[1] Having fifteen paragraphs, it is even longer than "On Socrates and the Prophets," the entire second part of "Jerusalem and Athens." Thus, simply in terms of space, Strauss dedicates more time to the consideration of the Bible than to any other source. In "The Biblical Account of the Beginning," Strauss provides a careful retelling of specific events in Genesis and, as in Strauss's other exegetical works, this version sometimes leads to surprising results. Strauss's discussion of the Bible is narrative in style. With one important exception in the final paragraph of this section, Strauss once again allows himself to fade into the background. Unlike the section on social science, however, his account of the Bible is far from dry. Strauss covers the events recounted in Genesis from the creation to Abraham's sacrifice of Isaac. He ends with a consideration of who the God of Abraham, Isaac, and Jacob is through an examination of God's revelation of His name to Moses. In imitation of Genesis, man becomes the focus of Strauss's analysis of the Bible. Hence, Strauss lets us learn about the biblical God through His interaction with man.

The subjects covered in this section are listed below:

The Biblical Account of the Beginning

1. The First Creation Account (paragraphs 10–11)
2. The Second Creation Account (paragraphs 12–14)
3. The Fall (paragraphs 15–17)

4. Cain and Abel (paragraph 18)
5. Noah and the Flood (paragraphs 19–20)
6. The Curse of Canaan, Nimrod, and Babel (paragraph 21)
7. Abraham (paragraphs 22–23)
8. God's Name (paragraph 24)

It is important to note that there are, in a sense, two middle paragraphs in this section. Not only is there a middle paragraph for the section itself, but the middle paragraph of the entire essay falls within "The Biblical Account of the Beginning" as well. Strauss considers the sin of Cain in the central paragraph of the section. In that paragraph, we learn that the foundations of civilization are all laid by the sons of Cain; they are laid in blood. What the sons of Cain bring to the world is contrary to what Strauss repeatedly implies is the central teaching of the Bible, i.e., that man is meant to live in simplicity. In contrast, the central paragraph of "Jerusalem and Athens," at first glance, appears to be simply a transitional one, bridging the gap between Noah and Abraham. Closer examination, however, reveals it as a further commentary on politics and civilization or man's constant attempt to overcome his own limitations.

With the close of the last section, Strauss indicated that reason and revelation may not be the absolute antagonists he had first said they were. Indeed, with the last paragraph, he was compelled to admit that the Bible at least begins reasonably. In this section, the case will be made for revelation, although Strauss does not openly present it as his defense of Jerusalem. All cursory indications would suggest that, if anything, Strauss is hostile to Jerusalem, but there is evidence that this is not his last word on the subject. By his own admission, in order to defend Jerusalem, he will need to demonstrate that the Bible is not filled, as Spinoza claims, with self-contradictions, ancient prejudices, and superstitions; it is not simply the "outpouring of an uncontrolled imagination" that is "poorly compiled and poorly preserved."[2] In analyzing this section, it will be interesting to see if Strauss answers all of Spinoza's challenges.

Strauss does not present his defense of revelation here in the same terms as he does elsewhere. Although we know that revelation is connected somehow with obedience, we are not given much information in "Jerusalem and Athens" on what revelation is exactly. All we know thus far is that, according to revelation, wisdom begins with fear of the Lord. Strauss does not speak of what revelation means. This omission is important because, as Strauss makes clear elsewhere, revelation means different things to different religions. In *Persecution and the Art of Writing*, for instance, Strauss is careful to distinguish between Christian revelation, on the one hand, and Jewish and Islamic revelation, on the other:

> Revelation as understood by Jews and Muslims has the character of Law (*torah, shari'a*) rather than of Faith. Accordingly, what first came to the sight of the Islamic and Jewish philosophers in their reflections on Revelation was not a creed or a set of dogmas, but a social order, if an all-comprehensive order, which regulates not merely actions but thoughts or opinions as well. Revelation thus understood lent itself to being interpreted by loyal philosophers as the perfect law, the perfect political order. Being philosophers, the *falasifa*, as they were called, attempted to arrive at a perfect understanding of the phenomenon of Revelation. Yet Revelation is intelligible to man only to the extent to which it takes place through the intermediacy of secondary causes, or to the extent to which it is a natural phenomenon. The medium through which God reveals Himself to man is a prophet, i.e., a human being.[3]

As we shall see, Strauss too will follow the loyal philosophers by interpreting revelation as the perfect law. Be that as it may, Strauss says little directly about law in "Jerusalem and Athens." His focus is instead on the lessons of Genesis.

It is unclear why Strauss deviates here from his normal method of careful differentiation. One possibility is that he intends to blur the lines distinguishing Judaism and Christianity. Elsewhere, Strauss makes it clear that Christianity, in contradistinction to Judaism, is even open to philosophy:

> Christianity, and not Judaism, is based on the most perfect divine revelation. Both its universalist and its spiritual character, as contrasted with the particularist and carnal character of Judaism in particular, explain why the ascent to philosophy is easier or more natural for the Christian than for the Jew, who as such "despises" philosophy.[4]

Thus, it is clear that Strauss understands the distinctions regarding revelation. It is, therefore, strange that he makes no such distinctions in the present essay. One possible reason is that what he speaks about in "Jerusalem and Athens" holds for both traditions, because it is undeniable that both Christianity and Judaism share the biblical account of the beginning. Another possibility is that for the purposes of this work Strauss wants all revealed religions to stand together against modernity, as he suggests elsewhere they must do in order to fight communism; in doing so, they do not deny their disagreements but only obscure them so that they may stand against a graver threat: "Their union requires that they conceal from themselves and from the world that they are incompatible with each other—that each regards the other as indeed noble, but untrue."[5] Strauss's intention will become clearer as we proceed.

Strauss accords the author of the Bible the same regard that he would any great writer; the implicit assumption of this entire section is that the author wrote carefully. An underlying, if unstated, assumption of the upcoming analysis is that the Bible is a coherent whole, not a poorly compiled account. Although the question of authorship is uncertain, Strauss treats Genesis as if it is the work of one mind, of one who does not say anything without a purpose. Thus, from the beginning, Strauss is on the attack against Spinoza's claims. Spinoza himself, however, will not be mentioned again.

Strauss does not consider the question of what the Bible is at this point but saves his analysis until the next section, where he compares the Bible to Hesiod's *Theogony*. We are simply presented with the Bible as *the* authority for Jerusalem. Consequently, we are presented with arguments in the Bible before we consider the fundamental question of what the Bible is. In other words, we are not told why it has authority or why we should consider the Bible as the exposition of Jerusalem's defense.

Strauss does not turn to tradition for guidance on interpreting any given passage of the Bible. Remember his critique of the biblical critics: they failed to understand the Bible as it was understood by its immediate addressees. This allows him an advantage that is not insignificant. He can quite rightly assume his audience's ignorance of anything more than the most basic outline of Genesis. By sticking to the text of the Bible itself, Strauss is able to retell those events and make them new for us. And of course, much that most think is in Genesis is actually derived from tradition. As we will see, Strauss often deviates from tradition; he often interprets the text in a manner that strikes the reader who is unfamiliar with his method as peculiar. But the result of his exegesis is to get the reader to consider Jerusalem seriously.

It is helpful to compare his treatment of the Bible here with his treatment of it in "On the Interpretation of Genesis." For instance, we learned at the close of the last section that the Bible begins reasonably because it begins at the beginning. "On Genesis" gives us further illumination on the reasonableness of the beginning of the Bible. The Bible begins reasonably because it "begins with an articulation of the permanently given whole."[6] Thus, the Bible begins as philosophy would dictate it should. Remember that philosophy is the "quest for the 'principles' of all things, and this means primarily the quest for the 'beginnings' of all things or for 'the first things.'"[7] Although the Bible and philosophy may give different accounts of the whole, the author is aware of the importance and necessity of giving an account of the whole and of the first things.

Although the presence of Umberto Cassuto is relegated to two footnotes, Strauss draws heavily from his work. As a biblical scholar, Cassuto set himself against biblical scholarship's documentary hypothesis, the modern derivative of Spinoza's critique of the Bible. Although Cassuto did not live to finish his project of writing a line-by-line commentary on the Torah, we do have his extensive commentaries on Genesis and Exodus, which serve not only as a devastating critique of biblical criticism but also as illuminating and careful exegetical works in their own right. Cassuto's main thesis can be summarized as follows: he grants that the Torah, and specifically Genesis, may be a retelling of existing folklore, but it is a careful retelling, one that painstakingly avoids all vestiges of idolatry and anything else that is not in accord with the precepts handed down from Mt. Sinai. Cassuto insists that Genesis is the work of one author who was more than a compiler. What appear as strange repetitions or remnants of superstitious beliefs to modern eyes appear so only to those unfamiliar with the ancient Israelites' manner of thinking and writing.[8] We are reminded of Strauss's cautionary note in the previous section that biblical criticism fails because it does not attempt to understand the various layers of the Bible as they were understood by the immediate addressees. This monumental flaw does not escape Cassuto. Cassuto also points out that the Torah, in contrast to other works in the Old Testament, cannot be understood as poetry, although it may have borrowed from existing poetic tradition. The Torah held itself to much stricter standards. Cassuto explains:

> The prophets and the Biblical poets, who were accustomed to clothe their ideas in poetic garb and to elucidate them with the help of similes, and generally to employ the familiar devices of poesy, were not, to be sure, deterred from using what they found to hand in Israel's epic poetry. But the Torah, which is not written in verse but in prose, and employs as a rule simple, not figurative, language, and weighs every word scrupulously, was careful not to introduce ingredients that were not completely in accord with its doctrines. Nay more, whenever necessary it voiced, in its own subtle way, its objection in principle to concepts suggestive of an alien spirit. . . .[9]

Upon reading Cassuto's *Commentary on the Book of Genesis, Parts I and II*, it is easy to see Strauss's indebtedness to Cassuto's exacting scholarship. As Strauss's examination of Genesis will demonstrate, he too finds Genesis to be the work of one mind.

With Cassuto's help, we can also begin to see the distinction that Strauss drew earlier between poetry and song. Remember that Strauss has insisted that the Bible is not poetry, i.e., it does not have a mythical character to it.

Although Strauss follows Cassuto's lead in many respects, he does not always agree with him. An important example is found in both authors' account of creation. Cassuto affirms the traditional understanding of the first chapter of Genesis.[10] In contrast, Strauss does not find support for creation *ex nihilo* within the text itself, as we shall soon see.

The question of the authorship of the Bible will arise early in Strauss's examination of Genesis. One question that Strauss does not explore, however, is the question of inspiration. If anything, he appeared to have rejected the idea of inspiration at the end of the last section when he said that the Bible does not proclaim itself to be miraculous. It could be that this is simply in accord with his purpose to settle in advance with Athens. However, I think it could be more accurately argued that he proceeds in this manner to get the reader to see the coherence of the account of the beginning first. By leaving the question of God's inspiration aside, he allows the listener to acquire an admiration for the coherence of the text itself: to see that it is not an irrational account, that to consider revelation seriously does not require choosing between following reason and following an irrational call to blind obedience. Furthermore, this understanding of his method is in accord with the change that we noted earlier, i.e., that to focus our attention on the author instead of the addressees of the Bible would be impious. Thus, his exegesis of the Bible does not allow us to bring with us any assumptions or prejudices, good or bad.

The First Creation Account:
The Heavens Fall (paragraphs 10–11)

In the first paragraph of this section (paragraph 10), Strauss begins by quoting the beginning of Genesis. He next questions its authority by asking who said it. Although he doesn't consider the question of what the Bible is here, he at least hints at the problem by considering the question of authorship. We cannot know who said the opening sentence because Genesis does not tell us. The question then becomes whether or not it is important for us to know who said it. Strauss suggests that if we look at the matter philosophically, it does not matter who said it: what matters is the truth of the statement.[11] But, apparently, we are not going to consider the matter philosophically because Strauss continues his consideration of who is speaking. Perhaps we cannot consider the matter philosophically because of the nature of the statement: whether or not God created the heavens and the earth cannot be verified; it must be either believed or discounted. Nevertheless, Strauss insists that we have no right to assume it is God who is speaking because the Bible does not say "God said." Thus, from the beginning, Strauss draws our attention to how precise the author of the creation account will be: if a word or phrase is missing, then it is missing for a reason; we cannot assume it was forgotten. To draw our attention to the problem further, he adds wryly that only God was an eyewitness to the beginning.[12] Strauss refers us outside the Torah to Job 38:4 in a footnote. There God asks Job: "Where were you when I laid the earth's foundations? Tell me, if you know and understand." Strauss says that we must assume it is some nameless man that is telling us about the first things. What remains unspoken is whether or not we can trust this nameless man. Trust in the source is vital because we cannot independently confirm whether or not the world was created: someone had to be told about it. Thus, Strauss leads us to wonder on whose authority the writer knows about creation.

Strauss reminds us that tradition says that Moses was the author of not only the creation account but all that follows it. He cites Deuteronomy 34:10: "there did not arise in Israel a prophet like Moses whom the Lord saw face to face."[13] Because Moses spoke to God face to face, he is in a position to speak from authority. But by referring us to this passage in Deuteronomy, Strauss points to a parallel problem. Some events recorded in the Torah occur after Moses's death. Even the passage Strauss cites suggests another author. Therefore, his unadulterated authorship is called into question.

Tradition is thus suspect from the beginning. We begin to see how problematic it is to consider the Bible as Jerusalem's sole line of defense. In this opening paragraph, Strauss has managed to weave all sorts of problems in, however subtly. We have the problems of authorship and prophecy as well as the authority of interpretation. He raises these issues for the careful reader to ponder but does not offer any obvious solutions, at least at this point.

Strauss does not settle the question of authorship here; he suggests that we simply call the unnamed person a "narrator." The narrator does not claim to have been told by God of what he relates. He could have heard it from other men; he could simply be retelling a tale. Although

Strauss allows the possibility that what is recorded in Genesis is simply a retelling of a tale, he treats it as more than that: he treats Genesis as if it gives a coherent account of man's condition, as if it might be speaking truthfully. In the beginning, however, Strauss encourages us to begin consideration of the Bible by being skeptical. As he will show, the beginning of the Bible can withstand such scrutiny. In "On Genesis" Strauss says, "The beginning of the Bible is not readily intelligible. It is strange."[14] Thus we learn our first lesson about the Bible and, hence, Jerusalem. We cannot approach the Bible in the same manner as we would a philosophic text: it may be reasonable but not immediately comprehendible to unassisted human reason. The Bible is enigmatic. As Strauss will demonstrate through his exegesis of Genesis, the biblical author provides the philosophically minded with a worthy alternative to Athens.

Strauss next considers the act of creation itself. The Bible says, "And the earth was unformed and void. . . ." Following the Bible literally, Strauss notes that it does not say that the earth was created out of nothing, but simply that it was chaotic; God's action is the providing of order. He states in "On Genesis": "It would appear, if we take this literally, that the earth in its primeval form, without form and void, was not created, the creation was formation rather than out of nothing."[15] Thus, from the outset, Strauss adheres to the text and not tradition. His discussion of creation could be called his first surprise. If Strauss sticks to this point, there might not be as much divergence between Jerusalem and Athens as it appeared at the beginning, that is, if, as Strauss suggests, creation *ex nihilo* is a later interpretation. Of course, the notion of a God capable of forming matter out of nothing is completely foreign to Greek philosophy.

It is interesting to compare his statement here with one from "Progress or Return" in which he seems to contradict himself. It arises from his discussion of Maimonides' analysis of the fundamental difference between Greek thought and the Bible:

> The issue as he stated it was as follows: philosophy teaches the eternity of the world, and the Bible teaches creation out of nothing. This conflict must be rightly understood, because Maimonides is primarily thinking of Aristotle, who taught the eternity of the visible universe. But if you enlarge that and apply it not only to this cosmos, to this visible universe in which we live now, but to any cosmos or chaos which might ever exist, certainly Greek philosophy teaches the eternity of cosmos or chaos; whereas the Bible teaches creation, implying creation out of nothing.[16]

In "Jerusalem and Athens," Strauss is silent about whether teaching creation makes creation *ex nihilo* implicit. Yet if we compare these two passages to one found within Strauss's introductory essay to the *Guide,* we find the following: "Maimonides does say that the Account of the Beginning is the same as natural science and the Account of the Chariot is the same as divine science (that is, the science of the incorporeal beings or of God and the angels)."[17] We are reminded of what Strauss says of Maimonides' intention in writing the *Guide*: "his intention is to show that the teaching of these philosophic disciplines [physics and metaphysics], which is presupposed, is identical with the secret teaching of the Bible."[18] To put it more simply, Maimonides, according to Strauss, worked from two assumptions: "that the Bible is an esoteric text, and that its esoteric teaching is closely akin to that of Aristotle."[19] How creation can be woven together with the Greek understanding of nature remains unspoken. We should keep this in mind to see if this is Strauss's view as well.

Earlier we wondered why Maimonides was absent from "Jerusalem and Athens"; it may be that he is absent in name only. Remember that Strauss begins this section with his own analysis of the "Account of the Beginning" and ends with a discussion of God's name, or the divine science. What is unclear is whether Strauss's final word on creation is that it was merely formation or that it was *ex nihilo*. He leaves it deliberately vague: he states that it "appears" as if the author implies formation and, then, only if the text is taken literally.

The next detail that Strauss notes is the demotion of heaven and the consequent elevation of the earth's status. He first observes that Genesis speaks of what the earth looked like but not the heavens. Strauss considers this an indication that the heavens are unimportant, an indication that will be reinforced in the creation account. The demotion of the status of heaven in the Bible will become crucial, especially when compared to both Greek poetry and philosophy.

Paragraph eleven is a further adumbration of the theme of the demotion of the heavens. It is a consideration of the six days of creation. Strauss is able to encapsulate the entire first account into one, albeit lengthy, paragraph of thirty-one sentences. Following what has now become a pattern, the middle sentence contains the lesson of the paragraph as well as the theme of the first creation account: "Heaven is lower than earth."[20]

In his consideration of the creation account, Strauss immediately confronts the difficulties that biblical critics use to support their thesis that Genesis is not a unified and coherent narrative. The first problem is that both light and vegetation are created before the sun. Considered from the point of view of nature, this is an impossibility.

But, as we have learned, nature is a concept foreign to the Bible. At this juncture, Strauss makes an intriguing suggestion in a footnote. He points to the possibility of philosophic agreement with the biblical account of the order of creation by referring his reader to both Plato's *Republic* and a fragment from Empedocles. Both references agree that vegetation is part of the earth. Empedocles, however, comes the closest to agreeing with the Bible. In the fragment, Empedocles claims that vegetation exists prior to the sun because plants are contained within the womblike earth.[21] Placing these two philosophers in a footnote serves to remind us of the presence of the philosophic account and, in this case, a point of potential agreement.

The problem of the order of creation, according to Strauss, is easily disposed of by stating that, although they may be related, "creation-days are not sun-days."[22] More telling however, is the argument he makes regarding the problem of vegetation preceding the sun. Again we are confronted with an aberration of nature, but Strauss shows us that this is anything but arbitrary. He effectively demonstrates that the six days of creation are not presented in random order. He argues that there is a progression in creation: God begins with the lowest matter and ends with the highest; He begins with inert matter and moves to those creatures with the power of motion. Thus, it is entirely reasonable that Genesis has vegetation, which is "rooted in the earth" and "the fixed covering of the earth," preceding the creation of the sun, which is capable of motion.[23] Fish, fowl, land creatures, and man are of higher rank than the heavens because these creatures, unlike the planets, can move where they will.[24] The most important thing is that, according to the biblical account of the beginning, the heavens lack life. Hence, they are not gods. He does not mention it here, but we know that the Bible stands in stark contradiction to the Greek understanding of the heavens in both poetry and philosophy. The Hebrew insistence that the heavens are not gods sets Israel apart from other nations.[25]

Another indication of the demotion in the status of the heavens is the use of different verbs to distinguish the different acts of creation. Genesis uses several verbs in the account. The heavenly bodies are "made" by God, whereas man, as befits a creature fashioned in God's image, is "created." It is worthwhile to quote Strauss at length here:

> What the heavenly lights lose, man gains; man is the peak of creation. The creatures of the first three days cannot change their places; the heavenly bodies change their places but not their courses; the living beings change their courses but not their "ways"; men alone can change their "ways." Man is the only being created in God's image.[26]

The Biblical Account of the Beginning 69

Note what Strauss says that man shares with God. He does not speak of man's endowment with reason, but rather his ability to change his "ways."[27] Thus, the creator God first appears as one who can change His ways. For Strauss, the God of the Bible is first and foremost an incomprehensible God who can and does change His "ways." Therefore, He cannot be known or understood because His "ways" are unpredictable. Strauss's interpretation of the events in Genesis serves also to confirm this understanding, as we shall see. Philosophy cannot touch the biblical God. As Strauss will tell us at the close of "The Biblical Account of the Beginning," the passage from the Bible that speaks most tellingly of the God of Abraham, Isaac, and Jacob is "I shall be gracious to whom I shall be gracious and I shall show mercy to whom I shall show mercy."[28] God is unpredictable, albeit in marvelous ways.

Strauss must dispose of another difficulty in the first creation account, one connected with man's creation in God's image. The Bible reads, "Let us make man in our image, after our likeness," suggesting a multiplicity within God.[29] This problem is much more difficult to answer than that of the order of creation. In imitation of his subject matter, this passage in "Jerusalem and Athens" is arguably one of the most difficult to understand. First, Strauss remarks that it is meant to illustrate that "bisexuality is not a preserve of man."[30] At the same time, he is quick to discount any possibility that the Bible has a polytheistic notion of gods and goddesses by reminding his audience that "there is no biblical word for 'goddess' and hence creation is not begetting."[31] What Strauss is suggesting is made a little clearer by turning to his commentary in "On Genesis" on this very difficult passage:

> The dualism of the male and female could well be used for the fundamental articulation of the world and it was used in this way in many cosmogonies—the male and female gender of nouns seems to correspond to the male and female gender of all things and this could lead to the assumption of two principles, a male and a female, a highest god and a highest goddess. The Bible disposes of this possibility by ascribing the dualism of male and female, as it were, to God himself by locating, as it were, the root of their dualism within God. God created man in his image and, therefore, he created him male and female. And also the Bible mentions the distinction of male and female only in the case of man, hence saying, as it were, that male and female are not universal characters. There are many things that are neither male nor female but all things are what they are by being distinguished from each other; and all things are either fixed to a place or capable of local motion. This latter dualism, distinctness-local motion, does not lend itself to the assumption of two gods. . . . Furthermore, it excludes the possibility of conceiving of the coming into being of the world itself as the progeny

of a male and of a female god. The dualism chosen by the Bible, the dualism as distinguished from the dualism of male and female, is not sensual but intellectual, noetic. . . .[32]

Here we find Strauss emphasizing the intellectual dualism in his explanation, a dualism he finds embedded in the very act of creation itself. In "Jerusalem and Athens," however, he chooses to leave his readers puzzled.

Strauss is silent in "Jerusalem and Athens" regarding the intellectual character of the biblical account, but he does insist, against the biblical critics, that this passage in the creation account is in agreement with the Bible elsewhere on a most important point: the oneness of God. It is not a superstitious fragment that was accidentally preserved; it is there for a purpose. Instead of being a remnant of polytheism, it is a subtle teaching against those who worship other gods: a warning that they are either worshipping something that they fashioned themselves, i.e., idols, or they are worshipping lifeless beings, the heavens, creatures that are, in fact, lower in the order of creation than man himself. In making this point, Strauss does clarify it to a certain degree. In a footnote, he suggests that we temper this point with a consideration of Deuteronomy 4:15–19, in which the Lord assigns the heavens for the heathens to worship. Thus, it would seem that the worshipping of false gods is not completely forbidden for all men, but only for those to whom He has revealed Himself. In fact, the worship of the heavens is in some sense natural. In "On Genesis," Strauss provides further illumination of the verse in question:

> All nations, all men as men cannot help but be led to this cosmic religion, if they do not go beyond the created things. "But the Lord has taken you and brought you forth out of the iron furnace out of Egypt, to be under Him a people of inheritance as you are this day." In other words, the fact that the world has a certain structure is known to man as man. That the world is created is known by the fact that God speaks to Israel on the Horeb; that is the reason why Israel knows that sun and moon and stars do not deserve worship, that heaven must be depreciated in favor of human life on earth, and ultimately, that the origin of the world is divine creation. There is no argument in favor of creation except God speaking to Israel. He who has not heard that speech either directly or by tradition will worship the heavenly bodies, will remain, in other words, within the horizon of cosmology.[33]

This will not be the last time Strauss will draw our attention to the heathens' worship of the cosmic gods.

At this juncture in his retelling of the biblical account, Strauss begins to imitate biblical writing. In affirming the coherence of the biblical account, Strauss writes dramatically that the Bible is not contradictory but instead affirms silently what it proclaims loudly elsewhere, i.e., that "there is only one God, the God whose name is written as the Tetragrammaton, the living God Who lives from ever to ever, Who alone has created heaven and earth and all their hosts; He has not created any gods and hence there are no gods beside Him."[34] It may be that Strauss resorts to dramatic writing in recognition of the weakness of the argument that he presents here. One lesson is clear: the Bible is indeed cryptic, for it takes an exceptional man to see this scriptural passage as an affirmation of monotheism. The Bible requires a guide to interpret it. Just as Maimonides served as that guide in the Middle Ages, Strauss does so now.

Strauss reminds us of the distinction between myth and history at the end of the paragraph. The creation account, although not historical in the strictest sense, does not include any mythical creatures.[35] In that sense, it is an account of the whole that is comprehensible to man as man. Strauss then returns to the earlier theme of polytheism in making this odd remark: "All non-polemical references to 'other gods' occurring in the Bible are fossils whose preservation indeed poses a question but only a rather unimportant one."[36] We are not told what that question is, nor are we told where those fossils are. This is the first admission that there may be some passages in the Bible that are inadvertent. Strauss is silent about what those passages might be. It should be pointed out, however, that so far he has not ignored any of the difficult passages in Genesis. Instead, he has made them seem sensible.

The Second Creation Account: The Problem of Knowledge (paragraphs 12–14)

In paragraph twelve, Strauss turns to a consideration of the Bible's teaching about evil. The first account ends after the creation of man with God declaring the entire work "very good." Thus, the question arises of why there is evil. Again, the Bible proceeds reasonably, although Strauss chooses not to remind us of this fact. Because the world was just declared very good, the author must now account for the presence of evil.

Strauss is not immediately satisfied with what he says is the biblical answer to the presence of evil in creation, i.e., that evil originates with man. First, he makes the tentative suggestion that "perhaps creation as a whole cannot be 'very good' if it does not contain some evils."[37] He supports this suggestion by paraphrasing Isaiah 45:7, "There cannot be light if there is not darkness, and the darkness is as much created as light: God creates evil as well as He makes peace."[38] The biblical God is certainly worthy of fear if He has this much power. Yet, it cannot be coincidental that Cassuto also cites this passage in his commentary. Cassuto argues that the declaration that light is good in Genesis 1:4 is there specifically "to prevent the misconception that the darkness is also good. It is the light that God created; the darkness is only the absence of light, and therefore is not good (the declaration, *I form light and create darkness*, in Isa. xlv 7, is directed against the dualistic doctrine of the Persians)."[39] The question that must be asked is whether Strauss, because he understands the God of the Bible as one who changes His ways, thinks that the biblical God can or does create evil. He certainly suggests this possibility here. Before answering that question, however, it would be necessary to define what evil is. Strauss does not do so, which makes this passage difficult to understand. Evil, in philosophic terms, is a lack or an absence. It is something that is missing and, therefore, to attribute to God the power to create it is, at the very least, problematic. To understand just how radical this suggestion is, it is helpful to turn to a more traditional understanding of evil.

In *The Politics of Heaven and Hell*, James Schall, in his discussion of St. Augustine's contribution to the debate on evil, makes the following argument. Although Plato and Augustine agree in many respects, there is a profound disagreement as well: "The Platonic notion that to escape evil one has to escape matter also . . . was necessarily rejected by St. Augustine, who posed another, now classical theory that evil was not itself a substance, but a lack of what ought to exist in a good subject or substance."[40] This distinction is a necessary result of the doctrine of creation in which matter, God's creature, is repeatedly pronounced good. There is no hint in "Jerusalem and Athens" that Strauss agrees with this traditional account of evil as the profound absence of good, but a hint of just the opposite. By suggesting that God has the power to create evil, Strauss makes the biblical God even more mysterious.

Strauss does not settle the question of evil here; instead he says that the evil that the Bible is concerned with after creation is particular: the Bible addresses the problem of the evil that afflicts man. This kind of evil is decidedly not present at creation. To account for this kind of evil requires a retelling of the creation account that is focused on man. And that is exactly what we find in the second account of creation. The evil that afflicts man, as we will soon learn, comes to man through the temptation of the woman by one of the creatures. Thus, the problem only appears to have gone away. However, this is not really a problem because, as Strauss continues, the second account may actually contradict the first account: "After all, the Bible never teaches that one can speak about creation without contradicting oneself. In post-biblical parlance, the mysteries of the Torah (*sithre torah*) are the contradictions of the Torah; the mysteries of God are the contradictions regarding God."[41] Strauss is much clearer about what this means in "Mutual Influence": "if the text is divinely inspired all those things mean something entirely different from what they would mean if we were entitled to assume that the *Bible* is merely a human book. Then they are just deficiencies, but otherwise they are secrets."[42] Thus, Strauss has an answer to Spinoza's critique regarding self-contradictions, an answer that is irrefutable. The answer comes from Maimonides.

Taking our bearings from Strauss's analysis of Maimonides, he says that Maimonides read the Torah "as the work of a single author, that author being not so much Moses as God Himself."[43] Understanding the Torah as a perfect book, Maimonides maintained that all of the obvious contradictions must be understood as intentional. Maimonides, Strauss suggests, saw the deficiencies of the Bible as "purposeful irregularities, intended to hide and betray a deeper order, a deep, nay divine meaning."[44] For Maimonides, and it seems for Strauss as well, the Bible is perhaps the most esoteric of all texts. By admitting that there are at least seeming contradictions in the Bible, Strauss shows the need for a guide. More important, Strauss admits the possibility that the Bible is inspired.

Strauss proceeds to the second creation account in paragraph thirteen. He devotes three paragraphs to the discussion of the second chapter of Genesis. The fall presents many lessons to those who study it with care. He begins by noting the distinctions, even contradictions, between the two accounts. In the first account, man alone is created in the image of God. Strauss's silence, therefore, leaves us to wonder about the status of woman, especially considering her part in the fall of man.[45] In the second account, man is made of two decidedly distinct elements: dust and the breath of life. There is no mention that he is made in the image of God. And, the second account does not have man and woman created together. Thus, at first glance, it would seem that the two accounts could not possibly fit together.

Before considering Strauss's interpretation of the second account, it is useful to see what Cassuto has to say about the two different accounts of creation. First, he grants that the two creation accounts were already extant in Hebrew oral tradition. The first account, being the more philosophical, held sway with the learned among the Hebrews; the second account, with the story of the Garden of Eden, is the more colorful and was the more popular account. The author of Genesis took the two different existing traditions and made them harmonious with Jewish belief.[46] Any apparent discrepancies arise only by assuming that the author did not intend for the two accounts to be read together:

> Relying on the account of the first stages of creation given above, our section does not recapitulate the story; it depicts simply the position as it was at the *closing phase* of creation when man alone was wanting. An incongruity presents itself only if we separate the conjoined passages and treat our section as an independent narrative; then, of course, we need to find in it the beginning of the creation story.[47]

Thus, the contradictions that Strauss mentions are not really contradictions at all. By pointing to Cassuto's work, Strauss lets us see this, although he does not say so openly. Also, in "Progress or Return," Strauss says directly that both accounts carry the same message, indeed, that they are in "perfect agreement."[48]

Strauss next considers the distinctions between life as we know it and life as presented in the second account of creation. As Strauss paints it here, the life of man as we know it is reminiscent of Hobbes's assessment: nasty, brutish, and short. Man is forced to rely upon nature for his needs, and nature is not beneficent; for example, man needs rain, which does not always come. Strauss calls the life of man "needy and harsh," one that requires hard work. If this is the original condition in which man is given to survive, Strauss speculates that "man would have been compelled or at least irresistibly tempted to be harsh, uncharitable, unjust; he would not have been fully responsible for his lack of charity or justice."[49] This theme of almost irresistible temptation will be in the background of Strauss's retelling of the fall of man. However, with the middle sentence, Strauss asserts man's responsibility for the harshness he must face. Man is responsible, the Bible tells us, because he was originally given a life of ease, as distinct from one of luxury. It was a simple life in which there was neither toil nor care, one in which man was given everything he needed and had only one prohibition, not to eat of the tree of knowledge; indeed he could have even eaten of the tree of life.[50] Strauss does not mention it, but the manner in which he describes man's original condition resembles nothing so much as Plato's "city of pigs" in Book II of the *Republic*.[51]

There is one notable exception in the Genesis account—man and woman do not even need to work.

Strauss explains that the prohibition against eating from the tree of knowledge does not mean that man was denied knowledge entirely, only knowledge of a specific kind. Strauss describes the kind of knowledge that man originally lacked as "knowledge sufficient for guiding himself, his life."[52] Although man was not a child, he was supposed "to live in child-like simplicity and obedience to God."[53] As Strauss paints the second account, God originally intended man to remain less than human. Strauss also suggests that there is a connection to be made between the simple life that God originally intended and the demotion of the heavens. The problem of what the forbidden knowledge of good and evil actually is becomes obscured in "Jerusalem and Athens," and deliberately so. If we turn to "Progress or Return," we learn that

> the knowledge of good and evil means, of course, not one special branch of knowledge, as is shown by the fact that in God's knowing of the created things, they always end, "And He saw that it was good." The completed thing, the complete knowledge of the completed thing, is knowledge of the good, the notion being that the desire for, striving for, knowledge is forbidden. Man is not meant to be a theoretical, a knowing, a contemplating being; man is meant to live in childlike obedience.[54]

The contrast between Strauss's interpretation of the Bible and Aristotle's discussion of the best life could not be more stark. In "Jerusalem and Athens," however, Strauss does not draw the contrast so explicitly. As we have discovered before, he is much clearer in "On Genesis." There he gives his explanation a different emphasis than he does in "Progress or Return." In "On Genesis," he states, "We may say that disobedience means autonomous knowledge of good and evil, a knowledge which man possesses by himself, the implication being that the true knowledge is not autonomous; and, in the light of later theological developments, one could say the true knowledge of good and evil is supplied only by revelation."[55] True knowledge of good and evil comes to man through the Ten Commandments; more explicitly, true knowledge comes through God's revelation.

Strauss only hints at these things in "Jerusalem and Athens"; in "On Genesis," he is more explicit. There, the question of why God forbids man moral knowledge, which Strauss connects with the Bible's demotion of heaven, is stated openly. It is worth repeating here:

> the crucial thesis of the first chapter, if we approach it from the point of view of Western thought in general, is the depreciation of heaven.

> Heaven is a primary theme of cosmology and of philosophy. The second chapter contains this explicit depreciation of the knowledge of good and evil, which is only another aspect of the thought expressed in the first chapter. For what does forbidden knowledge of good and evil mean? It means ultimately such knowledge of good and evil as is based on the understanding of the nature of things, as philosophers would say; but that means, somewhat more simply expressed, knowledge of good and evil which is based on the contemplation of heaven. The first chapter, in other words, questions the primary theme of philosophy; and the second chapter questions the intention of philosophy.[56]

Thus, the heavens are not a worthy object of man's contemplation: God alone is. We do not know why Strauss is more explicit in "On Genesis" than he is here. What is clear is that, for Strauss, the knowledge that Adam and Eve lacked was moral knowledge received either from God or through independent contemplation. Once fallen, man is allowed moral knowledge, but it is given to him by God.

Robert Sacks gives further illumination as to what might be behind Strauss's understanding of the knowledge of good and evil. In Sacks's discussion of the fall, he points out that the same phrase "knowledge of good and bad" occurs in only two other places in the Old Testament (II Samuel 14:17 and I Kings 3:9) and "In all these cases the knowledge of good and bad seems to be knowledge appropriate to political life."[57] The first reference is to the kind of wisdom that a king would have. The second is to the gift of wisdom, which Solomon chooses over all else.[58] So far in Genesis, no political life exists. Therefore, there would be no need for such knowledge.

As a contrast, it is helpful to compare Strauss with Cassuto here. Cassuto writes that what our two original parents lacked was simple objective knowledge. This, he thinks, is indicated by their first discovery, their nakedness. Upon eating of the fruit, they learn that in fact they are naked, not that nakedness is good or bad. It is only upon their discovery of this fact that they are ashamed. Cassuto writes, "there is no suggestion here of discernment, judgement or choice, between good and evil, but of the objective awareness of all things, both good and bad."[59] He suggests the following interpretation with regard to the serpent's temptation:

> In the ultimate analysis, we have here an allegorical allusion to the craftiness to be found in man himself. The man and his wife were, it is true, still devoid of comprehensive knowledge, like children who know neither good nor bad; but even those who lack wisdom sometimes possess slyness. The duologue between the serpent and the woman is actually, in a manner of speaking, a duologue that took place in the woman's

mind, between her wiliness and her innocence, clothed in the garb of a parable.[60]

Although he surely knew Cassuto's argument, we find nothing in Strauss to suggest that he agrees with Cassuto.

Strauss continues the discussion of man's original condition in the next paragraph. Because man lacked the knowledge sufficient to guide his life, he did not even realize that he was lonely. God, because He does have knowledge of good and evil, understood man's incompleteness and gave him an appropriate helpmate. Strauss makes an interesting point here: even though the man welcomes the woman and delights in her, he does not call her good because he does not have moral knowledge. This is another indication of the care with which the author has rendered the story. Strauss once again demonstrates that, upon close examination, Genesis is not simply a loosely gathered collection of tales and scraps of tales: each word, and each omission of a word, has a purpose.

The Fall: A Reckoning with Evil (paragraphs 15–17)

Paragraph fifteen presents the story of the fall, to which Strauss gives a unique and decidedly untraditional interpretation. Strauss's retelling of the seduction of Eve and what follows is intriguing. His discussion of the fall is much less dependent on the text than his discussion of the first creation account. In fact, Strauss inserts more of his own interpretation here than he did in his analysis of the first creation account.

The next few paragraphs will concentrate on the mystery of the fall. The mystery, as Strauss presents it here, is that the fall was inevitable, at least in some sense. The opening sentence sets the tone for what follows: "Thus the stage was set for the fall of our first parents."[61]

Just as Strauss's understanding of what was forbidden does not follow tradition, neither does he follow the traditional interpretation of crediting the devil with seducing our first parents.[62] If one looks at Genesis, there is actually no mention that the serpent is possessed. Strauss, therefore, is simply keeping to what is in the text. He begins by stating that the serpent was a beast of the field, although the most cunning. The Bible, he does note, is silent about why the serpent behaved as it did. Strauss posits the following: "It is reasonable to assume that the serpent acted as it did because it was cunning, i.e., possessed a low kind of wisdom, a congenital malice; everything that God has created would not be very good if it did not include something congenitally bent on mischief."[63] This is another assertion that some evil must be inherent in creation itself. Again, this assertion is unsubstantiated. Strauss does not tell us why congenital malice is necessary; we are left to assume that it is another contradiction or mystery of the Torah.

Emil Fackenheim writes of this passage that it is a symptom of Strauss's restraint: "I think there is a restraint in him *vis-a-vis* evil altogether."[64] What we are to make of it is hard to tell. Perhaps we are meant to think no more than this regarding the problem of evil: "the notion that evil is a correlative of freedom in a creature and [is], therefore, in a very real sense, a sign of man's exaltation by God, not God's lack of concern for him."[65] This certainly would be in accord with Strauss's interpretation of creation, i.e., that man is the being who can go where he will, who is free because he is created in the image of God. What is clear is that Strauss is being deliberately obscure. We can at least say that Strauss follows Cassuto in staying away from what Cassuto would call poetic or mythical interpretations, although, of course, a talking beast certainly falls within the category of mythical beings. Nevertheless, Strauss has made it clear that at least a portion of the created world was originally hostile to man.

The serpent begins his seduction by suggesting that God acted maliciously in forbidding the fruit of only this particular tree. The woman is not impressed by the serpent's arguments and corrects the serpent by repeating God's prohibition. But, as Strauss points out, she does not get it quite right. She adds to the prohibition by saying that they are not even allowed to touch the tree. Strauss is silent as to why she would make this mistake, although he does suggest an answer in the middle sentence: "She surely knew the divine prohibition only through human tradition."[66] We are thus confronted with a not so gentle reminder of the problem that has been present in "Jerusalem and Athens" from the beginning, i.e., the problem of tradition in general: how do we know it is true, or how can we trust tradition? Here, with the first recorded instance of tradition, something is lost in the transmission from one person to the next. If tradition only once removed proves unreliable, how are we to trust it from generation to generation? Of course, if Strauss's interpretation is correct, this problem with oral tradition did not escape the author's notice either. It may be why the writing of the Bible itself is necessary. Strauss, however, only alludes to the problem here.

It should be noted that, even if the woman did make a mistake re-

The Biblical Account of the Beginning   79

garding the prohibition, she succeeded only in making the prohibition more demanding than it originally was. But this, according to Strauss, was only coincidental: because the woman refers only to "the middle tree," Strauss suggests that she could have even been mistaken as to which tree was forbidden. Oral tradition is, therefore, on decidedly shaky ground.

The serpent next accuses God of lying, by saying that the man and the woman will not die but instead will become like God if they eat of the forbidden tree. God acknowledges later, in Genesis 3:23, which Strauss will even quote, that "they have become like us," drawing our attention to the problem further. The question thus becomes whether or not the serpent was correct or, to put it impiously, was God lying? Perhaps the serpent's lie is that even if man had both the forbidden knowledge and immortality, he would only be like God, similar but still a fundamentally limited being. He would remain a creature.

It seems clear that Strauss wants us to ask such impious questions, and it is just such questions that lead to the accusations of nihilism against him. For instance, Shadia Drury argues that, for Strauss, the serpent tells the truth but only part of it: "Crime and suffering are the price man must pay for the love of knowledge. . . . As a seeker after wisdom, man sets himself up in permanent opposition to God; an opposition that is identical to the conflict between the love of knowledge and the love of God, Athens and Jerusalem."[67] While this may be Strauss's first word on the subject, it is certainly not his last.

What follows next in "Jerusalem and Athens" is most intriguing. Strauss has the woman forget the divine prohibition; she does not choose disobedience. In her forgetfulness, she contemplates the tree and sees that the tree is good. She is, therefore, no longer completely ignorant of good and evil. Strauss does not consider the question of what would have happened if she had simply stopped at this point: presumably, she would have gained the forbidden knowledge, but not through disobedience. Instead, having seen the good, she immediately sets out to acquire it.

In Strauss's retelling of the fall, it is hard to blame the woman for her transgression: first, she could not remember the law correctly, even if there was only one rule to remember; then, through the serpent's cunning, she forgets it entirely. Second, if she knew of it only through tradition, isn't her culpability lessened? Third, according to Strauss's interpretation, the woman saw that the tree was good; how can it be wrong to pursue the good? Strauss leaves us with these ambiguities and continues his interpretation of the fall.

Following the woman's example, man succumbs too. Strauss states that after woman's fall, man's was inevitable: "The man drifts into disobedience by following the woman."[68] It is difficult to see how culpable man could be, given this interpretation. Of course, the whole idea of the woman having forgotten the prohibition, even if she couldn't remember it accurately, is without support in the text of Genesis itself. All that Genesis says is that "When the woman saw that the fruit of the tree was good to eat, and that it was pleasing to contemplate, she took some and ate it" (Gen. 3:6). As our biblical guide, this is Strauss's second adaptation of the account; his first is the suggestion that evil is inherent in good.

The sixteenth paragraph continues this theme, as Strauss considers the pair's disobedience. Again he insists, "they drifted into disobedience."[69] Strauss cautions against using the term "rebellion" because it is too strong a word, implying a certain degree of high-handedness. There is nothing to suggest that they rebelled out of a desire to rule themselves. Despite this, God's punishment is severe—both for them and the serpent. God does not, however, take away the consequence of their action; our first parents keep the knowledge that they have gained by their disobedience. Strauss points out that man is allowed to remain God-like: God admits that "man has become like one of us, knowing good and evil" (Genesis 3:22). Instead of stripping this knowledge away, God simply prevents Adam and Eve from gaining immortality by expelling them from the garden, so that they cannot reach the tree of life. Strauss notes that until then they could have eaten of it at any time. He speculates that the divine prohibition distracted man from the tree of life: we are drawn to what we are forbidden, but we do not take full advantage of our opportunities.

Another problem with Genesis 3:23 is, of course, God's use of the plural in reference to Himself. This time, however, Strauss remains silent about it. By quoting the passage directly, he nonetheless draws our attention to it. Could this be one of the nonpolemical references to other gods that he referred to earlier?[70] It is unclear.

At this juncture, Strauss has managed to arouse a certain amount of disquiet. Although he has convinced us that the Bible is not simply a collection of tales, he has replaced that problem with another that is even worse: a sense that man has been dealt with unfairly by being expected to behave in an impossible manner. Strauss accomplishes this feat by making man's fall a drifting into disobedience, a device that is surely intentional. He downplays man's ability to choose by seeming to deny him any knowledge. In the following paragraph, Strauss makes sure that the unease continues with his account of what occurs after the fall. The problem of man's fall is compounded by the fact that Strauss has made it clear that he thinks that the author of Genesis was completely aware of this difficulty.

In paragraph seventeen, Strauss summarizes the lessons we have learned so far. The first lesson is that God intended man to live simply, without knowledge of good and evil. Strauss then reminds us of the narrator by suggesting that the narrator had to know that in order to be forbidden to attain knowledge of good and evil, one must necessarily possess some degree of knowledge, if only the knowledge that knowledge of good and evil is evil. Thus, he seems to retract his earlier position that man lacks all moral knowledge. We are puzzled by this and are meant to be. As Strauss says, "This story partakes of the unfathomable character of God."[71] The beginning is shrouded in mystery, which cannot be fully understood. Nevertheless, man is caught by a desire to live without evil. Genesis shows him that God once gave him that very opportunity and that "his deepest wish cannot be fulfilled."[72] In order to have knowledge, man must suffer the consequences of evil. According to Strauss, this is man's first lesson at the hands of God.

Cain and Abel:
The Political World (paragraph 18)

Paragraph eighteen, the central paragraph of this section, encompasses the events from the appearance of the first brothers until the time of Noah; thus we have a gloss on life prior to the Flood. Strauss first considers Cain and Abel. The story of Cain and Abel gives the first indication of the results of the fall. Strauss tells us that Cain, in contrast to his shepherd brother, was a farmer, an occupation that Strauss had earlier described thus: "The life of man as we know it, the life of most men, is that of tillers of the soil; their life is needy and harsh; they need rain which is not always forthcoming when they need it and they must work hard."[73] Cain, then, is like most men. But God prefers Abel's sacrifice from his flock to Cain's fruits of the field. Cassuto attributes God's preference to the fact that the Bible singles out Abel's sacrifice by saying he brought the best of his flock.[74] In contrast, although Strauss admits that God's preference has more than one reason, he only mentions one: God prefers the pastoral life because it more closely resembles the original simplicity of the Garden of Eden. Strauss, therefore, chooses to ignore the reason explicitly given in Genesis for God's preference.

Strauss mentions that God warns Cain against "sinning in general."

God's warning is in Genesis 4:7: "If you do well, you are accepted; if not, sin is a demon crouching at the door. It shall be eager for you, and you will be mastered by it." Nevertheless, Cain ignores God's warning. As Strauss notes, Cain's punishment is relatively mild, despite the fact that he killed his brother and denied his guilt afterwards. Man punishes murder with death; God does not: a reminder that God's ways are not our ways.[75] Strauss compares Cain's punishment with that of his parents. Cain, who has knowledge of good and evil, receives a much lighter sentence than his parents did. Moreover, his parents, unlike Cain, did not attempt to deny their guilt. The corruption implicit in the fall seems to be progressive: man has acquired more knowledge, but his heart has grown more evil. Strauss explains that we should not be shocked by this light punishment; instead, we should simply assume that in the beginning punishments were milder, although we are not told why this should be so. Strauss does say, "The relatively mild punishment of Cain cannot be explained by the fact that murder had not been expressly forbidden, for Cain possessed some knowledge of good and evil, and he knew that Abel was his brother, even assuming that he did not know that man was created in the image of God."[76] According to Strauss, Cain had sufficient moral knowledge to know that what he did was wrong. Yet he still seems struck by the light punishment Cain receives at God's hands, or he wants us to be struck by it.[77]

Strauss does admit that Cain, unlike his parents before him, is cursed by God. The fact of the curse seems to negate Strauss's argument that Cain received a mild punishment. Surely, it is not a mild thing to be cursed by God. This is, in fact, God's third curse. He also cursed the serpent and the ground. As Cassuto notes, "Because of the first man's sin, the soil was cursed; Cain's transgression, which is far graver, brings down a curse on the transgressor himself."[78] Cain is the first being made in God's image to be cursed.

With Cain's murder of his brother, Strauss leads us to speculate about what man can know on his own. At least at the beginning, it can be said that man's moral knowledge is incomplete. It must be remembered that there are as yet no commandments, only God's admonition to Cain to avoid sin. If this is an accurate interpretation, then Cain still retains some resemblance to his parent's original condition of childlike simplicity. Cain is, then, not quite like "most men," unless "most men" are not completely culpable for their misdeeds. Yet by this very statement, we are again led to speculate about the degree of Cain's guilt. If he did not possess complete knowledge of good and evil, to what degree can he be held accountable? And what are we to make of God's warning against "sinning in general"? Does Strauss think that Cain could have understood it completely? These are just a few of the questions that Strauss suggests to the careful reader. The answer could be that until the complete revelation of law, man is unaware of the moral law in its fullness.

Strauss takes relish in pointing out that Cain and his descendants founded a city and practiced the arts. Strauss notes that Cain shares with Romulus both the crime of fratricide and the distinction of founding the first city. Strauss's mention of Romulus is the first nonbiblical reference in this section, and it is not coincidental that it is his first mention of politics as well. The least that can be said is that, according to Genesis, civilization is not an unqualified good. The difference between the Bible's first discussion of politics and, for instance, Aristotle's assertion that man is political by nature is astonishing. From the biblical perspective, political life is alien to man's original simplicity. Yet Strauss has been preparing us for this, because it would seem that the knowledge that man was originally forbidden, according to Strauss, could be considered political knowledge. Strauss, however, does allow that this is only the first thing that the Bible says about the political realm; it is not the last.

Strauss is not alone in pointing out this dichotomy. According to biblical scholars Isaac Kikawada and Arthur Quinn, the Bible stands out against other ancient texts because

> Civilization requires population control, and thereby regards human life as just a qualified good. How appropriate then to attribute the origin of the city to the murderer Cain, and other civilized arts to his descendants. And lest we think that these descendants might not be as bad as Cain, the author inserts the taunt of Lamech, who prides himself on valuing human life even less than Cain.[79]

At this point it is worth mentioning that Strauss does not include God's commandment to our first parents, i.e., to be fruitful and multiply, which is yet another indication that for the Creator God all life is unqualifiedly good. This omission cloaks an important contrast between the biblical God and His other counterparts.

The Bible apparently teaches different things at different times. Strauss draws our attention to an example of this: "One is also tempted to think of the difference between the first word of the first book of Samuel on human kingship and its last word."[80] When we turn to Samuel, we discover that the Israelites' request for a king was an implicit rejection of God, as He alone is the true king of Israel (1 Sam. 10:18). However, the book of Samuel ends with the reign of

David, who is chosen by God to rule over Israel. In "Progress or Return," Strauss expands on his allusion to changes within the Bible. First, he notes that the first word in the Bible on the city and the arts is that these things come from Cain, who is cursed. But this is not the last word on the city and the arts, as he reminds us that Jerusalem becomes the holy city and the Temple is constructed through art. He explains:

> Fundamentally, the institution of human kingship is bad—it is a kind of rebellion against God, as is the *polis* and the arts and knowledge. But then it becomes possible by divine dispensation that these things, which originate in human rebellion, become dedicated to the service of God, and thus become holy. And I think that this is the biblical solution to the problem of human knowledge: human knowledge, if it is dedicated to the service of God, and only then, can be good, and perhaps, in that sense, it is even necessary. But without that dedication it is a rebellion. Man was *given* understanding in order to understand God's commands. He could not be freely obedient if he did not have understanding.[81]

Thus, the reason for the change in the status of the political is made explicit in "Progress or Return" but is only alluded to in "Jerusalem and Athens." This "biblical solution" to the problem of human knowledge leads Strauss to consider again the problem of wisdom that started his inquiry. In "Jerusalem and Athens," Strauss asserts that, similar to the scriptural contradiction regarding monarchy, "the prohibition against eating of the tree of knowledge is, as one may say, its first word simply and the revelation of the Torah, i.e., the highest kind of knowledge of good and evil that is vouchsafed to man, is its last word."[82] Thus, Strauss presents the first indication since the introduction that according to the Bible, revelation and philosophic contemplation are incompatible. But it is only a hint; he never argues their opposition as forcefully as he does in other texts.

The last word we hear of Cain's descendants is that Lamech boasted of his superiority to God as an avenger. Lamech revels in telling his wives, "I kill a man for wounding me, a young man for a blow, Cain may be avenged seven times, but Lamech seventy-seven" (Gen. 4: 23–24). Lamech is decidedly a political man, as vengeance is a political passion. Yet this passion leads him to attribute a divine superiority to himself. Fittingly, Cain's line will soon die out; only Seth's line continues after the Flood. In contrast to the sons of Cain, Seth's descendants were not noted for their achievements. Instead, they are remembered for their piety: Enoch "walked with God and Noah was a righteous man and walked with God; civilization and piety are two very different things."[83] Again, it must be remembered that this is not the Bible's last word on the subject.

Noah and the Flood: The Experiment that Failed (paragraphs 19–20)

In paragraph nineteen, Strauss bring us to the Flood. The story of Noah takes up two paragraphs. It is an important story because after the Flood there is, in a sense, a new creation; man begins again and with his fresh start comes the first covenant between God and man.

It would seem that we were correct in our assessment that the degree of culpability and evil is progressive, since "by the time of Noah the wickedness of man had become so great that God repented of His creation of man and all other earthly creatures, Noah alone excepted."[84] This wickedness was already anticipated by what we learned about Lamech. Strauss does not, however, dwell on God's regret, or the possibility of a perfect being having regret. He only mentions it, leaving it to the reader to contemplate on his own.

Before continuing with the story of the Flood, Strauss digresses with a discussion of antediluvian longevity. The remarkable life spans of those who lived before the Flood could be considered another superstitious relic; however, Strauss is able to give us a reasonable account of why they lived so long. The longevity of the children of Adam and Eve is a reflection of man's original condition, a reflection of their lost immortality. After the beginning, man is in decline. An indication that this is what the Bible means to teach us is another obscure passage in the Bible that Strauss mentions but does not explain. He refers to when the sons of God consorted with the daughters of man and bore them the mighty men of old (Gen. 6:1–4). Cassuto himself refers to this passage as "one of the obscurest in the Pentateuch."[85] Yet the only thing that Strauss says about this episode is that it indicates that we are looking at a decline after the Flood. Surely this race of giants is worthy of comment. But Strauss chooses to gloss over this passage.

Cassuto argues in his *Commentary on Genesis, Part II*, that the sons of God are not human beings, but angels of low rank.[86] The Torah's purpose for including this passage is to disabuse the Israelites of heathen notions. Cassuto says that the author's intention is to say, "Do not believe the heathen tales about human beings of divine origin, who were rendered immortal; this is untrue, for in the end every man must die, *in as much as he, too, is flesh*."[87] The Torah is expressly clear that God himself did not consort with the daughters of man; the God of the Israelites is not like Zeus in any respect. There is no possibility of a race of demigods, no men such as Achilles. According to Cassuto, despite its appearance to the contrary, the Torah includes this race of giants to disabuse the Israelites of pagan notions. It is not a "misplaced anachronism. On the contrary, the Torah's intention is to counteract the pagan legends and to reduce to a minimum the content of the ancient traditions concerning the giants."[88] Thus, it is quite odd that Strauss does not discuss this passage.

Robert Sacks, in his commentary on Genesis, makes the following interesting remark, which may be what Strauss had in mind: "From all one can see, the corruption of the earth begun in the days of Noah seems to be associated with the rise of the heroic. But the heroic, the desire to make a name for oneself, presupposes an awareness of death."[89] Noah, as he also points out, is the first man to be born in a world in which it was understood from birth that man must die.[90] Man now knew what death was and that it was inevitable.

Although Strauss says that the sons of God wedding the daughters of men indicates a decline, he notes that the fall cannot be understood simply in terms of decline, because that fall made necessary the revelation of the Torah. The Flood can also be understood as a preparation for this revelation; hence, Strauss notes, there is a certain ambiguity in the fall.[91] The theme of the fundamental inscrutability of God continues. First, man cannot understand the punishments God metes out, as witnessed in the discrepancy between Cain's mild punishment and his parents' severe one. Our wonder at God's ways will continue to grow, especially with the Flood, where we will learn that God comes to regret His creation. And more important, after the Flood, God makes a covenant with one of His creatures, an extraordinary occurrence.

Strauss proceeds to the account of the Flood in paragraph twenty. He pronounces the Flood as the "proper punishment for the extreme and well-nigh universal wickedness of antediluvian men."[92] This should be compared to his statement on the punishment of Adam and Eve, which he pronounced harsh, and that of Cain, which he pronounced mild. Apparently, the farther away from the original simplicity we get, the more responsible we are for our actions and, therefore, the more deserving of severe punishment.

Another theme that Strauss has been hinting at is now explicitly stated: "The ambiguity regarding the Fall—the fact that it was a sin and hence evitable and that it was inevitable—is reflected in the ambiguity regarding the status of antediluvian mankind."[93] Notice that

Strauss tells us the reason that the fall was evitable but not why it was inevitable.

At this stage it is clear that the author of Genesis, as Strauss has stated elsewhere quite openly, understands what he is doing. His express purpose, according to Strauss, is to reject the philosophic understanding of man. Thus, we have an inevitable fall, a need for revelation because man cannot discover the moral code on his own. Yet there is this twofold strain: on the one hand, what caused our original parents to fall, Strauss has insisted, was not high-handed rebellion; on the other hand, the great temptation that faces man after the fall is the desire for independence, be it by Lamech's sin or through philosophy. Man is tempted by both the high and the low. But Strauss has yet to present us with any biblical example of high-handed rebellion.

There are problems that Strauss avoids considering; after spending a great amount of time on the first few chapters of Genesis, Strauss now becomes cryptic. We have already noted his omission regarding the race of giants. Now we see that in his discussion of the Flood, he covers every aspect of it but the Flood itself. He did allude to the problem earlier in his reference to Machiavelli's *Discourses*, but he took some pains to hide that reference. The Flood is surely looked on by biblical critics with a great degree of skepticism, although they must admit that periodic cataclysms do occur. Indeed, there are many differing Flood myths. But, as with all else, the event recorded in Genesis stands out against all mythic accounts. Just to name one difference: the Flood is not the gods' answer to the problem of overpopulation.[94] Another important distinction to make is that Noah is chosen by God not out of some sort of capriciousness, as the hero is chosen in other myths, but because of Noah's righteousness.[95] Strauss, however, does not consider the problem of the Flood here.

Another theme that comes to the fore has been implicit since his discussion on the fall but not explicitly stated, i.e., the problem of law. Before the Flood, man lived without law: God gave man neither laws nor judges. Although man did not drink wine or eat meat, this was not due to any explicit prohibition, but was instead a relic of his original simplicity. The only law we are told existed was the prohibition against eating from the tree of good and evil. There is also what Strauss calls God's general warning to Cain against sin. Strauss calls man's state before the Flood God's second experiment that ended in failure: "This experiment just as the experiment with men remaining like innocent children, ended in failure."[96] God's first experiment was the attempt to have mankind live in childlike innocence. According to

Strauss, neither experiment was a mistake of God's; they were for the purpose of teaching man. The lesson is that "fallen or awake man needs restraint, must live under law."[97] After the fall, man needs the political art. Perhaps that is why Cain and his descendants are the first political men: because they were the most in need of it; they were the most in need of law.

Here Strauss gives us the unique teaching of Genesis: the law that man needs must not be simply imposed but rather part of a covenant between God and man. This covenant, which is a partnership between two unequal parties, occurs after the Flood. God's promise never to destroy all life on earth again is not even conditional upon whether all obey the laws after the Flood: "God's promise is made despite, or because of, His knowing that the devisings of man's heart are evil from his youth."[98] The episode that began with God's regret of His act of creation ends with a magnificent, and undeserved, gesture from Him. Through Noah, man begins again. It is "to some extent a restoration of mankind to its original state; it is a kind of second creation."[99] Thus, postdiluvian man is, in a decisive respect, superior to antediluvian man. Strauss also stresses the importance of God expressly prohibiting murder after the Flood. Murder is forbidden and punishable by death because man is created in God's image. Thus, he says, the covenant brings an increase in both hope and punishment. God will never destroy almost all of mankind, regardless of whether he becomes "well-nigh universally wicked"; however, man must now be justly punished for his misdeeds. Therefore, murder requires the punishment of death. Moreover, after the Flood, man's dominion over animals is now accompanied by the animals' fear of man. Strauss does not suggest whether or not this is an improvement; Cassuto notes that the "attitude of fear and dread may be due to the fact that the creatures were saved from the Flood on account of man and through his action; from now on they would realize more clearly the superiority of the human species."[100] After the Flood, the world becomes recognizably similar to the way it is now; for instance, there are no longer any talking beasts.

Canaan, Nimrod, and Babel:
Blessings and Curses (paragraph 21)

Paragraph twenty-one sets the stage for the covenant with Abraham. Although a relatively short paragraph—six sentences—it is the central paragraph of the entire essay. Strauss singles out three events between the two covenants for our consideration: Noah's curse of his grandson

Canaan, the excellence of Nimrod, and the destruction of the tower of Babel. It is unclear at the beginning of the paragraph how the three events are connected; however, as we will see, each demonstrates man's attempt to circumvent fundamental laws.

Canaan is cursed because his father, Ham, sees Noah's nakedness. Ham, unlike his two brothers who averted their eyes, transgressed "a most sacred, if unpromulgated, law."[101] Strauss's silence as to the nature of this sacred law leads us to wonder about Ham's deed. Rabbinic scholars suggest that Ham committed incest with his mother.[102] This interpretation makes the most sense because we wonder about Noah's righteousness if he punishes Canaan for his father's misdeeds. If Canaan is the result of Ham's misdeed, however, Noah's curse makes perfect sense. This passage is reminiscent of Strauss's earlier comment that the honoring of father and mother is a fundamental tenet of the Jewish religion. This creates an interesting problem, because as Strauss admits, Ham transgressed a "sacred, if unpromulgated, law." Because incest was not expressly forbidden by the covenant, its sacredness leads us to reconsider what we have learned from Strauss about the biblical teaching on the nature of moral knowledge. There is the subtle suggestion that man is capable of reaching at least some moral judgments independent of God's revelation. Again, we are led back to Cain's crime: if the prohibition against incest does not need to be promulgated to be known, what of fratricide? Surely it is even more innate in man? Although Strauss is silent about the nature of Ham's sin, he does stress the fact that it leads to the first division of mankind: into the blessed and the cursed. This division, however, unlike the division that follows Babel and the one after the calling of Abraham, is brought about by man, for it is Noah's curse.[103]

Strauss next considers Nimrod, the mighty hunter. Nimrod is connected with the event that follows because his kingdom included Babel. Also, although Strauss fails to mention this fact, Nimrod is a descendant of Ham and therefore comes from the line of those cursed by Noah. Strauss has only this to say of Nimrod: "Nimrod was the first to be a mighty man on earth—a mighty hunter before the Lord; his kingdom included Babel; big kingdoms are attempts to overcome by force the division of mankind; conquest and hunting are akin to one another."[104] Again we have an indication of what the Bible has to say about politics: empires are built by the cursed. Yet with Strauss's comparison of hunting and conquest, we are reminded that this biblical teaching is not one that man would know by nature.[105]

The final incident that Strauss discusses in this central paragraph is connected with the second. Again it is a political problem: it is man's attempt to overcome his own limitations by building a worldwide kingdom. Here again, the Lord God is forced to intervene in the affairs of man, although, as Strauss says, the confounding of speech is a "milder alternative to the Flood."[106] God divides man into nations and therefore prevents Nimrod's empire from encompassing all of mankind. Strauss does not mention what is normally the focus of attention in this account: man's attempt to reach the heavens by his construction of the tower of Babel. Nor does he mention the potential problems of the account, for example, the fact that God comes down to investigate what His creatures are doing indicates a lack of knowledge (Gen. 11:5–7). From what we have learned from Strauss's biblical exegesis so far, the fact that God must come down to investigate His creatures may tell us more about His creation than about God: it may be an indication that they cannot be left alone to find the law themselves.

With the end of the central paragraph, human life has finally become as we know it now: men are divided into nations having different languages, their life spans are normal, and the animals live in fear of them. It is a world that we recognize.

Abraham and the Covenant
(paragraphs 22–23)

The next two paragraphs are dedicated to a discussion of Abraham and the covenant that leads to the election of Israel as the chosen people. Both are quite lengthy. Paragraph twenty-two is twenty-one sentences long, and the following paragraph is nineteen sentences long. Before he turns to Abraham, Strauss makes an interesting aside about how God will now deal with man, even if man is always bent on wickedness. After the dispersion at Babel, God will divide mankind into two distinct parts: those who are chosen and those who are not. This division will become a political division as well.

Strauss compares the two covenants as well as the two men who are singled out to be partners with God through the covenants. According to Strauss, Noah is selected because his own righteousness separated him from the rest of mankind. Abraham, in contrast, is separated from his kin at God's command. The Bible, Strauss notes, does not say that God chose Abraham for his righteousness. Strauss does not deny that Abraham was righteous, however, because he grants that Abraham demonstrates this virtue by the immediacy with which he answers God's first command: he leaves his home, and all that he knows, to set out for a strange land. Although God promises Abraham that he will be the father of a great nation, Abraham knows that he will not live to see this promise fulfilled, he therefore must give God his complete trust. This trust is made more impressive by the fact that Abraham and his wife are childless. As Strauss says, "It was Abraham's trust in God's promise that, above everything else, made him righteous in the eyes of the Lord."[107] Yet Abraham's righteousness appears laughable even to his own wife. The lesson is that trusting in God does not always appear sensible to others. Because "nothing is too wondrous for the Lord," Sarah becomes pregnant although she is well past child-bearing years.[108]

It is after God's promise that Sarah will bear Abraham a son that we learn of another essential difference between Noah and Abraham. God tells Abraham that He is worried about the people of Sodom and Gomorra: "God did not yet know whether those people were as wicked, as they were said to be. But they might be; they might deserve total destruction as much as the generation of the Flood."[109] Strauss reminds us that Noah did not question God's decision to send the Flood; Abraham, however, does question God. Strauss attributes Abraham's questioning of God to his "deeper trust in God, in God's righteousness, and a deeper awareness of his being only dust and ashes than Noah."[110] Abraham fears that God will destroy the righteous as well as the wicked, so he bargains with God. God concedes that He will not destroy Sodom if Abraham can find ten righteous men in the city. Strauss states that in allowing this concession, God allows Abraham to act as a "moral partner in God's righteousness." With the new covenant, Abraham has a "share in the responsibility for God's acting righteously."[111] This is an indication of the astounding nature of the new covenant. While focusing our attention on the distinction between Noah and Abraham, Strauss points to another problem: God's knowledge, and seeming lack thereof. Again we must wonder whether this tells us more about Abraham and his fellow creatures than it does about God. By not knowing whether Sodom and Gomorra should be destroyed, God involves Abraham in the moral dilemma: Abraham must determine their fate by determining who is righteous.

In paragraph twenty-three, the theme of Abraham's trust in God is continued and deepened. Strauss shows us how great Abraham's trust is when God asks him to destroy the one thing that seems to be the fulfillment of God's promise to him: his own son, Isaac. It is the final and "severest test of Abraham's trust."[112] We have already learned of the wondrous nature of his birth: Sarah was thought to be barren and becomes pregnant at age ninety. Now there will be another wonder as Isaac is saved from death at his father's hands. Strauss is quick to point out that God's demand goes against His express forbidding of murder, but he also reminds us that human and divine justice are two different things: "God alone is unqualifiedly, if unfathomably, just."[113] Although Abraham argued with God about the destruction of Sodom and Gomorra, he does not argue with God regarding his own beloved son. Strauss explains the difference in this way: Abraham bargains with God over the fate of Sodom and Gomorra because in that case he was not faced with a divine command. In this case, however, he is. Abraham is willing to give to God that which he holds most dear. In turn, Abraham is rewarded for his supreme trust: "Abraham's intended action needed a reward although he was not concerned with a reward because his intended action cannot be said to have been intrinsically rewarding."[114] We have yet another wondrous occurrence: Isaac, and thereby the chosen nation, is saved from destruction. The lesson we are to learn is this: the biblical God is to be placed above all else, as Abraham does so faithfully. As Strauss reminds us, we are even to choose God over His chosen nation.[115]

This is arguably one of the most difficult passages of the Bible to explain and Strauss does so beautifully.[116] The sacrifice of Isaac cannot be explained away as a superstitious relic, as central as it is to the election of Israel. Strauss writes, "Abraham did not argue with God for the preservation of Isaac because he loved God, and not himself or his most cherished hope, with all his heart, with all his soul and with all his might."[117] However, the greater problem is not so much with Abraham's action as it is with God's. God asks Abraham to do something intrinsically repugnant. For Strauss, the problem lies in the unfathomable justice of God. Earlier Strauss had wondered aloud if the children of Sodom deserved to be destroyed along with their parents. If the sacrifice of the children of wicked men gives us pause, then what of the only child of an innocent, even righteous man?[118] This, of course, assumes that everyone merits the gift of life, a great assumption in the Judeo-Christian conception of the universe. But God spares Abraham from committing the dreadful act.

God's Name (paragraph 24)

With paragraph twenty-four, the final paragraph of the "The Biblical Account of the Beginning," Strauss leaves Genesis for Exodus. He does not say why he leaves Genesis at this point. Perhaps after the election of the chosen nation, further consideration is not critical. What is clear, however, is that it is an ascent: at least part of mankind appears to learn from God's education. Noah was righteous; Abraham,

The Biblical Account of the Beginning   93

by his questioning of God, becomes God's moral partner; Moses is not afraid to speak with God and ask His name.

This last paragraph is a consideration of who the biblical God is. The opening sentence is once again an imitation of biblical writing, which ends with the rather impious question of what kind of God is the biblical God. Strauss opens by recalling all that we have learned about God thus far: "The God Who created heaven and earth, Who is the only God, Whose only image is man, Who forbade man to eat of the tree of knowledge of good and evil, Who made a Covenant with mankind after the Flood and thereafter a Covenant with Abraham which became His Covenant with Abraham, Isaac, and Jacob—what kind of God is He?"[119] Strauss then corrects himself, saying it is more reverent and more adequate to ask, "What is His name?"[120] We learn God's name when we turn to Exodus 3:14.

With the revelation of God's name comes the most striking passage in "Jerusalem and Athens." Strauss first lets his audience know that God's name is normally translated as "I am That (Who) I am." He even writes that someone whom he does not name calls this passage "'the metaphysics of Exodus.'"[121] This is the first time since the opening of this section that Strauss has referred us directly to tradition.[122] But he refers to tradition only in order to dispute it:

> we hesitate to call it metaphysical, since the notion of *physis* is alien to the Bible. I believe that we ought to render this statement by "I shall be What I shall be," thus preserving the connection between God's name and the fact that He makes covenants with men, i.e., that He reveals Himself to men above all by His commandments and by His promises and His fulfillment of the promises.[123]

This is the first and only time in the first part of "Jerusalem and Athens" that Strauss writes in the first person singular.[124] It is also important that Strauss speaks in terms of faith: he says "I believe" rather than "I know."

By changing the traditional interpretation of God's name, Strauss implies that he is being truer to the Bible's intention. His argument is based on the fact that ancient Hebrew holds no capacity for metaphysics. Because of this lack, Strauss implies, God would not reveal Himself in a manner that could be understood metaphysically. While it is true that the concepts of metaphysics and nature are alien to Hebrew Scripture, one can go even farther than that to say that it is difficult even to speak abstractly in Hebrew.[125] This fact, however, does not mean that God's revelation of His name might not go beyond the immediate addressees' understanding, i.e., that through "deepening meditation" those who contemplate His name may come to a fuller understanding of it in later ages. Of course, Strauss has avoided this problem by stating that he is limiting the discussion to the understanding of the Bible by its immediate addressees. There are two problems with that, however; first, what is the status of Strauss as biblical guide and, second, has there not been a certain "progress" in moral understanding from Adam and Eve to Noah to Abraham? If that is the case, is it not possible that an all-knowing God would reveal Himself in a way that would become clearer through "deepening meditation"?

Strauss maintains that "I shall be what I shall be" preserves the connection between the name of God and the fact that He chooses to make covenants with men and reveals Himself only to those He has chosen. But that is a failure to distinguish between God's being and His doing, which seems to be contradicted by the fact that God, through His covenants with Noah and Abraham, does give His people power over Him: He limits Himself in making these covenants, promising never to undertake the destruction of creation, promising to protect the chosen people.[126] Will, properly understood, is an exercise of choice. As G. K. Chesterton points out, "Every act of will is an act of self-limitation. To desire action is to desire limitation. In that sense every act is an act of self-sacrifice."[127] When one wills one thing, one excludes all else.

Another possible interpretation of "I Shall Be What I Shall Be," which Strauss does not mention, is that it could be a denial of Moses's request, because to know God's name is to have some power over Him. As Strauss notes elsewhere, "an omnipotent God who is in principle perfectly knowable to man is in a way subject to man, in so far as knowledge is in a way power. Therefore a truly omnipotent God must be a mysterious God, and that is, as you know, the teaching of the *Bible*."[128]

Strauss's decision to impose his own translation on God's name is in accord with the tenor of the essay so far: that God is essentially unknowable, that the gap between philosophy and theology is essentially unbridgeable. If God is Being qua Being, then He is *the* subject of metaphysics, even if we can only know Him incompletely through philosophy. But Strauss preserves God's essential incomprehensibility by making Him primarily a willing being: He is What He wills to be. The distance between this conception of God and the Aristotelian conception of thought thinking itself could not be greater. The God of Abraham, Isaac, and Jacob is essentially a God of mystery. Strauss's decision to use this translation of God's name is explained in "Progress or Return." There, he states that it is a necessary result of the Bible's contention that its God is the one true God:

> [T]he Bible, biblical thought, clings to this notion that there is one particular divine law; but it contends that this particular divine law is the only one which is truly divine law. All these other codes are, in their claim to divine origin, fraudulent. They are figments of man. Since, however, one code is accepted, then no possibility of independent questioning arises and is meant to arise. Now what then is it that distinguishes the biblical solution from the mythical solution? I think it is this: that the author or authors of the Bible were aware of the problem of the variety of the divine law. In other words, they realized, and I am now speaking not as a theologian but as an historian, they realized what are the absolutely necessary conditions if one particular law should be *the* divine law? The answer is: it must be a personal God; the first cause must be God: He must be omnipotent, not controlled and not controllable. But to be knowable means to be controllable, and therefore He must not be knowable in the strict sense of the term. Thus in the language of later thought, of already Graecified thought, God's essence is not knowable; as the Bible says, one cannot see God's face. But this is not radical enough, and the divine name given in Exodus, which literally translated means, "I shall be what I shall be," is the most radical formulation of that.[129]

Although Strauss makes this assertion in "Progress or Return," it is still a matter of faith in "Jerusalem and Athens." Just what a radical distinction the Bible's claim of God's omnipotence is will be demonstrated in his discussion of the Greek counterparts.

It should be relatively easy to determine which translation of God's name is correct. Strauss even provides us with the Hebrew word itself: "*Ehyeh-Asher-Ehyeh*." Unfortunately, it is not that simple. According to Cassuto, the verb used is the imperfect tense, which, in biblical language, can signify any tense, although it comes closest to the present tense in modern Hebrew.[130] Cassuto notes the importance of giving the God of Abraham, Isaac, and Jacob a name, because according to

> the conception prevailing in the ancient East, the designation of any entity was to be equated, as it were, with its existence: whatever is without an appellation does not exist, but whatever has a denomination has existence. The meaning of an object's name indicates its nature and determines its characteristics. . . .[131]

In his translation of God's name, Cassuto uses the present tense because he thinks it best encompasses the sense of the text, which he thinks is:

It is I who am with My creatures (compare B. Berakhoth 9 b) in their hour of trouble and need—as I have already declared to you: 'But I will be with you' (v. 12)—to help them and save them. And I am who I am, always, and just as I am with you, so am I with all the children of Israel who are enslaved, and with everyone who is in need of My help, both now and in the future. There is also implicit in this interpretation the thought of implementing the promises: I am who I am always, ever alike and consequently I am true to My word and fulfil it . . . .[132]

Interestingly, Cassuto links the name of God with His promises, too. There is this distinction, however, in Cassuto's interpretation—God is much less mysterious.

Strauss refers us to nine biblical passages as proof of his belief in his translation: Exodus 33:19; Exodus 19:9; Deuteronomy 4:12; Deuteronomy 5:4–5; Exodus 20:19 and 21, 24:1–2; Deuteronomy 18:15–18; and Amos 3:7. All but the last passage are from the Torah. Strauss does not turn to the prophet Ezekiel for illumination on his interpretation of God's name. Remember that Ezekiel is the prophet Maimonides credits with the divine science, i.e., the Account of the Chariot.[133]

Each verse cited speaks to the mysterious nature of the biblical God: "He cannot be seen; His presence can be sensed but not always and everywhere; what is known of Him is only what He chose to communicate by His word through His chosen servants."[134] In one example Strauss cites (Exodus 20:19), even the chosen people understand that it is impossible to see God, that is, to know Him, for they urge Moses to act as their mediator before God lest they see Him and die. The God of Israel is shrouded in mystery: He chooses to covenant with them, yet He is beyond their comprehension.

The final sentence of "The Biblical Account of the Beginning" summarizes beautifully the theme of the section: "For almost all purposes the word of God as revealed to His prophets and especially to Moses became the source of knowledge of good and evil, the true tree of knowledge which is at the same time the tree of life."[135] We should note, however, that it is not all purposes, but only "almost all." The ambiguity of moral knowledge is maintained at the close of this section. Thus we see why Strauss has let us learn about the biblical God by retelling the events in Genesis: because the God of the Bible forbids philosophy, it is possible to learn about an omnipotent God only through his interaction with man. We also begin to see why it is true for Jerusalem that wisdom begins with fear of the Lord. It is wise to fear a Creator Who reveals Himself only to those to whom He wishes and is gracious only to those to whom He wishes to be gracious.

Chapter Five

The Greek Counterparts

Strauss opens the fifth and final section of "The Beginning of the Bible and Its Greek Counterparts" in an odd manner. He begins by stating rather abruptly, "This much about the beginning of the Bible and what it entails."[1] Not only is this an incomplete sentence, the only one in the entire work, but it is also a rather sudden transition. It is as if Strauss is admitting that he has given an incomplete account of the case for revelation, as if he recognizes that he has left problems unsolved and things unsaid. For example, in an essay in which he spends a considerable amount of time reflecting upon the God of Abraham, Isaac, and Jacob, he discusses only Abraham's actions and interactions with God. Are Isaac and Jacob unimportant to the argument or is everything already present in the covenant with Abraham? Strauss does not say. The abbreviated argument is acceptable, given the format of a lecture; but it is worth drawing our attention to nevertheless.

The section covering the Greek counterparts is six paragraphs long. Strauss does not spend very much time on the Greek counterparts. He admits this by saying that he will only "cast a glance" at them.[2] The first paragraph compares the crucial difference between the Greek accounts of the beginning and the biblical one. The second paragraph is dedicated to the poetry of Hesiod. It is reasonable to compare Hesiod's work with the Bible because he, along with Homer, is said to have given the Greeks the gods. It is our first look at mythology. Elsewhere, Strauss has defined mythology as that which is "characterized by the conflict between gods and impersonal powers behind the gods."[3] We, therefore, have a sense of just how different the biblical universe and the Greek cosmos will prove to be. The third paragraph is dedicated to the Presocratics, in particular Parmenides and Empedocles. Because it is a rare occasion when Strauss devotes any time to the

Presocratics, this is the first thing that we notice. The next paragraph concerns Aristotle, followed by two paragraphs on Plato. Since Aristotle is the only Greek out of historical order, this too is of interest. Why does he consider Aristotle before Plato? It may be that this entire section is an ascent: the section moves from poetry to philosophy, from the mythology of Hesiod to the philosopher who Strauss considers closest to agreeing with the biblical account. Since the second part of "Jerusalem and Athens" is dedicated to a comparison of Socrates with the prophets, this solution seems the most probable.

The first paragraph of the section on the Greek counterparts is a lengthy one—nineteen sentences. In this paragraph, Strauss finally considers the question he has hitherto avoided, i.e., the question of what the Bible is. He answers the question by comparing the Bible to Greek poetry and philosophy: he is best able to describe the Bible by showing us what it is not. He begins by noting the first thing that distinguishes the Greek accounts from that of Genesis: the Greeks present themselves as human authors. He qualifies this statement somewhat, noting that Hesiod sings what the Muses tell him and both Parmenides and Empedocles claim to be imparting the teachings of a goddess. Despite this, the Greeks still take credit for their art: we know who wrote the work they left behind. Moreover, the Greeks present their works as true, even if that truth is received from a goddess, although, as Strauss notes, the Muses cannot always be trusted, as they sometimes tell lies that resemble the truth. Hesiod himself admits as much when he relays the first thing the Muses impart to him: "You shepherds of the wilderness, poor fools, nothing but bellies, we know how to say many false things that seem like true sayings, but we also know how to speak the truth when we wish to."[4] This reference is interesting for several reasons, not the least of which is the difference in status of the shepherd here in comparison to Genesis. There is no notion in Hesiod that man was meant for a simple life. Shepherds have a low status in Hesiod's poetry. But the first thing that strikes us is that Hesiod cannot vouch for the truthfulness of his account because he cannot trust the story that the Muses tell; Hesiod's poetry may only be a lie that seems true. The Bible, as we have seen, has no element of speculation about it; it is presented unqualifiedly as the true account.

The next distinction between the Greeks and the Bible that Strauss explicitly examines is that the Greeks composed books, that is, complete wholes; Strauss insists that the Bible cannot be considered a book. Here Strauss addresses the problem that he carefully avoided before he had discussed the biblical account of the beginning. Strauss defines

The Greek Counterparts 99

a book as a coherent whole: nothing is there that the author does not wish to be there; nothing is left out that the author wished to include. In contrast, the Bible, according to Strauss, is at best only a collection of books. But, as he asks in the middle sentence, "are all parts of that collection books?"[5] For example, can the Torah be considered a book? He does not think so: "Is it not rather the work of an unknown compiler or of unknown compilers who wove together writings and oral traditions of unknown origin? Is this not the reason why the Bible can contain fossils that are at variance even with its fundamental teaching regarding God?"[6] In his attempt to answer this basic question, Strauss gives suggestions but no definitive answers; we are thus confronted with a series of questions, answered only silently.

He is more explicit regarding the problem elsewhere. For example, in "Mutual Influence" he states:

> The question is, how do we know that the *Torah* is from Sinai or the word of the living God? The traditional Jewish answer is primarily that our fathers have told us, and they knew it from their fathers, an uninterrupted chain of reliable tradition, going back to Mount Sinai. If the question is answered in this form, it becomes inevitable to wonder, is the tradition reliable?[7]

He then proceeds to raise questions from the Torah that seem to contradict the reliability of this tradition. This problem, however, does not succeed in destroying the possibility of revelation for Strauss, but only in demonstrating the impossibility of proving revelation.

In "Jerusalem and Athens," Strauss contends that the compiler or compilers took pre-existent holy speeches and excluded only that which could not "by any stretch of the imagination" be construed as consistent with the tenets of the fundamental teaching of Judaism. He even suggests that the piety of these unknown compilers may have led them to make some changes in the holy speeches. It is no longer important, therefore, whether Moses was the author of the Torah because what we have is a compilation or, to borrow an earlier phrase from Strauss, "re-collections of re-collections, deepenings through meditation of the primary experiences."[8] But the status of these holy speeches is unclear. For instance, what makes them holy? If it is simply the people's regard for them, then it is only tradition; if it is something more than that, such as inspiration, why would the speeches need to be changed? Or is it the compilers who are inspired? Again, Strauss only points to the problems here.

The Bible, on the face of it, then, has many authors. The difficulty is how all of the different authors could have produced a book that is

100   *Chapter Five*

a coherent whole. Hence, there is a problem with the Bible that does not exist with any other book: there may be things there that were not intended by the original authors, i.e., contradictions and repetitions. Furthermore, any given book of the Bible may have one author or several, and a compiler as well. The very work of the compiler, Strauss insists, began the tradition of seeing the work as one coherent whole. Strauss ends his consideration of what the Bible is by stating, "The tendency to read the Bible and in particular the Torah as a book in the strict sense was infinitely strengthened by the belief that it is the only holy writing or the holy writing par excellence."[9] The question of how these came to be holy speeches is implied but not answered. Thus, in "Jerusalem and Athens," the question of inspiration is alluded to but not explicitly addressed. The problem of many authors disappears if the compiler or compilers had the authority to determine whether or not any given writing was inspired. To determine that, however, requires going outside the Bible itself, as Strauss pointed out earlier.

This argument that the Bible is a compilation of pre-existing holy speeches does not come as a surprise given Strauss's analysis of biblical criticism; however, it must be compared with his analysis of Genesis itself. Strauss does not leave any self-contradictory teachings unexplained in Genesis; at most, he only points to them. At this stage in his argument, he does not mention his unanswerable argument that the contradictions of the Torah are the mysteries of the Torah. It is helpful to recall that the point at which he says that there may be contradictions is in his comparison of the two creation accounts, and he shows us that these very contradictions fall away upon close scrutiny. Strauss also points us to the biblical scholarship of Cassuto, who establishes quite conclusively that Genesis is in fact a coherent whole, not a miscellany of tales and superstitions as Spinoza would contend. Again, we are confronted with a puzzle: Strauss has made the Bible appear less than he has already demonstrated it to be. And it is unclear at this point why he does so. This discussion concludes his consideration of the Bible. With the next paragraph, he turns to Hesiod.

Hesiod
(paragraph 26)

The twenty-sixth paragraph also has twenty-six sentences. Hesiod's poetry gets only one, albeit lengthy, paragraph. Here Strauss considers both *Theogony* and *Works and Days*: these two works give us Hesiod's account of the beginning of the gods and of man. This paragraph returns to the narrative style of the previous section on the Bible. In it, Strauss makes only one direct comparison between Hesiod's poetry and the Bible. But he does not need to make more because comparisons between the two are readily apparent now that we have spent so much time considering the claims of the Bible with Strauss as our guide.

Strauss begins with the *Theogony*. There Hesiod sings of the generation of the gods. We have already learned from Strauss that the biblical account of the beginning is not a song, or any other form of poetry. The Greek and biblical accounts of the beginning are different in all respects. The first thing to note is that man and his problems are no longer of primary consideration. As we discovered in "The Biblical Account of the Beginning," the Bible begins with a consideration of man and ends with a consideration of God, an ascent from creation to creator. The focus of attention shifts with the Greeks. Hesiod begins with the gods; man is not important. First, the gods are begotten, not made; the notion of creation is foreign to Hesiod. Heaven and earth are not lifeless beings but rather the progenitors of the gods. For Hesiod, there are no transcendent beings. There is nothing eternally preexistent in Hesiod's cosmos. According to Hesiod, "everything that is has come to be."[10] There is no notion of the radical contingency of the universe in Hesiod's poetry, or in any Greek thought for that matter. There is no consideration that the universe and all it contains did not need to exist, that it is a gift of creation. In imitation of the Greek understanding of the cosmos, Strauss begins with Hesiod's account of the gods before he considers his account of man.

Strauss recounts the different generations of the gods. With this recital, the comparison, although unstated, is obvious. Hesiod's *Theogony* presents the gods at war with one another. The killing of family members is not unusual. Indeed, Zeus becomes king by dethroning his father, Kronos, who castrated his own father and was thwarted in his attempt to murder his son, Zeus. Hesiod presents the Greeks with gods who are far from perfect. These gods can and indeed often do commit evil deeds. Thus when he speaks of Zeus, Strauss wryly notes, "Given his ancestors it is not surprising that while being the father of men and belonging to the gods who are the givers of good things, he is far from being kind to men."[11] The Greek gods' behavior can be wicked. The gods are thus very much like man, behaving badly at times and well at others. Strauss, however, shows us only the despicable side of the gods. We are therefore confronted with a marked contrast to the biblical God. The gods not only behave like man among themselves but to man as well. Strauss does say that they sometimes bring gifts

102   *Chapter Five*

by teaching man to imitate them: the Muses bring man the arts; Zeus brings man kingship. Hence they can still be considered the "givers of good things," but that is not all they give. Zeus, unlike the God of the Bible, does not care if man imitates him in political life through the imitation of kingship. Zeus is not a jealous god in the way that the biblical God is.

Strauss continues his analysis of Hesiod's work by comparing the relationship of song and kingship, and perhaps even of the Muses and their father, to the story of the hawk and the nightingale in Hesiod. Hesiod speaks of the two birds in *Works and Days,* in which he says that when a nightingale is caught by a hawk, she must go where he wills: he may eat her or not, as he so chooses.[12] The lesson, according to Hesiod, is that "he is a fool who tries to match his strength with the stronger. He will lose his battle, and with the shame will be hurt also."[13] This reference to the tale of the hawk and the nightingale is strange. Strauss does not tell us why he finds it necessary to remind us at this point of the precarious nature of art, i.e., that it must depend upon the good will of he who sponsors it. It may be that he is reminding us of the problem of persecution and the need to write with care. We wonder, as we did at the beginning, what one would need to hide today. One possibility is that this reference may be connected to his making the Bible appear less compelling than he has already demonstrated it to be.

Strauss next makes his only reference to the Bible in his discussion of Hesiod by commenting on the relationship of Zeus and Wisdom. He obliquely refers to the close relationship between Zeus and his first wife, Metis or Wisdom. He comments that it should be compared to the relationship between God and wisdom in the Bible, in particular in Proverbs 8. When we turn to the pertinent passages in *Theogony,* we find just how different that relationship is.

Hesiod says of Zeus's first mate that Metis was not only wiser than man but also wiser than all the gods, Zeus included. Fearing that any male offspring would follow his and his father's footsteps by overthrowing him, Zeus devours Metis before she can give birth to Athena. Zeus thus simultaneously secures his position as king of all and acquires the wisdom to remain there.[14] In contrast, Wisdom is the first creation of the God of the Bible, created even before heaven and earth (8:22).[15] Wisdom describes her relationship with God in Proverbs: "Then I was at his side each day, his darling and delight, playing in his presence continually, playing on the earth, when he had finished it, while my delight was in mankind" (8:30–31). Wisdom's delight in mankind leads her to share her gift with him: "for he who finds me finds life and wins favour with the Lord, while he who finds me not, hurts himself, and all who hate me are in love with death" (8:35–36). A sharper contrast could not be found. In the Bible, wisdom is God's creation and He wants this creation to be treasured by man. He delights in sharing her. No creator himself, Zeus covets Metis's gift. Strauss's comparison points to Zeus's fundamental incompleteness: amazingly, Zeus, king of the gods, did not always possess wisdom. Zeus is far from the eternal and perfect being who is outside of time, who intervenes in time when He wills, who covenants with His creation. Moreover, the difference between the jealousy of Zeus and the biblical God is now clear: Zeus is jealous of those who have wisdom because he is imperfect; the biblical God is jealous of our love, not out of need, but out of concern for us.[16] This difference between the Bible and the Greek counterparts is illustrated even by Aristotle. In the *Nicomachean Ethics*, Aristotle asks whether it is prudent to call a man happy until after he is dead so as not to provoke the envy of the gods.[17]

Shadia Drury cites this very passage as evidence that Strauss sees no real distinction between Zeus and the biblical God. She writes that for Strauss,

> Will and caprice rather than reason and wisdom are their distinguishing marks. Strauss comments that the relation of Zeus and Metis "may remind one of the relation of God and wisdom in the Bible." Metis (wisdom) is Zeus' first spouse, and she becomes inseparable, although not identical, with him. Characteristically, Strauss does not elaborate. What is implicit is that here, as in the Bible, wisdom is associated with woman. Love of wisdom or philosophy therefore is not love of God. On the contrary, it is a sort of competition with him, an attempt to possess Metis, who, being a woman, can be seduced. All this deepens the opposition of Athens and Jerusalem.[18]

While it is true that Strauss does not explain the distinction between Zeus's and the biblical God's relationship with wisdom, but he does not need to. By referring us to the pertinent passages, he shows us the vast distinctions to be drawn. The difference between cannibalism, on the one hand, and the delight of the Lord in His creation, on the other hand, could not be more profound. Moreover, Proverbs makes it clear that the Lord is pleased to share His creation with man, as the previously cited passages demonstrate. For those who fail to check the citation, the two may appear closer than they are in reality; but for those who do, the superiority of the biblical God shines through.

Man is the subject of *Works and Days*. In it, Hesiod presents us with his teaching on the just life. Hesiod opens his poem by asking the Muses to tell him of their father Zeus because "men are renowned or remain unsung as great Zeus wills it."[19] *Works and Days* is Hesiod's attempt to get his brother, Perses, to behave justly toward him. Strauss notes trenchantly that "the question of the right life does not arise regarding the gods."[20] Their deeds are simply recounted; the actions of man, however, are judged. The right life for man is one devoted to work, particularly to agriculture. Recall that Strauss considered Cain's tilling of the soil less pleasing to God. For Hesiod, work is good, even a "blessing ordained by Zeus who blesses the just and crushes the proud: often even a whole city is destroyed for the deeds of a single bad man."[21] Zeus, then, is not completely unconcerned with men. His interest, however, is unpredictable. The biblical God required well-nigh universal corruption before He repented of His creation. After the destruction of the Flood, He makes a covenant with Noah promising never to undertake such destruction again, even if man is universally wicked. Later, God confounds man's speech so that there cannot be well-nigh universal wickedness. In other words, God provides for His creation, even when His creatures are disobedient. In contrast, Zeus is unconcerned with sparing the righteous from destruction, much less with confounding the wicked. Furthermore, the notion that Zeus or any god would covenant with a mortal, or consider making him his moral partner as God did with Abraham, is completely unthinkable to the Greeks.

Strauss refers us to two different passages in *Works and Days* (35–36, 225–85) that demonstrate Zeus's relationship with man. In the first passage, we learn that Hesiod's brother has cheated him in dividing their inheritance. Thus, the first example is a personal one in which injustice is allowed to continue. Zeus apparently is not interested in Hesiod's plea for justice. We begin to see why Hesiod found it necessary to write this work in defense of the just life. The second and longer passage is an argument for behaving justly. It is in this passage that we learn that Zeus may destroy an entire city in order to punish one man. Hesiod claims that when cities are ruled justly, Zeus allows them to flourish, sending peace to them: they prosper, their women are fruitful, and life is good. When injustice prevails, however, Zeus is quick to punish: he sends war and famine and makes women barren. Although Strauss is silent, we must compare Zeus's behavior with the biblical God, who will spare a city for ten righteous men.

Hesiod tells us that Zeus knows of man's behavior because the gods, though they are invisible, mingle with men and keep watch for Zeus.

Indeed, Justice is Zeus's daughter. When she is abused, she pleads at the feet of her father for retribution. Moreover, Zeus himself can see and understand everything. Hesiod warns his brother,

> He is watching us right now, if he wishes to, nor does he fail to see what kind of justice this community keeps inside it. Now, otherwise I would not myself be righteous among men nor have my son be so; for it is a hard thing for a man to be righteous, if the unrighteous man is to have the greater right. But I believe that Zeus of the counsels will not let it end thus.[22]

Thus, Hesiod is forced to qualify Zeus's concern with justice somewhat: Zeus only watches when he wishes. For Hesiod, the just life is not only difficult; it is not intrinsically rewarding. Without the threat of punishment and the trust in Zeus to right wrongs, Hesiod would misbehave just as his brother has. The appeal to live justly is one of self-interest, but that appeal is not truly compelling because one can never know if his misdeeds have been noted. The passage ends with Hesiod telling his brother that justice is a gift from Zeus, the finest thing that man has. Yet, it is not much of a gift, since its reward is not reliable. Hesiod does not present the case for justice as a virtue with its own intrinsic reward.

Strauss next reconsiders his original statement that for Hesiod work is intrinsically good. Apparently, that is not Hesiod's final word on the subject. It now looks as if work is a curse instead of a blessing, since men are forced to work because the gods have kept the means of life hidden from them. This is man's punishment for accepting Prometheus's gift of fire. But, as Strauss is quick to point out, the very fact that man needed fire suggests that he was not adequately provided for in the beginning. Yet, despite the original adverse conditions, Zeus sends man Pandora and her box in order to punish him for Prometheus's crime. The lesson, according to Strauss, is that the harshness of man's life is not due to any sin on his part, for how does one turn down a gift from a god? Man's condition is fundamentally incomprehensible for Hesiod. In contrast, the Bible tells us why we must earn our bread through the sweat of our brow: it is our punishment for disobedience. In Hesiod's cosmos, man is merely a pawn in the ongoing battles between the gods.

This understanding of the human condition is reaffirmed by Hesiod through the account of the five races of men. The first race, the golden race, was made by the gods under Kronos's reign. The golden race lived a paradisiacal life, in which there was neither labor nor hardship; the earth poured forth good things. The race of men that Zeus makes, however, is not so blessed. Moreover, Strauss notes that Hesiod fails to say whether man's condition is due to "Zeus's ill-will or to his lack of power; he gives us no reason to think that it is due to man's sin."[23] Whatever the reason, each succeeding race is more miserable than the last. And there is no reason for hope, because there is no divine promise that man's status will ever change. Strauss's reference to hope reminds us that Hope is the only spirit not set loose from Pandora's box. This, according to Hesiod, is also in accord with Zeus's will; indeed, the lesson is that it is impossible to avoid what Zeus wills.[24] In Hesiod's world, the gods, as a rule, do not love man; Prometheus, in fact, is punished for his concern. The only thing consistent about the gods is their inconstancy. In Hesiod's poetry, there is no escape from the condition in which we find ourselves: fate controls us. When fate rules, the proper response is fear because of the unpredictable nature of the gods: our actions cannot control our fortunes; virtue is not intrinsically rewarding. In contrast, the biblical God provokes fear, or more appropriately, reverential awe, because of His goodness, i.e., because He is who He is and we are unworthy of His gifts. In the world of Hesiod, we are under the control of the gods: they may intervene to help us in our need or they may not, as it pleases them. As he writes, "the mind of Zeus of the aegis changes with changing occasions, and it is a hard thing for mortal men to figure."[25] Zeus is utterly unpredictable.

That is all the time that Strauss dedicates to Hesiod and, therefore, all the time that he spends on Greek mythology. We see that mythology does show conflict between the gods and man as well as the incredible difference between these gods and the God of Abraham, Isaac, and Jacob. These gods are not omnipotent. There is something higher than them that controls man. Fate plays a role in mythology and leaves man without hope. Or, as Strauss puts it in "Progress or Return":

> In all Greek thought, we find in one form or the other an impersonal necessity, higher than any personal being; whereas in the Bible, the first cause is, as people say now, a person. This is connected with the fact that the concern of God with man is absolutely, if we may say so, essential to the biblical God; whereas that concern is, to put it very mildly, a problem for every Greek philosopher.[26]

The reason for the biblical God's concern is because of the very act of creation, an action not of necessity but of love. The act of creation, as Strauss has presented it in "Jerusalem and Athens," is an act of formation from chaos, an act that brings order; in the Greek world of the poets, the only real order is that which man provides.[27]

The Presocratics
(paragraph 27)

Strauss now turns to Greek philosophy. In paragraph twenty-seven, a brief paragraph of four sentences, he looks at Parmenides and Empedocles. Two philosophers, who predate the Socratic turn toward investigating the human things and whose works we have only in fragments, are the first to speak for Athens, if Athens stands for philosophy alone. Although Strauss does not tell us why he chooses them, one can speculate. Parmenides is often credited as the first metaphysician, i.e., the first philosopher to distinguish between being and becoming. It is also interesting that he appears in three Socratic dialogues, one of which features him discoursing on metaphysics with a young Socrates present.[28] It is unclear why Empedocles is of interest, except that Empedocles, along with Plato, was referred to earlier as being in substantial agreement with the Bible's presentation of vegetation as coming forth from the earth.[29] Strauss does not remind us here that both philosophers claim to be imparting the teaching of a goddess.

Interestingly, Parmenides communicates his philosophy through poetry. Perhaps it is related to his claim to be relaying the speech of a goddess, or it might be due to the nature of first philosophy itself, that it is difficult to speak about without poetry. In his poem "On Nature," of which we have only fragments, Parmenides is led by maidens to the gates of the paths of Night and Day. Once the gate is opened, a goddess tells him of the two roads, only one of which leads to knowledge:

> the one, that (it) is, and that (for it) not to be is not possible; this is the way of conviction, for it follows truth: the second, that (it) is not, and that (for it) not to be is of necessity, which is a path, I tell you, that is entirely outside the scope of inquiry; for you could neither recognize (that which) is not, for this is not possible, nor could you express it. For that which it is possible to think is the same as that which can be.[30]

The goddess continues, telling Parmenides that to know and to be are the same.[31] According to Parmenides' account, being is completely separate from becoming. This makes the status of mankind problematic. Most men do not know; they are lost in the realm of opinion; they are left helpless, unable to reach truth, and remain mired in nonbeing. Man's ability to know is highly questionable without the aid of a goddess. It should also be noted that the primary concern of Parmenides is with the attainment of wisdom, not with obedience.

Empedocles, too, chooses to communicate the revelation of his Muse through the medium of poetry. Of his work, we have only the fragments of two poems, "On Nature" and "Purifications"—the first being an explanation of the cosmos, the second, an explanation of the divine. In "On Nature," Empedocles posits that there are four eternal elements (air, earth, water, and fire) of which all things are composed; these elements, in turn, are the only things that have real being.[32] What looks like a constant coming-into-being in this world is only an appearance; the only things that have permanence are the four elements that intermingle to form all living things. Although men speak of nature, it is an illusion. As he writes, "And I shall tell you something more. There is no birth in mortal things, and no end in ruinous death. There is only mingling and interchange of parts, and it is this that we call 'nature.'"[33] Empedocles accounts for change, or the intermingling of the elements, by attributing change to the warring of the two principles of love and strife, good and evil.[34] Aristotle, in discussing Empedocles' work in his *Metaphysics*, writes:

> For if one were to follow up and attend to the *thought* intended rather than to the vague expression of Empedocles, he would find *Friendship* as the cause of good things and *Strife* as the cause of bad things. Thus, if we were to say that in a sense Empedocles both mentions and is the first to mention *Badness* and *Goodness* as principles, we might perhaps be right, if indeed the cause of all good things is *Goodness* itself and of all bad things *Badness* itself.[35]

Perhaps this is why Strauss includes this Presocratic philosopher in "Jerusalem and Athens," although his conception of good and evil is certainly different than the biblical one.

In the text of "Jerusalem and Athens" itself, Strauss dedicates very little time to these two Presocratics. Parmenides is only mentioned, and all that we learn of Empedocles is that he maintained that there are four eternal elements, one of which he called Zeus. Strauss remarks that Empedocles' Zeus and Hesiod's Zeus bear little in common. He is silent, however, about the comparison between the Presocratic philosophers and the Bible. Despite the earlier reference to Empedocles' agreement with the Bible in the discussion on creation, there is little that the biblical account shares with the Empedoclean account.

The Greek Counterparts 109

Strauss states that the crucial distinction between the poet Hesiod and these two philosophers is their disagreement regarding being and becoming. For the philosophers, "that which truly is, has not come into being and does not perish."[36] Strauss reminds us that this does not mean that what truly has being is necessarily a god or gods. Even if there are gods, they bear little resemblance to what Hesiod depicts or to what the Greeks generally understand the gods to be.

It is worth remarking that as it is rare for Strauss to consider the Presocratic philosophers, it is just as rare for him to consider questions of metaphysics. Strauss is usually content merely to point to the subject, so it is interesting that he considers metaphysics here, no matter how briefly. Note also that these two philosophers' teachings, unlike that of Hesiod, have no bearing on the life of man: they have no political or moral teaching. This is not unrelated to the fact that that which is cannot be created or destroyed. For the Presocratics, man is far removed from that which truly has being.

Aristotle
(paragraph 28)

In the twenty-eighth paragraph, Strauss comes to Aristotle. Again, it is a short paragraph of only five sentences. The poetry of Hesiod and the philosophy of Parmenides and Empedocles fade into the background. The subject of metaphysics, however, continues. Aristotle's metaphysics is decidedly not based on the revelations of a god or goddess: what he tells us, man can know on his own. The middle sentence describes the definitive distinction between the Aristotelian god and the God of the Bible: "Only by thinking himself and nothing but himself does he rule the world."[37] But before he turns to Aristotle, Strauss begins with a reference to the Middle Ages. In the twelfth and thirteenth centuries, he says, Jerusalem and Athens "reached the level of what one may call [their] classical struggle."[38] This is the first allusion to the title since his first discussion of wisdom. However, he does not dwell on the medieval period but refers to it only to say that at the time of the classical struggle between Jerusalem and Athens, Aristotle was *the* philosopher. Aristotle's god shares some things in common with the biblical God: both are thinking beings.[39] But for Aristotle, that is all that god is: pure thought thinking itself and nothing else. The Aristotelian god rules the world but does not provide law. Aristotle's god does not create the world but is co-eternal with it. This difference in the conception of the deity is also reflected in man. Far from being created in God's image, man is lower in rank than the heavens. The notion of providence is so far removed from the Aristotelian conception of god that Strauss ironically describes it as blasphemous for Aristotle to consider the idea of thought thinking itself as being just. Instead, Aristotle's god is "above justice as well as injustice."[40] He is above the concerns of mere mortals. Unlike in his brief discussion on the Presocratics, however, Strauss does refer the reader in a footnote to six crucial passages in the Aristotelian corpus.

The first two passages to which Strauss refers us are from the *Metaphysics*.[41] In the first passage, Aristotle has been discussing the final cause. He next presents his argument that the highest being is pure intellect and the object of pure intellect must necessarily be itself. Pure intellect has no potency, because that would imply change in the highest being. But pure intellect does share something in common with the biblical God, as Aristotle writes: "We say that God is a living being which is eternal and the best; so life and continuous duration and eternity belong to God."[42] In the next passage that Strauss cites, Aristotle considers the possibility that god could think about something other than himself. Since this activity would require change, it is impossible for Aristotle to entertain the possibility. Aristotle's god does not have a providential nature, for that would require a composite nature. He states, "Would it not be absurd to be thinking of certain things? Clearly, then, He is thinking of that which is most divine and most honorable, and He is not changing, for change would be for the worse, and this change would then be a motion."[43]

From *De Anima*, we learn that in order to know, the intellect cannot be mixed.[44] Strauss next refers to two passages from the *Nicomachean Ethics*, in which we learn that there are many things more divine than man, the planets, for example.[45] The second passage is from Book X, where Aristotle discusses man's highest activity, i.e., contemplation. Aristotle makes it clear that he thinks it petty and unworthy to attribute justice to the gods, the most blessed and happy beings:

> We assume that the gods are in the highest degree blessed and happy. But what kind of actions are we to attribute to them? Acts of justice? Will they not look ridiculous making contracts with one another, returning deposits, and so forth? Perhaps acts of courage—withstanding terror and taking risks, because it is noble to do so? Or generous actions? But to whom will they give? It would be strange to think that they actually have currency or something of the sort. Acts of self-control? What would they be? Surely, it would be in poor taste to praise them for not having bad appetites. If we went through the whole list we would see that a concern with actions is petty and unworthy of the gods.[46]

Interestingly, in the passage to which Strauss draws our attention, Aristotle addresses only the question of interaction between the gods themselves and not between gods and men. Furthermore, in this passage, Aristotle is not speaking of the prime mover, but of the Greek gods.

Finally, Strauss cites a passage from the *Eudemian Ethics*. This reference is strange because it doesn't have any obvious connection with the previous discussion. It is the only reference that has nothing to do with either the Aristotelian god or the traditional gods; instead, its focus is on man. It is entirely concerned with the distinction between the noble and good man's ability to use natural goods well as opposed to other men's ability. Only the truly good and noble man will know how to use things well. Aristotle writes in the passage Strauss references:

> . . . for things absolutely good are not good for [the many] as they are for the good man; to the noble and good man they are also noble, for he does many noble deeds by reason of them. But the man who thinks he ought to have the excellences for the sake of external goods does deeds that are only noble *per accidens*. Nobility and goodness, then, is perfect excellence.[47]

Thus Strauss points to a reiteration of Aristotelian virtue to remind us that for Aristotle virtue is an end in itself; to be virtuous for any other reason than for the sake of virtue, e.g., a reward, is not a truly virtuous act. Wealth and beauty are better used by a good man than a base one. And finally, for Aristotle, a truly virtuous man does not behave well out of fear of the Lord, but for virtue's sake.

Here Strauss is quite willing to raise questions openly that he kept hidden in his discussion of the Bible. The references to Aristotle all show the impossibility of the prime mover having any knowledge of anything but itself. Hence, the question of the possibility of providence is raised in the context of philosophy, for it is not impious to deny such attributes to the Olympian gods. This is not an unusual strategy for Strauss, as can be seen in his essay on Plato's *Euthyphron*. In his discussion of Plato's dialogue on piety, Strauss asks,

> But can one return to orthodoxy? Can one accept a position which is based on mere tales? Yet, if we abandon the tales, what can we say about the gods and about piety? Still, we divine that the gods are superhuman beings, and therefore that the highest human type gives us an inkling of what the gods might be.[48]

It does not take much imagination to ask the same questions regarding the Torah, and it looks like Strauss wants us to ask just such questions. At this point, it appears as if Athens has once again gained ascendancy. Of equal interest, however, is the fact that Strauss mentions the biblical God in terms of intellect here as he did not do in the section on the Bible.

Strauss does not explicitly draw our attention to the distinctions between Aristotle and the Bible, but the comparisons are obvious. Of equal importance is the distinction between Aristotle and Hesiod. From the last citation of the *Nicomachean Ethics*, it is clear that Aristotle is contemptuous of Hesiod's portrayal of the gods.

Plato
(paragraphs 28–29)

In paragraph twenty-eight, Strauss turns to Plato. He spends the next two paragraphs on Plato's teaching; of all the Greeks, Strauss dedicates the most attention to him. Except for a brief reference to the ideas, Strauss drops the discussion of metaphysics once he turns to Plato. Instead, theology replaces metaphysics. At this point, it is unclear whether we are meant to see this as an ascent or a descent.

Strauss draws from three dialogues in these two final paragraphs of "The Beginning of the Bible and its Greek Counterparts": the *Republic*, the *Timaeus*, and the *Laws*. The first open reference is to Plato's *Laws*. Socrates is absent from this dialogue. Moreover, although he is present in the *Timaeus*, Socrates is, for the most part, silent. Surprisingly, of the three Platonic dialogues to which Strauss refers, Socrates, who figures so prominently in the second part of "Jerusalem and Athens," speaks in only one—the *Republic*. As Strauss writes in *The City and Man*, "by failing to present a conversation between Socrates and the Eleatic stranger or Timaeus, he indicates that there is no Platonic dialogue among men who are, or could be thought to be equals."[49] In the *Timaeus*, the sequel to the *Republic*, the interlocutors are supposed to discuss the just city in motion, i.e., at war; but it quickly turns into a discussion of the beginning, or the first things. Timaeus himself gives an account of creation. The *Republic* contains the Socratic discussion on justice. A principal teaching from this dialogue, according to Strauss, is that "in a well-ordered society it is required to tell untruths."[50] The *Laws*, Strauss tell us, "is the most political work of Plato. One may even say that it is his only political work, for in it the chief character, the Athenian stranger, elaborates a code for a city about to be founded, i.e., he engages in political activity."[51] It is also interesting that what Strauss has called Plato's most political work is a discussion of a city that is supposed to have been founded by a god. The *Laws* is a dialogue about Crete, a regime founded by Minos, who is said to have received the laws from Zeus.

Strauss opens paragraph twenty-eight by referring again to the medieval debate between Jerusalem and Athens. During that struggle, Strauss tells us, Plato was often referred to as the philosopher who is closest in agreement with the Bible. This method is distinct from Strauss's treatment of Aristotle, who is simply "the philosopher." Strauss begins by considering the similarities between Plato and the Bible. Immediately we see the difference between Plato and Aristotle. Plato even has a theology—something that Strauss would say Aristotle decidedly does not have. For Strauss, Plato has many teachings in accord with the Bible. He teaches that the heavens and the earth had a beginning, that they were made by a father god who is invisible, and that their continued existence depends upon this god's will. The Platonic god is both eternal and good. Creation is good as well. Strauss describes two elements of Plato's theology: first, that God is good and not the cause of evil; second, that God is simple and therefore, unchangeable. Interestingly, he gives us no references for these assertions. With the next sentence, the middle one, Strauss states that "On the divine concern with men's justice and injustice, the Platonic teaching is in fundamental agreement with the biblical teaching; it even culminates in a statement that agrees almost literally with biblical statements."[52] The accompanying footnote refers the reader to Plato's *Laws*, Amos 9:1–3, and Psalm 139.

In the passage noted from the *Laws*, we learn that there is no escape from the retribution of the gods. Man must pay either here or in Hades or, should he deserve it, in someplace even worse. In Amos, the Lord tells the prophet, "No fugitive shall escape, no survivor find safety; if they dig down to Sheol, thence shall my hand take them; if they climb up to heaven, thence will I bring them down" (Amos 9:1–2). Psalm 139:7–10 echoes this theme: "Where can I escape from thy spirit? Where can I flee from thy presence? If I climb up to heaven, thou art there; if I make my bed in Sheol, again I find thee . . . even there thy hand will meet me and thy right hand will hold me fast." Unlike Zeus, whose concern with the affairs of man is unreliable, both the Platonic god and the biblical God know all that men do and mete out justice accordingly. Strauss emphasizes the connection between the act of creation and the resulting concern God has for His creatures.

After his discussion of the Platonic creation account, Strauss considers the disagreements between Plato and the Bible, which, he says, are "no less striking."[53] The first problem is that Plato grants that his account of creation is only a likely tale. Moreover, his creator god creates other gods as well. These gods, unlike Hesiod's gods, are visible and living beings; in fact, they are the heavenly beings. These are the ones who create all other living beings including man. Furthermore, the Platonic god is not the highest thing; the eternal ideas are higher. Strauss writes, "The Platonic god does not create the world by his word; he creates it after having looked to the eternal ideas which therefore are higher than he."[54] An element of necessity seems to be implicit in the Platonic god's creation, an element decidedly not present in the biblical God's act of creation. Strauss tells us that Plato gives his explicit teaching on theology in his discussion of education in the *Republic*. This is not Plato's final word on the subject, however, because, as Strauss also states, Plato exchanges theology with the "doctrine of the ideas" in his discussion of the education of the philosophers.

In "Jerusalem and Athens," Strauss gives us no hint that he finds Plato's "doctrine of the ideas" less than compelling, although his use of the word "doctrine" is revealing. In a lengthy passage in his essay on the *Republic*, however, Strauss appears completely unpersuaded:

> The doctrine of ideas which Socrates expounds to his interlocutors is very hard to understand; to begin with, it is utterly incredible, not to say that it appears to be fantastic. Hitherto we had been given to understand that justice is fundamentally a certain character of the human soul or of the city, i.e. something which is not self-subsisting. Now we are asked to believe that it is a self-subsisting being at home as it were in an entirely different place from human beings and everything else participating in justice (cf. 506 d 1–510 a 7; *Phaedrus* 247 c 3). No one has ever succeeded in giving a satisfactory or clear account of this doctrine of ideas.[55]

In "Jerusalem and Athens," the only indication that Strauss does not take Plato's ideas seriously is his use of the word "doctrine." This is an indication that the ideas are still in the realm of theology. Strauss has already admitted that this is no more than a likely tale, by Plato's own account. Moreover, we learn that providence becomes the subject of the *Laws* only in the discussion of criminal law. Strauss therefore leaves the impression that Plato's likely tales of providence and theology are not his final word on the subject but rather noble lies. These noble lies not only are in sharp contrast to the Presocratic accounts and Aristotle's presentation of god, but they also ought to be distinguished from Hesiod's poetry. Both Plato and Hesiod grant that they might only be presenting likely tales, but Plato's tales buttress arguments that virtue is its own reward; Hesiod must appeal to self-interest alone. He must try to convince his brother to behave well out of fear of Zeus's ire. Remember that a key question animating the *Republic* is whether the just man can be happy, even if he is subject to utter ruin. For Plato and for the Bible, the answer is yes.

Before proceeding any further it must be noted that Strauss, in other works as well as later in this essay, argues that we cannot assume that the interlocutors that Plato presents in his dialogues are in agreement with him. Therefore, it is unclear how definitive a treatment of Plato's theology this discussion is. In fact, Strauss commits what he calls a mistake in his discussion of Cohen: he presumes to draw a line between Plato's teaching and Socrates' teaching.[56] One thing should be considered, however: the three interlocutors, Timaeus, Socrates, and the Athenian Stranger, are all wise men. Strauss does not refer us to the teaching of Thracymachus, for example.

The final paragraph of "The Beginning of the Bible and its Greek Counterparts" has seven sentences. It begins with an important distinction that Plato draws between the two kinds of gods: there are both visible or cosmic gods and gods of tradition, the gods of Hesiod and Homer. The visible gods can be seen regularly; the traditional gods, only when they wish to be seen. The visible gods "are accessible to man as man—to his observations and calculations—, whereas the Greek gods are accessible only to the Greeks through Greek traditions."[57] For Plato, these visible gods are at least of higher rank than the traditional gods, if not the only real gods. Strauss then reminds us of what the Bible has to say about the visible gods: worship of the planets is not forbidden for other nations, but it is for Israel, because cosmic gods are not really gods; there is only one God.

Strauss refers us in a footnote to three different works: Plato's *Timaeus*, Aristophanes' *Peace*, and Deuteronomy 4:19. In the passage from the *Timaeus*, the participants have just concluded a discussion on the visible gods and have turned their attention to the gods of tradition.[58] We learn that we cannot know the origins of the traditional gods but must rely on the tradition of those who claim to be their offspring; we ought not doubt the word of the children of gods. Timaeus says,

> To know or tell the origin of the other divinities is beyond us, and we must accept the traditions of the men of old time who affirm themselves to be the offspring of the gods—that is what they say—and they must surely have known their own ancestors. How can we doubt the word of the children of the gods? Although they give no probable or certain proofs, still, as they declare that they are speaking of what took place in their own family, we must conform to custom and believe them.[59]

It goes without saying that it would be in the interest of such persons to claim to be the descendants of gods. Again we have an instance of Strauss pointing to a problem of revelation surreptitiously by allowing it to come out in the context of the Greek pantheon, although it is certainly a different thing to claim to be a descendant of a god than it is to claim to be a chosen nation.

The reference to Aristophanes is the only one that comes as a surprise; it is the only comedy referred to in the entire essay. Aristophanes is perhaps best known for laughing at convention and showing a passionate concern for justice. Strauss has this to say about Aristophanes' comedies:

> Comedy rises high in order to bring down the high. This would not be possible if it did not presuppose the distinction between what is truly high, high by nature, and what is high only by convention: Comedy rises to what is highest by nature in order to lower what is high only by convention.[60]

Thus, with the central citation, Strauss points to the central question: how seriously are we to take the Greek pantheon? He answers this question through Aristophanes. Aristophanes shows the traditional gods to be ineffectual; they do not care for the Greeks. As Strauss says in his conclusion to *Socrates and Aristophanes*:

> The Aristophanean comedy certainly presupposes tragedy; it builds on tragedy; in this sense, at any rate, it is higher than tragedy. It conjures up for us, within the limits of that possibility which it must respect, a simply pleasant falsehood: a life without war, law courts, terrors caused by gods and death, poverty, and coercion or restraint or *nomos*. The falsehood points to the truth; the truth is the inevitable suffering, coeval with man, that is caused by both *physis* and *nomos*. That harsh truth is indicated but also obfuscated by what human beings say about the gods; yet the hostile power of the gods—as distinguished from the harshnesses due to *nomos* proper and to *physis*—can be easily overcome . . . . One could say that both tragedy and comedy present the transgressions of sacred law, tragedy presenting such transgressions as acts of *hybris*, and comedy presenting them as acts of *alazoneia* (boasting).[61]

As we will see in *Peace*, transgression of sacred law does not lead to punishment but to peace.

The Aristophanean comedy *Peace*, Strauss writes, "presents a clear case of the triumph of madness."[62] *Peace* is set during the Peloponnesian war. Trygaios, the hero whom Strauss takes to be the comic poet in disguise, has ridden up to heaven on a dung beetle to rail at Zeus because of the war ravaging Hellas.[63] Strauss states that the importance of Trygaios's journey is that "he surely is open to the possibility that he might have to act against Zeus, and he takes it for granted that Zeus has obligations to the Greeks."[64] Upon his arrival, Trygaios finds the halls empty; the gods have left because they are angry with the Greeks. He soon discovers that Zeus has allowed War to place Peace into a deep pit. It thus becomes clear that if Trygaios is to save Greece, he must go against Zeus's expressed will. When Trygaios tries to remove Peace with the help of Attic farmers, Hermes, catching him, says he must die for thwarting the will of Zeus. Trygaios gains his life back through bribery. He warns Hermes that the moon and sun are going to give Hellas to the barbarians in an attempt to uproot the traditional gods of Greece; if Hermes saves him, he will ensure that Greece worships Hermes above all other gods. The moon and sun are going to give Greece to the barbarians because the barbarians, unlike the Greeks, worship them. Hermes agrees to the bargain and Peace is set free.

As we have seen, the traditional gods prove not only undependable but completely useless in a crisis. Trygaios himself must ride up to heaven in order to restore Peace to Greece. Aristophanes lets his audience see how easily the power of the gods is overcome; the cunning of one man is all that it takes. Moreover, by pointing to the cosmic gods, Aristophanes also points to that which is high by nature.

This discussion of the revolt of the cosmic gods is, of course, the passage to which Strauss refers us.[65] In his discussion of the play in *Socrates and Aristophanes*, Strauss makes an interesting comment regarding the reason for the worship of the heavens. The sun and moon "come to sight as self-moving (hence living) beings of utmost splendor, which are visible to all men at regular intervals and thus reveal themselves to men without ever descending to earth or men's ascending to heaven."[66] The cosmic gods can be the subject of science, i.e., they do not need to reveal themselves to be known. Neither the traditional gods nor the biblical God can be known in that manner. We begin to see why the God of Abraham, Isaac, and Jacob would allow those to whom He has not revealed His splendor to worship the lowly substitute of the heavens.

The third reference to which Strauss directs us is the now familiar passage from Deuteronomy in which God tells the Israelites that they are forbidden to bow down before the heavens. Strauss's insistence on taking the worship of the cosmic gods seriously becomes particularly interesting when we compare his statements here with what he says is Maimonides' teaching in the *Guide for the Perplexed*. In his introductory essay to the *Guide*, Strauss argues that "according to Maimonides, the Law agrees with Aristotle in holding that the heavenly bodies are endowed with life and intelligence and that they are superior to man in dignity; one could say that he agrees with Aristotle in implying that those heavenly bodies deserve more than man to be called images of God."[67] In "Jerusalem and Athens," Strauss has demonstrated just how much liberty one would have to take with the Bible for this to be true.

The Bible, in contrast to Plato, does not ascribe the heathen's worship of the cosmic gods to their use of reason but instead to God's dispensation; they are allowed to worship the heavens only because He wills it. Despite the fact that God allows others to worship the sun, moon, and stars, the God of the Israelites is the only true God. Strauss does not explain the reason for this dispensation here; the explanation belongs to the prophets. God's plan for Israel, and indeed for all mankind, will be made clearer by the prophets. All we know now is that the biblical God only "manifests Himself as far as He wills."[68]

In the final sentence of the first part of "Jerusalem and Athens," Strauss points out that if we compare the Platonic with the biblical understanding of the worship of the heavens, we find "the fundamental opposition of Athens at its peak to Jerusalem: the opposition of the God or gods of the philosophers to the God of Abraham, Isaac and Jacob, the opposition of Reason and Revelation."[69] Plato, unlike *the* philosopher according to the Middle Ages, is Athens at its peak. Notice that Hesiod's poetry, which opened the section on the Greeks, has completely disappeared. Strauss does not say here what the peak of revelation is. However, at the close of the section on the Bible, he implies that it is "the word of God as revealed to His prophets and especially to Moses."[70]

Thus, Strauss ends "The Beginning of the Bible and Its Greek Counterparts" with what appears, at first glance, to be the triumph of reason. But deeper consideration reveals that the movement of the final section of the first half of "Jerusalem and Athens" is from mythology to the philosophy that most closely resembles Jerusalem. And it is clear that for Strauss it is an ascent. Strauss begins with the gods of Hesiod. There are two problems with them: they are insufficiently concerned with man and they are unworthy of imitation. Indeed, imitation of the gods is forbidden to man. After a brief look at the Presocratics, Strauss turns to Aristotle, whose god is certainly worthy of imitation. Indeed, the imitation of the divine is the best life. Aristotle's god, however, is not and cannot be concerned with the affairs of men. Thus Strauss ends with Plato, whose likely tales present a god who is both providential and worthy of imitation, in other words, a god who is most like the biblical God. In commenting on the lesson of the *Euthyphron*, Jaffa makes the following comment, which seems to sum up what we have learned thus far from Strauss:

> There is nothing about the [traditional] gods that enables them to solve the question of the right way of life for man. Only as the gods become the exoteric names for the permanent and unchanging attributes of nature—above all of the sun, the moon, and the stars—can they supply such guidance. Then they become but the names for the intelligible necessities which are not gods, but ideas. But it is precisely on this issue that the Bible differs both from Plato and the Greek poets; for the Bible affirms the unity of God and denies that this unity is subject either to multiplication or division. Why this is so is a mystery. There is no intelligible necessity that accounts for God, and hence there can be no "science" of God. "I shall be that I shall be" is Strauss's translation of the name of God. God is not bound by anything other than His own will. Hence the highest "science" is not metaphysics, but Torah: the study of God's promises to man, as the ground of the knowledge of the right way of life.[71]

Chapter Six

"On Socrates and the Prophets"

We turn now to the second part of "Jerusalem and Athens," where Strauss explores the distinction between Socrates and the biblical prophets. "On Socrates and the Prophets" is decidedly shorter than the first part. Although it has only eleven paragraphs, it can be divided into four different sections, as listed below. The first four paragraphs are a consideration of the work of Hermann Cohen; the second two paragraphs look to the prophets; the next two paragraphs consider Socrates' mission; and the final three paragraphs consist of a comparison between Socrates and the prophets. The outline is as follows:

II. "On Socrates and the Prophets" (paragraphs 31–41)
    A. Hermann Cohen (paragraphs 31–34)
    B. The Prophets (paragraphs 35–36)
    C. Socrates (paragraphs 37–38)
    D. A Comparison of the Two Missions (paragraphs 39–41)

Although there is no middle section of the second part of "Jerusalem and Athens," there is a middle paragraph, the thirty-sixth paragraph, which is dedicated to the distinction between true and false prophets. It is important that Socrates, and not the prophets, has pride of place in the title, in contrast to the first part of the essay; that order, however, is reversed in the essay itself. Before turning to an exegesis of "On Socrates and the Prophets," it would be best to make a few general remarks regarding the second half of the essay.

The second part of "Jerusalem and Athens" returns to the style of the introduction. Having abandoned the narrative style, Strauss once again becomes compelling. We are even reminded, through his analysis of Cohen, of the devastation of which he spoke so hauntingly in the opening of the essay. Strauss's presence once again becomes conspicuous in the essay as he returns to the use of the first person.

Strauss ended "The Biblical Account of the Beginning" with the assertion that all of the prophets, and in particular Moses, are believed to have given man the word of God, the true source of the knowledge of good and evil. He even called this knowledge from the prophets the true tree of knowledge and the tree of life.[1] Therefore, it is only natural that he consider the prophets and their contribution to Jerusalem before ending his discussion on Jerusalem and Athens. However, beyond the paragraph on God's name and the earlier discussion of who the narrator of Genesis is, Strauss does not consider the prophet Moses in "Jerusalem and Athens," an important omission. In other works, Strauss is not reticent about comparing Moses and the prophets, so it is unclear why he is now. Instead, he considers the later prophets: Isaiah, Jonah, Amos, Jeremiah, and Micah. Moreover, he concentrates his analysis not so much on their mission as on their call from God.

Perhaps it would be useful to turn again to Strauss on Maimonides' *Guide for the Perplexed* for illumination regarding the difference in status between Moses and the prophets. In "How To Begin To Study *The Guide for the Perplexed*," Strauss considers the superiority of Moses's prophecy. Its superiority consists in its being the only legislative prophecy: Moses gives the Jews the Torah, the Law.[2] Although he does not mention it, surely it is important that Moses had witnesses to the revelation on Mt. Sinai (Exodus 24). Indeed, the traditional argument in support of the Mosaic revelation is that it has come down to us through an unbroken chain from father to son going back to those who witnessed the events in the desert.[3] Yet, as Strauss points out by way of Maimonides, Moses's prophecy may not be unqualifiedly superior. Because it is legislative in nature, it is limited to actions or to behavior.[4] The prophets' contribution is one of furthering knowledge about God and hence it is, in some sense, contemplative in nature. As Strauss says, "The Account of the Beginning occurs in the Torah of Moses, but the Account of the Chariot, which is identical with the divine science or the apprehension of God (I 34), occurs in the Book of Ezekiel and in its highest form in the sixth chapter of Isaiah."[5] Therefore, it would seem that the prophets are in some sense superior to Moses. On the other hand, as Strauss consistently points out, the Messianism of the prophets is traditionally understood as a return to the beginnings: the Messiah in Jewish tradition will herald a return; hence, "the Messiah is inferior to Moses."[6] It is also interesting to note that in his introductory essay to Maimonides' work Strauss describes Maimonides work, not once but twice, as "a delight to the eyes. For the tree of life is a delight to the eyes."[7] This description is interesting given Strauss's ascribing the tree of life to the prophets' work in "Jerusalem and Athens." These thoughts should be kept in mind when considering Strauss's brief look at the prophets in the present essay. The question remains whether we are to consider the second half of "Jerusalem and Athens" as a continuation of the ascent.

Hermann Cohen
(paragraphs 31–34)

The final paragraph of "The Beginning of the Bible and Its Greek Counterparts" ended with Strauss claiming Plato as the peak of Athens. It is therefore no surprise that he dedicates a part of the second half of "Jerusalem and Athens" to an analysis of Plato's teacher, who is also known as the founder of political philosophy. To borrow a familiar phrase, Strauss proceeds reasonably in the second half of this essay.

Strauss chooses to open the second part of "Jerusalem and Athens" in a surprising way. Similar to the manner in which he began "The Beginning of the Bible and Its Greek Counterparts" with a discussion of social science, he starts "On Socrates and the Prophets" with a discussion of Hermann Cohen. Both parts of the essay, then, open with a discussion of something modern before turning back to more ancient and grander themes. Strauss began with a critique of social science because social science claims that the question of Jerusalem and Athens is no longer important: it is simply a matter of choosing between two different cultures; there is no difference between these two or any other culture; all cultures are limited. In order to turn to Jerusalem and Athens, Strauss had to show the vacuity of cultural relativism. In a similar way, Strauss opens "On Socrates and the Prophets" with an examination of Hermann Cohen and thereby returns to the theme with which he began "Jerusalem and Athens": the problem of placing one's faith in the inevitable march of history toward progress. Although both social science and the ideas of Hermann Cohen are fundamentally defective, when Strauss reaches Cohen, it is an ascent: an ascent because, as Strauss will show, Cohen—unlike the nameless social scientist presented earlier in the essay—at least understands the importance of Jerusalem and Athens, although he misunderstands their nature.

Strauss elsewhere describes Cohen as one who "surpassed all other German professors of philosophy of the period between 1871 and 1925 by the fire and power of his soul."[8] Strauss is not one to bestow praise lightly. Cohen was the founder of the Neo-Kantian school at Marburg. Strauss himself was a student at Marburg, although he came after Cohen's death. As he states in "A Giving of Accounts," "Cohen attracted me because he was a passionate philosopher and a Jew passionately devoted to Judaism."[9] Thus, with Hermann Cohen, Strauss presents a figure who stands for both Jerusalem and Athens; Strauss not only acknowledges him as a distinguished advocate of the Jews, but he also credits him with greatness in the field of philosophy. And this is how Cohen understood himself as well. Cohen's concern with and influence upon Judaism would certainly make him of interest to Strauss. Yet of equal importance is Cohen's concern with what Cohen would call the "social ideal." In other words, he took politics seriously. Strauss acknowledges this in the title essay of *What Is Political Philosophy?* when he contrasts Cohen's work with that of the next generation: "As regards the philosophers, it is sufficient to contrast the work of the four greatest philosophers of the last forty years—Bergson, Whitehead, Husserl, and Heidegger—with the work of Hermann Cohen in order to see how rapidly and thoroughly political philosophy has become discredited."[10] Cohen, then, was the last philosopher to consider politics a subject worthy of consideration. This seriousness, we are led to suspect, was a result of his dual concern with philosophy and Judaism.

Several questions are raised by Strauss's reference to Cohen: why does Strauss consider Cohen's understanding of the problem of Jerusalem and Athens relevant? Why did he not choose someone from what he has already called the "classic struggle" between Jerusalem and Athens, i.e., someone from the Middle Ages? Has he not already destroyed the modern answer? We are not told immediately why Strauss begins with Cohen, but his reason is not completely mysterious because Cohen too, according to Strauss, considered the grand questions of Jerusalem and Athens. And on reading Cohen, one can see the contribution he made to Strauss's formation. As Kenneth L. Deutsch and Walter Nicgorski ask in their introduction to *Leo Strauss: Political Philosopher and Jewish Thinker*:

> According to Strauss, Cohen "sometimes writes like a commentator on a commentary on an already highly technical text and hence like a man whose thought is derivative and traditional in the extreme; and yet he surprises time and again with strikingly original and weighty thoughts." Does Strauss imitate Cohen's example?[11]

From a cursory glance at Cohen, it would seem that the answer is yes. An indication of Cohen's importance to Strauss's thought is revealed by the amount of time that Strauss spends discussing him in his "Introductory Essay" to *Spinoza's Critique of Religion*. In that essay, Strauss credits Cohen with standing against the popular movement to rehabilitate Spinoza—indeed, with beginning the attack on Spinoza. Strauss characterizes Cohen's indictment of Spinoza as follows:

> [Spinoza] opposes spiritual and universalistic Christianity to carnal and particularistic Judaism: the core of Judaism is the Mosaic law as a particularistic not to say tribal law that serves no other end than the earthly or political felicity of the Jewish nation; the Torah does not teach morality, i.e. universal morality; the Mosaic religion is merely national; Moses's God is a tribal and in addition a corporeal God. By denying that the God of Israel is the God of all mankind Spinoza has blasphemed the God of Israel. He reduces Jewish religion to a doctrine of the Jewish state.[12]

Although Cohen's critique of Spinoza is useful, Strauss shows that it is not complete. Part of the problem, Strauss points out, is that Cohen himself does not remain faithful to the Torah because he fails to see the importance of the Account of the Beginning and what it implies about man's nature.

Cohen's failure is that although he "claims to be inspired by Biblical prophecy and hence is Messianic," he relies too much upon Kant, and makes a radical distinction between

> nature and morality, the Is and the Ought, egoism and pure will. The state is essentially moral, and morality cannot be actual except in and through the state. The difficulty presented by the fact that morality is universal and the state is always particular is overcome by the consideration that the state is part of a universal moral order . . . . The radical difference between nature and morality does not amount to a contradiction between nature and morality: nature does not render impossible the fulfillment of the moral demands. The morally demanded infinite progress of morality, and in particular the "eternal progress" toward "eternal peace" . . . is secured by the idea of God. . . .[13]

Cohen, as we will soon see, was a quintessential modern, seeking redemption through the state.

Cohen is best known for his work *Religion of Reason Out of the Sources of Judaism*. In 1972, Strauss wrote the introduction to the English translation of Cohen's *Religion of Reason*, which is reprinted as the last essay in his *Studies in Platonic Political Philosophy*. In it, he credits this work as "the crowning part of Cohen's *System of Philosophy*."[14] Cohen's intent was to distill a religion from Judaism based on the principles of reason alone. For Cohen, Judaism is inadequate in and of itself. Judaism's importance is due to its accomplishment of a historic task: gaining the "recognition of the world for the One God."[15] As Strauss writes in his introduction to the English translation, Cohen understands the Jewish contribution in the following light:

> This is the meaning of Israel's election: to be an eternal witness to pure monotheism, to be *the* martyr, to be the suffering servant of the Lord. The misery of Jewish history is grounded in messianism, which demands humble submission to suffering and hence the rejection of the state as the protector against suffering. Israel has the vocation not only to preserve the true worship of God but also to propagate it among the nations. . . . For the prophets and by the prophets Israel became the rest or remainder of Israel, the Israel of the future, that is to say, the future of mankind. The patriotism of the prophets is at bottom nothing but universalism.[16]

This vocation was made possible, Cohen teaches, in part by the diaspora. As a result of the loss of Israel, the prophets were able to shift their focus from seeing their God as the God of Abraham, Isaac, and Jacob to seeing Him as the God of all mankind. Therein lies the greatness of the Jewish religion for Cohen. Most important, Cohen contends that reason and not obedience must be the ground of religion. Of course, Cohen's insistence on this point goes against all that Strauss has maintained to be the root of revelation throughout "Jerusalem and Athens." As Strauss notes, "The religion of reason leaves no place for absolute obedience or for what traditional Judaism considered the core of faith."[17] Thus, for example, Abraham's willingness to obey God's command to sacrifice Isaac becomes incomprehensible under the religion of reason. Cohen's interest, therefore, is focused on the prophets, not the Torah, and this is not accidental.

Strauss's focus in the second half of "Jerusalem and Athens" is on an essay Cohen wrote entitled "The Social Ideal in Plato and the Prophets" and the similarities between the two essays are intriguing. Both were given as lectures. Strauss even remarks that Cohen repeated this lecture shortly before his death. We are thus reminded that Strauss too saw fit to include "Jerusalem and Athens" as the central chapter of the book he was compiling at the time of his death. Strauss says that Cohen's lecture is his "final view on Jerusalem and Athens and therewith on *the* truth."[18] Hence, we at least learn the reason why Strauss singles out this particular essay of Cohen's. We are led to wonder whether this lecture may be Strauss's final view on *the* truth as well. It is also interesting to note that Strauss, in using the Christian term of the Bible, is merely imitating Cohen, who uses such Christian terms as the Old Testament for the Hebrew Bible, for example.

One possible reason that Strauss begins the second half with Hermann Cohen is that we are meant to compare Strauss with Cohen; we are meant to see that Strauss was also both "a passionate philosopher and a Jew passionately devoted to Judaism," but more importantly, one who transcended historicism, and therefore went beyond Cohen's achievement.[19] Even the similarities in the title of the second part of "Jerusalem and Athens" and Cohen's title suggest that such a comparison is meant to be drawn. Cohen's understanding, as Strauss will show, is fundamentally flawed by its historicist outlook. This, too, may be the reason that Strauss chose to focus on Cohen, that is, to show that a return to Jerusalem or Athens must be unequivocal, that it must not be tainted with anything modern because the modern enterprise is hopelessly defective.

Strauss dedicates the first four paragraphs of the second part of "Jerusalem and Athens" to Hermann Cohen. Simply in terms of space, Cohen gets the most attention in the second part of the essay, while the discussions on the prophets and Socrates each get two paragraphs, and their comparison, three. Strauss describes Cohen here as "the greatest representative of German Jewry and spokesman for it, the most powerful figure among the German professors of philosophy of his time."[20] That time was the middle of the first world war; Germany, and the world, had yet to be devastated by the conflict and destruction of the Third Reich, not to mention Communist Russia. By considering Strauss's other comments regarding Cohen, we have begun to see why Strauss found it necessary to include him in his analysis of Jerusalem and Athens: he must demonstrate that a synthesis of Jerusalem and Athens is impossible.

The first paragraph of "On Socrates and the Prophets" has nineteen sentences. The middle sentence speaks of Cohen's understanding of the distinction between knowledge according to the prophets and knowledge according to science: "The prophets are very much concerned with knowledge: with the knowledge of God, but this knowledge as the prophets understood it, has no connection whatever with scientific knowledge, it is knowledge only in a metaphorical sense."[21] With some qualification, I think this can be said to be Strauss's view as well. Both men insist that prophetic and scientific knowledge are decidedly different things. At the very least, it can be said that both acknowledge Judaism's antagonism to philosophy.

Before looking at Strauss on Cohen, it will be helpful to look at Cohen's essay first. In "The Social Ideal in Plato and the Prophets," Cohen is quite emphatic regarding the prophet's lack of scientific knowledge: "Not even in Babylonia did he come under its spell, and in Palestine he certainly felt no inclination to lift its veil. The host of stars is of interest to him only because of the God who brought them into being, counted, and named them."[22] Even more stridently, Cohen states that the biblical mind "can barely cope with the concept of chaos, let alone conceive of some primeval matter."[23] As we have seen, Strauss's view of the creation account in the Bible would differ from Cohen's; Strauss sees it as an explicit rejection of and counter to the philosophic understanding. According to Cohen, the prophets' contribution to world history is their cosmopolitanism, their sense of compassion for their fellow man, and hence their keen sense of justice as shown by their concern for the unfortunate: widows, orphans, and the poor. Cohen's quarrel with the prophets is that they did not take that sense of compassion and conceive of trying to obliterate "the metaphysics of death."[24] While the prophets believed in the possibility of progress, they did not take their ideal to its ultimate consequences. This was because their insight into the human condition was not based on knowledge but simply on intuition.[25] For Cohen, a believer in progress, thought that "without philosophy, mankind's suffering cannot be ended; knowledge must become the cornerstone of the world's structure."[26] The prophetic insight into the necessity of compassion needs Platonic science to complete it. Plato, in turn, is equally flawed because he refused to recognize the equality of man. He could not conceive of a world in which there was not a division between rulers and ruled, and this failure Cohen found appalling.[27] Thus, we see just what a product of modernity Cohen is. By combining the social ideals of Plato and the prophets, he envisioned a world of the future in which there would be no suffering, and no distinctions among men.

Strauss begins his analysis of the essay with a synopsis of Cohen's understanding of Jerusalem and Athens. Cohen can first of all be credited with recognizing that "'Plato and the prophets are the two most important sources of modern culture.'"[28] We note that with the use of the term "culture" we are once again in the realm of social science. It is also at this point that we find Strauss's single reference to Christianity that we noted earlier: "Being concerned with the 'social ideal,' he does not say a single word on Christianity in the whole lecture."[29]

In exploring this comment, and seeming critique of Christianity, the first thing we notice is that Christianity is not social, i.e., it is not political. The Greek religion was inextricably linked with the political; he who conquered a city conquered its gods as well. And to a certain extent, Judaism, whose revelation is law, is bound up with the political too. Remember the distinction Strauss makes between the first and last word the Bible speaks about monarchy. With Christianity, however, there is a great change. Revelation is a person, not a law, and this person is also *logos* itself.[30] For further illumination we turn to Ernest Fortin's discussion of Strauss's distinction between Christianity and Judaism, a distinction between revelation understood as faith and revelation understood as law. Fortin writes, in his essay "Rational Theologians and Irrational Philosophers: A Straussian Perspective,"

> Anyone who takes the trouble to read the New Testament attentively from this point of view cannot help being struck by its all but total indifference to problems of a properly political nature. It will soon be discovered that it shows no awareness of the distinction between regimes, does not indicate any preference for one over the others, imposes none of its own, and makes no concrete recommendations for the reform of the social order. It was meant to be preached to all nations but was not destined to replace them or meant to compete with them on their own level. It simply takes for granted that Christians will continue to organize their temporal lives within the framework of the society to which they happen to belong and, while it strenuously opposes all forms of injustice, it leaves the administration of public affairs to the authorities whom God has ordained for this purpose. Its dominant theme is not justice but love, and love as a political principle is at best a pretty fuzzy thing. Accordingly, it does not tell us *who* should rule, but in general *how* human beings, be they rulers or subjects, ought to behave toward one another, which is a different matter altogether.[31]

James Schall puts the matter succinctly: Christians "must not confuse politics with salvation. States are not saved. Persons are."[32] As both Fortin and Schall suggest, this has a profound effect upon the political realm. But it should be emphasized that this theme of love and salvation was never intended as a political principle. It also must be remembered that the New Testament was built upon the Old: "Do not suppose that I have come to abolish the Law and the prophets; I did not come to abolish, but to complete. I tell you this: so long as heaven and earth endure, not a letter, not a stroke, will disappear from the Law until all that must happen has happened" (Matt. 5:17–18).

At its best, Christianity lets politics be politics and not metaphysics. As Schall writes,

> To state the case differently, I noticed that one of the primary effects of authentic revelation on political philosophy itself seemed to be, paradoxically, to free the city from the burden of becoming itself an ontology When religion remained itself—if and when it did—it allowed politics to be only politics, but on the condition that the questions posed about the highest things were themselves properly formulated and freely addressed in their own order, which was not necessarily or exclusively

political. I was always struck by the extreme, quasi-religious character of political philosophy when it claimed for itself something more than its limited competence. On the other hand, politics did have its own legitimacy, which made it something more than a mere tool of metaphysics or theology, however valid these latter might also be. I found, in other words, that often when the political philosopher thought he was talking about political philosophy, he was in fact speaking of revelation or metaphysics.[33]

It is true, and Strauss understood it, that to a certain degree, modernity's crisis is a result of an attempt to realize the other-worldly goals of Christianity in the here and now. Man forgot that "the Christian solution to the problem of the locus of man's ultimate happiness has been the cause of why men could participate in the public order for its own sake and not as some kind of surrogate for beatitude."[34] But it is also important to note that this attempt is heretical by its very nature, a perversion of Christianity. As G. K. Chesterton puts it forcefully:

> The modern world is not evil; in some ways the modern world is far too good. It is full of wild and wasted virtues. When a religious scheme is shattered (as Christianity was shattered at the Reformation), it is not merely the vices that are let loose. The vices are, indeed, let loose, and they wander and do damage. But the virtues are let loose also; and the virtues wander more wildly, and the virtues do more terrible damage. The modern world is full of the old Christian virtues gone mad.[35]

This diagnosis is one with which I think Strauss would agree. Try as one might, it is hard to find an explicit critique of Christianity by Strauss in "Jerusalem and Athens" or elsewhere.[36] Indeed, as John East has stated, "Although his personal heritage was Jewish, there is not a trace of antagonism in Strauss's writing toward Christianity; indeed, probably the most moving dimension of Strauss's thinking was his effort to afford 'recognition of that common ground' between Judaism and Christianity."[37]

After his sole remark on Christianity, Strauss begins with Cohen's analysis of Plato in "The Social Ideal of Plato and the Prophets"; he proceeds therefore in exactly the opposite way that Cohen does. Strauss says of his synopsis of Cohen that it is crude but not misleading. According to Cohen, we learn from Plato that truth is found in science. Plato also understood that science is incomplete and must be supplemented with the idea of the good, which, Strauss is quick to point out, should not be mistaken for God. For Cohen, Strauss explains, the idea of the good means a rational or scientific ethics. Scientific knowledge is the highest human achievement, according to Cohen. As Strauss suggests, "It is perhaps with a view to this fact that Cohen speaks once of the divine Plato but never of the divine prophets."[38] When we turn to this passage we find that Cohen states that "all moral cognition must also be scientifically or philosophically substantiated. And here the divine Plato, admonishing us to pursue the eternal verities, remains forever the guardian of the scientific approach to knowledge as the only infallible guarantee of truth."[39] Science is the divine pursuit.

But Plato's science is fundamentally insufficient and therefore requires supplementing from the prophets. Plato's imperfection is rooted in his understanding of the unchanging nature of man. As Strauss reminds his audience, the best regime is only possible if philosophers are given the power to rule, an unlikely occurrence at best. Philosophers must rule because only philosophers have knowledge. But philosophers by nature are few and far between. Hence, there will never be a race of philosophers; wars and warriors will always be with us; and there will always be classes, or a distinction between the rulers and the ruled. The best regime will be one that is ruled by a philosopher, necessarily the rule of one or only a few over many. This, for Cohen, is the "dark side of Platonism."[40] As he notes, "The flaw in a system which regards intellect and reason as the sole principles of cognition here becomes so manifest that one feels tempted to resort, after all, to the frail principle of compassion."[41] This "frail principle of compassion" is supplied by the prophets.

It is interesting that Strauss does not reveal what exactly Cohen held to be the crucial insight of the prophets; he only hints at it by saying that for Cohen, the prophets supply what is lacking in Plato only because of the prophets' ignorance of science and, therefore, of nature. All Strauss says regarding the prophets is that they are very much concerned with knowledge of a specific kind, knowledge of God. When we turn to Cohen we see that the prophets "discovered man's innate worth, and it is to their social conscience that we owe this discovery."[42] The prophets "regard man neither as the sons of gods nor as a demigod or hero. Their image of man is one of human weakness. And inasmuch as this weakness is primarily a moral inadequacy, the sinner is seen as the archetypal man."[43] All men are flawed. But more important, despite their imperfection, all are loved by the God of Israel: "Man's horizon widens as soon as he realizes that his own God also loves the barbarian and even declares that the hostile nations are quite as much His precious possession as is Israel itself."[44] This understanding led to a further insight: the belief that suffering is not a punishment or a result of guilt. This realization, for Cohen, is the distinction between religion and mythology; as Cohen writes, "wherever man associates suffering primarily with death, mythology still reigns supreme."[45] Just as philosophy is foreign to the prophets, so too is tragedy. But despite this advancement, compassion is inadequate because by itself it is not a sufficient motivation for social action. Plato supplies that impetus through science because "without philosophy, mankind's suffering cannot be ended."[46] For Cohen, there is no redemptive quality to suffering; it is something to be overcome. Thus, in Cohen, we have a true wedding of religion and the Enlightenment: a union of morality and science for the relief of man's estate. Having gone through the biblical account of the beginning with Strauss, we already know what a perversion of biblical thought Cohen's understanding is, but Strauss has yet to teach us what the prophets say.

Strauss begins his critique of Cohen with the second paragraph. Cohen deserves praise for showing us the fundamental "antagonism between Plato and the prophets."[47] However, that is insufficient because Cohen thought that this antagonism could be overcome. Strauss offers the first proof of Cohen's failing with a historical argument: Cohen was trapped by the time in which he lived. This allowed him more faith in the possibility of man's progress than the events that have taken place since would allow a reasonable man to hope. Although we are not bound by history, we can learn from it: "Catastrophes and horrors of a magnitude hitherto unknown, which we have seen and through which we have lived, were better provided for, or made intelligible, by both Plato and the prophets than by the modern belief in progress."[48] It should be noted that Strauss becomes quite personal here; there are six uses of the first person in this paragraph alone. We are reminded that Strauss, unlike Cohen, lived through such horrors. For Strauss, the fundamental flaw in Cohen's understanding is that he fails to see that there is a problem in combining Jerusalem and Athens and his failure is one of naiveté. It is unwise to place your faith in man, as it results in a misunderstanding of Jerusalem as well as Athens, and therefore a misunderstanding of man. As Strauss writes in his "Introductory Essay," Cohen placed his trust of the "infinite progress or of his belief in history, of his 'optimism,' of his certainty of the ultimate victory of the good: 'there is no evil.'"[49] In contrast, Strauss had lived through a vivid demonstration of the evil of which man is capable. Cohen did not see the need for the Torah or the Law, but only the prophets. But, as we have seen, in attempting to overcome the need for the yoke of the Law, the moderns only succeeded in unleashing a level of malevolence hitherto unknown.

In the third paragraph, we discover Cohen's cardinal mistake. He failed to see that the fundamental quarrel is between the moderns and the ancients and not between Plato and Aristotle or Kant and Hegel. This mistake led Cohen to misunderstand Plato and Aristotle, not to mention Kant and Hegel.

The fourth and final paragraph dedicated to Cohen is a transitional one. It begins the movement away from Cohen and back to Plato and the prophets themselves. Once again, we are finding modern answers to our questions woefully inadequate. Strauss begins this move by suggesting that it is more accurate to speak of Socrates and the prophets rather than of Plato and the prophets as Cohen did. Strauss bases his case on the fact that it is unclear how to differentiate between Plato and Socrates. He points out that in proceeding in this manner he separates himself from tradition. Thus, just as he became the interpreter for Jerusalem, so too is he for Athens. The decisive issue for Strauss is that Plato "points away from himself to Socrates."[50] If we are to take Plato seriously, he argues, we must look to Socrates. The first thing Strauss teaches us is that, unlike Plato, Socrates had a mission. But before considering Socrates, Strauss turns first to the prophets.

The Prophets
(paragraphs 35–36)

The section on the prophets begins abruptly. For the second time in "Jerusalem and Athens," Strauss uses the first person singular. And the contrast could not be more startling. Here Strauss states: "I cannot speak in my own words of the mission of the prophets. Surely here and now I cannot do more than remind you of three prophetic utterances of singular force and grandeur."[51] His first use of the first person singular was bold, even willful: "I believe that we ought to render this statement by 'I shall be What I shall be'. . . ."[52] With his second use of it, he speaks only of his inadequacy, his inability to use his own words when speaking about the prophets. And in fact, this paragraph consists mostly of passages from the Bible. We should compare this confession of inability with his comments in the introduction of "Jerusalem and Athens," where he reminds his audience that "it is better to fail nobly than to succeed basely."[53] Surely his first admission is meant to be ironic; the second does not appear to be. Strauss's inability to speak about the prophets should be compared with the skill with which he led us through the beginning of the Bible. Why is there a difference? Is it the difference already alluded to between speaking about the Account of the Beginning and the Account of the Chariot, between natural and divine science? between speaking about man and speaking about God? Perhaps it is not fitting to speak of the divine science in a lecture.

Strauss does not raise considerations of whether or not the prophets' works are compiled carefully, a question he considered paramount in relation to the Account of the Beginning. Again we note that Strauss chooses not to include Ezekiel among the prophets he mentions, even though Ezekiel is the prophet who reveals the Account of the Chariot. Strauss does include Isaiah, the prophet who has given us the divine science in its "highest form."[54] Another curiosity regarding this section is that while Strauss speaks about how the prophets receive their mission, he says very little about what it is exactly.

The fifth paragraph of "On Socrates and the Prophets" (paragraph 35) has twenty-six sentences. Strauss quotes from Isaiah, Jonah, Amos, and Jeremiah, all prophets with a mission. Each prophet, we learn, is like Plato's philosopher described in the *Republic*: he is compelled to carry out his mission. God compels the prophets to do His bidding. What compels the philosopher to return to the cave? Whatever it is, it is certainly not God. It should also be noted that there is one more passage from the Bible than his opening statement indicated. Thus, one of the passages does not speak with force and grandeur of the prophetic mission. Apparently, Jonah, the prophet who tries to refuse the mission that God has set before him, does not speak with the same force and grandeur as the other prophets.

Strauss begins with Isaiah. Isaiah, perhaps the greatest of all the prophets, has the pride of place. Strauss quotes from Chapter 6, which he has elsewhere called the most fundamental articulation of the divine name.[55] Strauss therefore is beckoning us to compare this articulation with the Mosaic revelation of God's name. But the fundamental articulation of the divine name is even more mysterious than the Mosaic revelation. Strauss gives no explanation of it. The citation from Isaiah is the longest (v. 1–8). It is also interesting that the passage from Isaiah is the only one for which Strauss does not give the pertinent verses; he only indicates the chapter to which we should turn. Curiously, he spends little time in explaining Isaiah's words. The quotation describes Isaiah's vision of the Lord God. Isaiah immediately recognizes that he is unworthy to see God. An angel purifies him with a burning coal and thereupon, as Strauss notes, Isaiah "volunteers" to be sent.[56]

Isaiah stands in marked contrast to his fellow prophet, Jonah. Jonah's first reaction is to flee from the Lord and his mission. Strauss states only that God does not allow Jonah to refuse his mission; he refrains from mentioning Jonah's stay in the whale. Jonah is simply forced to go to Nineveh, a pagan city. God sends Jonah to the capital of Assyria to stop those unchosen ones from persisting in their wickedness. If they do not cease, God will destroy them. Jonah is successful in his mission, despite his initial reluctance. God spares the city because the king orders public fasting and sacrifice; the city atones for its sins. The Lord God is apparently not completely uninterested in pagans. It is interesting to note, as the Biblical scholar Nahum Sarna does, that

> The sins of the generation of the flood are subsumed under the term *hamas*, the definition of which is "injustice, lawlessness, social unrighteousness." This is the same sin for which the heathen city of Nineveh was to be destroyed and for which "sulphurous fire" rained down upon Sodom and Gomorra."[57]

Sarna mentions this in the context of the God of Israel holding both individuals and societies culpable for their actions. Strauss, however, as has already been noted, focuses his attention only on the prophets receiving their mission. It is also interesting that Strauss does not cite the source for his quotation from the Book of Jonah.

Amos and Jeremiah, according to Strauss, also speak of being forced to act for God in their missions. Here he gives the second and third prophetic utterances. Amos, a shepherd of the southern kingdom of Judah, cries "'The lion hath roared, who will not fear? the Lord God hath spoken; who will not prophesy?'"[58] He who hears the word of God must act. As Strauss explains the prophets' compulsion, "The prophets overpowered by the majesty of the Lord, by His wrath and His mercy, bring the message of His wrath and His mercy."[59] This is the closest he comes to revealing the prophetic mission. Strauss says nothing in regard to Jeremiah, who prophesied after the Babylonians destroyed the Temple, but is instead content to quote verses 1:4–10. On being told that he was chosen even before his conception to serve God, Jeremiah protests that he is like a child, incapable of carrying out such a task. Feeling woefully inadequate to act for God, Jeremiah is told not to fear because God has put words in his mouth· "'See, I have this day set thee over the nations and over the kingdoms, to root out, and to pull down, and to destroy, and to throw down, to build, and to plant.'"[60] This is one more indication of the prophetic mission through the prophet's own description. Thus Strauss ends the first paragraph on the mission of the prophets.

The second and final paragraph on the prophets is the central paragraph of "On Socrates and the Prophets." It deals with the critical question of revelation itself, i.e., the distinction between false and true prophets. It is fifteen sentences long. The middle sentence is a biblical quotation regarding true prophets: "Or, as Jeremiah put it when opposing the false prophet Hananiah: 'The prophets that have been before me and before thee of old prophesied both against many countries, and against great kingdoms, of war, and of evil, and of pestilence.' (28.8)"[61] Like the previous paragraph, it is heavily interspersed with biblical quotations, but this time they all come from Jeremiah. Indeed, this time Strauss tells us that we will understand the distinction between false and true prophets only if "we listen to and meditate on" Jeremiah's words that "'cursed is the man, that trusteth in man, and makes flesh his arm. . . .'"[62]

Here Strauss admits that not only true prophets have claimed to be sent by God. Most men are, therefore, left in a quandary over whom to believe. Even those who have heard both are unsure to whom they should turn. The Bible's answer to the problem is simple: false prophets lie; they tell the people that which they most want to hear. False prophets promise peace. Citing the prophet Jeremiah, who struggled against the false prophet Hananiah, "The false prophets are 'prophets of the deceit of their own heart' (Jeremiah 26)."[63] The true prophet brings the word of God, which is "like a hammer that breaketh the rock in pieces."[64] Strauss sums up the difference beautifully:

> The false prophets trust in flesh, even if that flesh is the temple in Jerusalem, the promised land, nay, the chosen people itself, nay, God's promise to the chosen people if that promise is taken to be an unconditional promise and not as part of a Covenant. The true prophets, regardless of whether they predict doom or salvation, predict the unexpected, the humanly unforeseeable—what would not occur to men, left to themselves, to fear or to hope.[65]

Again we are reminded of Strauss's change of God's name to "I shall be What I shall be," which keeps the God of Israel radically free. He even uses the Hebrew word for God's name in the next sentence to ensure that we see the connection. It is interesting that Strauss fails to make the traditional arguments for distinguishing false from true prophets: first, that false prophets are those who contradict Mosaic law; and second, that true prophets demonstrate the veracity of their calling through miracles.[66]

Socrates
(paragraphs 37–38)

In the seventh paragraph of "On Socrates and the Prophets," Strauss finally gets to the subject of Socrates. Strauss insists that the only place to learn of Socrates' mission is in Plato's *Apology of Socrates*. The two other sources for Socrates are omitted at this point. Strauss did refer to Aristophanes in the last section, but not to his *Clouds*—the Aristophanean critique of the Socratic enterprise. And Strauss will end "Jerusalem and Athens" with a quote from Xenophon's *Memorabilia*. At this point, however, Plato is the only source. Yet Strauss qualifies his initial statement by declaring that the *Apology* "presents itself as the speech" that Socrates gave to the city of Athens, a careful reminder that we must take Plato at his word that he provides a true account.[67] Trust is also necessary, at least in some respect, regarding philosophy. Socrates is charged with denying the existence of the gods of Athens and with corrupting the young. What Strauss first singles out from this dialogue is that Socrates denies that he has anything more than human wisdom. This contrasts with the prophets, who decry their own abilities. They make no claim to wisdom: "Then said I, Ah, Lord God! behold, I cannot speak; for I am a child" (Jer. 1:6). But while God inspires the prophets, Socrates has no such inspiration or guide. Indeed, as Strauss will soon point out, Socrates' guide only serves to keep him from action, never to spur him toward it.

Strauss's next citation, Halevi's *Kuzari*, comes as somewhat of a surprise. The *Kuzari*, a classic medieval defense of the faith of Israel, is a dialogue between the heathen king of the Khazars and a rabbi who converts the king, but not before the king first converses with a philosopher, a Christian scholastic, and an Islamic doctor. The king becomes interested in conversion after an angel appears to him in a dream and reveals that "Thy way of thinking is indeed pleasing to the Creator, but not thy way of acting."[68] So our first glimpse of Socrates is through the eyes of a Jewish writer, one who takes great pains to place himself against philosophy. According to Halevi, Socrates never denies the possibility of divine wisdom, only that he has it. In the footnote that follows this discussion, Strauss refers us to two different passages in the *Kuzari*.

In the first passage, the rabbi tells the king of the distinction between the philosopher and the religious man.[69] Both are interested in God, but not for the same reasons. The philosopher is seeking knowledge. For him, someone's ignorance about God is no more harmful than his ignorance about the earth's shape. The philosopher seeks knowledge not in order to worship, but in order to imitate the Active Intellect. In the second and lengthier passage, the rabbi argues with the king about the philosophic quest for wisdom regarding the universe.[70] This quest is unimportant in light of creation. Through his argument, the rabbi demonstrates his complete familiarity with philosophic arguments. He ends this passage by saying this regarding the philosophic pursuit:

> All these things are still less satisfactory than the "Book of Creation." They are full of doubts, and there is no consensus of opinion between one philosopher and another. Yet they cannot be blamed, nay, deserve thanks for all they have produced in abstract speculations. For their intentions were good; they observed the laws of reason, and led virtuous lives. At all events, they have earned this praise, because the same duties were not imposed on them as they were on us when we were given revelation, and a tradition which is tantamount to revelation.[71]

In both passages, Halevi paraphrases Socrates' disclaimer of anything more than human wisdom.

In referring us to Halevi's *Kuzari*, Strauss also refers us to *Persecution and the Art of Writing*, the first and only time he will refer to a work of his own. The passage is from his essay "The Law of Reason in the *Kuzari*." It is well worth citing at length. Strauss is discussing Halevi's supposition that it is impossible to be both a philosopher and a believer in any revealed religion. He writes:

> For, according to him, a genuine philosopher is a man such as Socrates who possesses "human wisdom" and is invincibly ignorant of "Divine wisdom." It is the impossibility of converting a philosopher to Judaism which he demonstrates *ad oculos* by omitting a disputation between the scholar and the philosopher. Such a disputation, we may say to begin with, is impossible: *contra negantem principia non est disputandum*. The philosopher denies as such the premises on which the demonstration of the truth of any revealed religion is based. That denial may be said to proceed from the fact that he, being a philosopher, is untouched by, or has never tasted, that "Divine thing" or "Divine command" (*amr ilahi*) which is known from actual experience both to the actual believer, the Jewish scholar and the potential believer, the king. For, in contrast with the philosopher, the king was from the outset, by nature, a pious man: he had been observing the pagan religion of his country with great eagerness and all his heart; he had been a priest as well as a king.[72]

Strauss continues his argument by taking the comparison between the king and Socrates further. Socrates does not himself receive word from the oracle, whereas the king has a dream in which an angel appears. Both these occurrences, however, change both men's lives. Socrates begins to examine other people's claim to knowledge; the king examines the various religions. Socrates verifies the truth of the oracle; the king obeys the angel. Strauss ends his discussion by stating that "Halevi makes clear the natural limits of his explicit arguments: these arguments are convincing, and are meant to be convincing, to such naturally pious people only as have had some foretaste of Divine revelation by having experienced a revelation by an angel or at least a rudimentary revelation of one kind or another."[73] We are once again reminded of Strauss's cautionary note regarding miracles, i.e., that they are not for the purpose of convincing those who do not believe in the possibility of God.

In "Jerusalem and Athens," however, Strauss maintains that Halevi is not quite correct because he goes too far in attributing only human wisdom to Socrates. As Strauss points out, Socrates tells the Athenians about the origin of his mission: Chairephon's trek to Delphi, where he asks the oracle of Apollo if anyone is wiser than Socrates. The oracle tells Chairephon that no one is wiser than Socrates. Strauss shows us how strange, in comparison to the prophets, Socrates' reaction is:

> Socrates takes it for granted that the reply given by the Pythia was given by the god Apollo himself. Yet this does not induce him to take it for granted that the god's reply is true. He does take it for granted that it is not meet for the god to lie. Yet this does not make the god's reply convincing to him.[74]

We are reminded of the Platonic distinction between the visible and hence knowable gods and the gods of tradition. Socrates is skeptical of the Athenian god's ability to know the truth; the Athenian gods, then, cannot be the highest gods.

There are other interesting comparisons to be made. First, in contrast to the prophets, Apollo does not speak directly to Socrates. Nor does he really give him a mission. Socrates' mission is the result of his doubt of the god's knowledge. Even though he doubts the god, Strauss shows us that Socrates' carrying out of his mission proves a vindication of the god. The god did indeed speak truthfully: Socrates is the wisest because he knows that he is ignorant about the most important things. Socrates claims that the oracle actually wanted him to lead a life that examined himself and others. Thus, in an unexpected twist, Socrates has become the gift of the god Apollo to the city of Athens. Strauss makes this interesting comment regarding Socrates in *The City and Man*: "The gods do not approve of man's trying to seek

140   *Chapter Six*

out what they did not wish to reveal, the things in heaven and beneath the earth. A pious man will therefore not investigate the divine things but only the human things, the things left to man's investigation."[75] Socrates seeks wisdom by asking questions of his fellow citizens. He is, according to Strauss's definition, a pious man.

The contrast between Socrates and the prophets could not be more stark. In "Progress or Return," Strauss puts the difference in these terms:

> Contrast the account of the *Akedah*—the binding of Isaac—in the story of Abraham. There the crucial point is that Abraham obeys an unintelligible command, the command being unintelligible because he has been promised that his name would be called through Isaac and in the descendants of Isaac, and now he is asked to slaughter that son. Yet Abraham obeys the command unhesitatingly. The only analogy in Greek philosophy of which I can think would be the example of Socrates who is or believes at least that he has been, commanded by Apollo to [do] something, and yet the action consists not in unhesitating obedience, but in examining an unintelligible saying of Apollo.[76]

In paragraph thirty-eight, Strauss continues his examination of Socrates. In this short paragraph of three sentences, Strauss considers Socrates' daimonion. Although Socrates did not speak with Apollo, he does claim to hear a divine voice from time to time. In contrast to the Delphic oracle, which Socrates understands as urging him on to a philosophic life that examines the opinions of others, his daimonion only keeps him back: it keeps him from mortal danger by stopping him from entering politics. Strauss ironically points out that it is Socrates' obedience to the Delphic oracle that gets him into trouble. We are thus led to wonder how well the Athenian gods take care of their citizens. If they offer up the wisest, how well do the rest fare? Of course, Socrates was well advanced in years by the time he was put to death. We also wonder why his daimonion, which had hitherto protected him, was silent at his trial. Socrates takes its silence to mean that what has occurred is good.[77] Moreover, if Socrates is truly Apollo's gift to the city, then at least one of the gods cares for Athens because he wants them to be exhorted to virtuous activity.

One question should be raised before turning to the final section of "Jerusalem and Athens": how seriously are we to take this discussion of Apollo? Is this yet another likely tale? The issue will become clearer in the final section, but it would help to refer to Plato's "Second Letter to Dionysius." In his "Second Letter," Plato tells the tyrant Dionysius that he wrote dialogues in order to present philosophy, through

Socrates, as something new and beautiful; Socrates on his own is not either of these things, but through the Platonic art, he becomes compelling; the dialogues make Socrates, and through him, philosophy, attractive.[78] Perhaps, in order to make Socrates attractive, and thereby the pursuit of virtue attractive, Plato presents Socrates as Apollo's gift to Athens.

Comparison of the Two Missions
(paragraphs 39–41)

We have now reached the concluding section of the essay. In the final three paragraphs, Strauss compares the two missions of Socrates and the prophets: it is a comparison of the summits of Athens and Jerusalem. Having spoken of how they received their missions, he turns to what their missions are. In the first paragraph on the two divine missions, Strauss echoes the themes with which he began "On Socrates and the Prophets." He discusses the possibility of human nature changing and of a world without war.

Strauss begins by stating that because both Socrates and the prophets have divine missions, they are therefore concerned with justice or, more exactly, "the perfectly just society," one that is free from evil.[79] Again the contrast is marked. The God of Israel is concerned with justice, which, according to Aristotle, is the paramount political virtue.[80] Thus, Socrates and the prophets are in agreement about what is important. They disagree, however, about how the perfectly just regime will come to be. The prophets, of course, predict a Messianic age, i.e., something dependent upon divine intervention. For Socrates, the best regime is possible but completely dependent upon chance, i.e., the unlikely circumstance that a philosopher will have political power. According to Socrates, divine intervention is not required for the perfectly just regime to exist; it is within the capacity of human nature without changing that nature. In other words, if it occurs, it will not mean that men have become a race of philosopher kings, but only that a particular philosopher will rule. The prophets, however, predict divine intervention, which will result in drastic changes to all of nature. Strauss cites two passages from Isaiah. In Isaiah 11:9, the prophet writes that all the earth will become full of the knowledge of God. Thus, all creation will participate in the highest good. The Messianic age, moreover, will herald an unprecedented age of universal peace. Knowledge of God will no longer be the preserve of the chosen nation. The rest of mankind will no longer be left with only the sun and moon to worship. Citing the often quoted passage of Isaiah 2:2–4, Strauss shows how different the two visions are as he contrasts this universal age of peace with the Socratic ideal in which the best regime will be limited to one city and will still require a warrior class.[81]

Remember that Strauss has called the perfectly just society one that is free from evil. But Socrates and the prophets have a different understanding of evil. For Socrates, evil is somehow rooted in matter. As Strauss points out in "Progress or Return," "Man's guilt was indeed the guiding theme to tragedy. Hence Plato rejects tragedy from his best city."[82] From the standpoint of revelation, however, evil does not stem from matter; matter is good. Instead, evil is rooted in will. This distinction is important. As Schall explains,

> This means that real evil *need* not exist. Perhaps a cosmos without it is conceivable. When evil does appear, however, it is chosen. This is what gives the true dramatic, both tragic and comic, noble and ordinary qualities to existence. . . . Since evil is chosen, then, it can likewise be "unchosen," except to the degree free choice can permanently fix itself in its own selected world, a world discussed under the scriptural rubric of hell, as we have seen.[83]

After examining the perfectly just society according to both Socrates and the prophets, Strauss next considers the just man with the following paragraph. It is a short paragraph of five sentences. For Socrates, the just man is the philosopher. His life is dedicated to searching for the good. More important, virtue is not his end but only the means used to reach his goal, which is knowledge. For the prophets, a search for the good is unnecessary. It has already been provided by God Himself. Strauss quotes the prophet Micah as a summation of what Jerusalem requires: "God 'hath shewed thee, o man, what is good; and what doth the Lord require of thee, but to do justly, and to love mercy, and to walk humbly with thy God.' (Micah 6:8)"[84] Thus Strauss argues that virtue is of higher rank than knowledge in the Bible, and is accessible to all men, wise or not.

Strauss next contends that it is precisely because of this distinction that the prophets address a people, even all peoples, whereas Socrates normally speaks with only one man. The prophets are orators, whereas Socrates "engages in conversations with one man, which means he is addressing questions to him."[85] The search for knowledge is necessarily a private enterprise, but instilling virtue in a people is necessarily public. But this sentence is still unclear. In a letter to Alexander Kojéve, Strauss sheds some light on this distinction: "I do not believe in the possibility of a conversation of Socrates with the *people* (it is not clear to me what you think about this); the relation of the philosopher to the people is mediated by a certain kind of rhetoricians who arouse fear of punishment after death; the philosopher can guide these rhetoricians but can not do their work (this is the meaning of the *Gorgias*)."[86] From Socrates' and therefore philosophy's perspective, the prophets have a beneficial purpose. And as we have seen from the passages from the *Kuzari*, at least from Halevi's perspective, philosophy, too, can be understood as a good: "Yet they cannot be blamed, nay, deserve thanks for all they have produced in abstract speculations. For their intentions were good; they observed the laws of reason, and led virtuous lives."[87]

The final paragraph of "Jerusalem and Athens" opens with what Strauss calls a "striking example" of a prophet talking to a single man, or engaging in conversation with one man as Socrates did.[88] That example is the one of Nathan speaking to King David (2 Sam. 12:1-7), the same citation that Strauss uses as a preface to *Natural Right and History*. Nathan relays the parable of the stolen lamb to David, who is eager to see justice done against the perpetrator. Strauss compares this exchange to one that Xenophon records about Socrates and Critias, a former companion of Socrates who became one of the Thirty Tyrants.

Although the prophet and Socrates say similar things, the circumstances differ vastly. Socrates compares Critias's ability as a statesman to a cowherd whose cattle decrease and go bad. Strauss notes the distinctions: Socrates does not confront his former companion directly, but the word does get back to Critias. Both men reprimand men in positions of political power. One rebukes a king who takes advantage of his authority to pursue private pleasures: David murders Uriah the Hittite in order to take Bathsheba as his wife. The other rebukes a man for harming the citizenry in general. Strauss does not tell us either man's reaction to his rebuke. Elsewhere, Xenophon relays that Critias was scolded by Socrates on an earlier occasion for having an uncontrolled appetite.[89] This reprimand earned Socrates the dislike of Critias. According to Xenophon, this hatred led him to enact a law directed against Socrates that forbade teaching the art of debate; later, he went further and directly forbade Socrates from asking questions of the young.[90] Whereas David accepts Nathan's, and thereby God's, rebuke and even accepts the punishment—the loss of his and Bathsheba's first-born son—Socrates is not successful in stemming the tyrannical desire of his former companion. David repents because he loves God. Critias remains unrepentant, affected by neither philosophy nor the gods of tradition.

Strauss elsewhere compares this conversation between Nathan and

David to the one between the tyrant Hiero and the poet Simonides, in which the poet playfully argues with Hiero that moderation is more pleasurable than giving in to his tyrannic impulses. Simonides must proceed gently, whereas Nathan shows no fear in severely castigating David for his misdeeds.[91] Strauss also compares the two kings' crimes: David killed only one man, Hiero, countless. It is interesting that both Greek examples—Critias and Socrates and Hiero and Simonides—come from Xenophon. Socrates, in contrast to Simonides, makes an enemy; he did not proceed cautiously enough with his rebuke. In "Progress or Return," Strauss tells us the reason for the difference in success between the philosopher and the prophet: "The force of the moral demand is weakened in Greek philosophy because in Greek philosophy this demand is not backed up by divine promises."[92] Strauss has demonstrated already that the traditional gods of the Greeks give man no reason for hope. Now we know that philosophy, too, is limited in its appeal.

This paragraph is remarkable for many reasons. Continuing in the style of the last several pages, Strauss himself writes only two sentences; the rest are quotes from the two sources. He ends the paragraph abruptly in the middle of a quotation from Xenophon. By ending with ellipses it is as if he is again admitting that his account is incomplete. It is also important that Xenophon, the gentleman philosopher, is the last to be quoted. We might have expected Plato, as the peak of Athens, to have had the last word. Nevertheless, philosophy does have the last word, leading us to think that philosophy triumphs. But, as we have seen, reason's last word only demonstrates philosophy's ineffectiveness in the face of evil.[93] The God of Israel, on the other hand, punishes David for something that would appear trivial when compared to the crimes of the average Greek tyrant. Thus Strauss brings us to a close of "Jerusalem and Athens."

Strauss ends "Jerusalem and Athens" in a surprising manner, with what can be called a critique of philosophy: it lacks teeth. Yet that argument, of course, is based only on utility. It also sets aside the question of the possibility of philosophers ruling. There is no question that revelation is a more effective basis for morality. For example, there is no need to invent likely tales such as the myth of Er.[94] In "Progress or Return," Strauss puts it in more striking terms, calling it a "philosophic lack of depth":

> Greek philosophy has frequently been blamed for the absence from it of that ruthless examination of one's intentions which is the consequence of the biblical demand for purity of the heart. "Know thyself" means

for the Greeks, know what it means to be a human being, know what is the place of man in the universe examine your opinions and prejudices, rather than "Search your heart." This philosophic lack of depth, as it is called, can consistently be maintained only if God is assumed not to be concerned with man's goodness or if man's goodness is assumed to be entirely his own affair. The Bible and Greek philosophy agree indeed as regards the importance of morality or justice and as to the insufficiency of morality, but they disagree as to what completes morality. According to the Greek philosophers, as already noted, it is understanding or contemplation. Now this necessarily tends to weaken the majesty of the moral demands, whereas humility, a sense of guilt, repentance, and faith in divine mercy, which complete morality according to the Bible, necessarily strengthen the majesty of the moral demands.[95]

As Schall explains, "Strauss detected a certain lack of depth in the philosopher because the philosopher did not see how the object of contemplation, God, was concerned with the individual man."[96] At the end of "Jerusalem and Athens," it is clear that there are profound differences between Jerusalem and Athens—even in the case of Plato, the peak of Athens, the philosopher who comes closest to agreeing with the Bible.

Chapter Seven

Conclusion

Conclusion

We have come to the close of "Jerusalem and Athens: Some Preliminary Reflections" and have found it a most exacting essay filled with many allusions and many difficulties. After going through "Jerusalem and Athens" in exhaustive detail, it is now possible to begin to draw the strands of Strauss's argument together to weave at least some preliminary conclusions regarding what Strauss wants to teach us about reason and revelation. Careful examination of the essay reveals little about it that is simple. Strauss makes us work to understand the problems behind reason and revelation. Everything important is understated and the conclusions are often left unsaid. To say the least, "Jerusalem and Athens" is not without ambiguity. Yet it is not impossible to come to some determination of Strauss's purpose.

It is helpful to remind ourselves of the obvious first. "Jerusalem and Athens" is a relatively short piece, forty-one paragraphs in all: an amazingly compact discussion, which presents a coherent case for a return either to classical philosophy in the form of Socrates or to biblical revelation. Remember what Strauss had originally presented as the problem in his introduction: "In order to understand ourselves and to illuminate our trackless way into the future, we must understand Jerusalem and Athens."[1] Having listened to Strauss, we can say that he has accomplished his task. With Strauss as our guide, we can at least say that we are no longer lost on a trackless way; we have two clear choices set before us. And we even understand, at least on some level, what those choices are. The question is, what does the future hold now that we understand our past? The debate centers on which way he suggests we should go—to Jerusalem or to Athens?

Earlier in our examination of this essay, we asked the question if, after understanding these two cities, Strauss would suggest a progress or a return. One thing seems clear: to Strauss, a desirable future has more the character of return than of progress. But at the same time, it appears that he leaves it open as to which city to look for guidance, in other words, to which city we should return. Remember that Strauss made the strange remark that "to speak of Jerusalem and Athens seems to compel us to go beyond the self-understanding of either."[2] Although he qualifies that statement by the use of the word "seems," and later by substituting this with a search for wisdom, his allegiance remains uncertain throughout the essay. Of course, this is not unintentional. His failure to come down clearly on one side or the other may at times be frustrating, but the result is not: by refusing to stand with either Athens or Jerusalem, he saves both possibilities. His concluding remarks in "Progress or Return" bear witness to this: "No one can be both a philosopher and a theologian nor, for that matter, some possibility which transcends the conflict between philosophy and theology, or pretends to be a synthesis of both. But every one of us can be and ought to be one or the other, the philosopher open to the challenge of theology or the theologian open to the challenge of philosophy."[3] Strauss may resemble Nietzsche in this essay, i.e., he may simply be a beholder of Jerusalem and Athens. But, if this is so, he is one with an essential difference from Nietzsche: he shows the impossibility of uniting Jerusalem and Athens, even at their highest level. He does not foretell the solution of a superman.

Strauss always cautions us to approach any thoughtful writing with care. Therefore we can make this general remark about this particular essay: the manner in which he writes also indicates his purpose. Alan Udoff, in an interesting discussion on the thought of Leo Strauss, suggests that, as a general rule, in Strauss's writing "the texts are cited without identifying their sources; that is to say, the authoritativeness of the texts is to rest on their instruction, not their authorship. For Strauss, anonymity is a sign and preserve of philosophy."[4] This observation about Strauss's style is particularly true of "Jerusalem and Athens." Strauss often fails to cite the source of a particular text. This is most noticeable in his discussions on the Bible and Plato. In "Jerusalem and Athens," however, he goes a step further: the authoritativeness of the texts he uses is based not only on the texts' instruction but also on his interpretation of them. Strauss thus makes himself the guide for perplexed moderns who are wandering their trackless way toward the future; he establishes himself as the new guide for those who wish to understand biblical teaching, as well as for those who wish to pursue the philosophic life. In keeping with this strategy, many times Strauss chooses to assert things in "Jerusalem and Athens" that he finds it necessary to demonstrate more forcefully elsewhere. Often, in order to understand his cryptic hints, we have had to turn to "On Genesis" or "Progress or Return" for illumination. In "Jerusalem and Athens," Strauss is the authority; his word alone is sufficient for the truth of any given statement. In fact, it is quite probable that this essay presents his authoritative view on the subject. That stated, what exactly has Strauss taught us in "Jerusalem and Athens"?

The first lesson is the most profound, and its profundity is not lessened by the fact that it is obvious. It is perhaps the only unqualified lesson in "Jerusalem and Athens." Above all, Strauss wants us to abandon any notion that a modern synthesis of reason and revelation is possible. Thus, he begins both parts of "Jerusalem and Athens" with devastating critiques of the modern solutions, the first with a denunciation of social science, which claims neither Jerusalem nor Athens to be important, and the second with an indictment of the possibility of a synthesis of the two through his analysis of Hermann Cohen.

The second lesson is not as obvious as the first but it is nonetheless profound, for Strauss has begun the recovery of Jerusalem, a task much more difficult than the recovery of Athens. It is more difficult because in some sense, Athens presents the possibility of a continued search, a constant questioning; it appeals to our modern souls more immediately than the life demanded by the Bible. A life of free and independent inquiry is certainly not as intimidating as a life of obedience, even if that life of questioning may eventually lead to virtue.[5] Earlier in our analysis, we had wondered if Strauss was intentionally cloaking the compelling nature of Jerusalem by making the case against revelation appear stronger than it actually is. Indeed, we noted several instances in which Strauss appears more impious on the surface than he is upon deeper examination, for example, his insistence that asking the very question of Jerusalem or Athens means an advance decision in favor of Athens, and his assertion that the Bible is the work of compilers, containing relics that were not intended.[6] Both arguments imply that Jerusalem is on very shaky ground. Yet his exegesis of Genesis belies this first impression and shows the inherent coherence of the text. The question thus becomes, why does Strauss appear to make the weaker speech the stronger?

I think the case can be made that he proceeds in this fashion in order to convince "those of us who cannot be orthodox" to listen to him.[7] Those who fall into that category are not simply secular Jews but those Christians who have abandoned their religion as well. He speaks to the lost souls of both traditions.

As argued earlier, atheism had become the reigning academic fashion. The problem then becomes how to get bright young students to consider the possibility of revelation, i.e., to consider the possibility that it might be true. To do so, one must proceed cautiously. James Steintrager has suggested that Strauss veils the case for Jerusalem in order to make those conventional students feel safe.[8] So, Strauss begins by granting the opposition's position: the Bible is a collection of "memories of memories"; it does not claim that the collection itself is miraculous; it may even contain unintended relics. By beginning with an advance decision in favor of Athens, he allows us to consider what the Bible has to say openly, without feeling threatened by the idea of God, especially that God which we thought we had outgrown and left behind in childhood.[9] As Schall writes in his penetrating analysis of Strauss, "Revelation, Reason and Politics: Catholic Reflections on Strauss":

> Strauss constantly, and rightly, worried that the fact of revelation might lead to the corruption or elimination of philosophy. The oft-quoted theological phrase—*credo quia absurdum*—would seem to lend strength to Strauss's worries. But likewise, Strauss also wondered that if revelation was indeed a fact, philosophers might well violate their vocation by refusing to consider even its possibility. Strauss's *secret writing* was thus sometimes necessary to protect philosophers, even philosophers from themselves.[10]

Strauss's method is ingenious, for he draws the reader into discovering the Bible only after he has sufficiently disarmed him by allowing him to hold on to his prejudices, at least temporarily. Then, through his exacting exegesis of the Bible, he brings the text to life, and the text itself demands that we respect it.

In order to succeed with this project, Strauss had to confront and answer the charges of Spinoza. We are now in a position to see that he has succeeded in destroying Spinoza's argument that "the Bible consists to a considerable extent of self-contradictory assertions, of remnants of ancient prejudices or superstitions, and of the outpourings of an uncontrolled imagination."[11] Strauss's use of Cassuto and his own analysis show that it is more than possible for an intelligent man to understand the Bible and learn from it, although it must be studied with care in order to see that it is God's wisdom before the nations. His greatest feat has been to demonstrate that, far from being a miscellany of superstitious tribal relics, Genesis provides a comprehensive account of the whole, and it can even be understood as a rebuke to philosophy. The Bible is not the work of a fevered imagination, but one of reason informed by faith.

Did Strauss leave no problems unresolved? Of course not. It might be helpful to consider again what Strauss fails to cover in this essay. We have already noted some of his omissions, but others only become clear after having gone through "Jerusalem and Athens." For instance, Strauss never discusses the anthropomorphisms in the Bible. He avoids discussing such things as God walking in the Garden of Eden or descending to earth to see what His creatures are doing in the kingdom of Babel. However, he does point to them. The question becomes, why is he silent? Is it because these things are inherently superstitious? That might seem to be the answer at first glance. However, there are other explanations that make more sense. The first one is that the problem of believing in corporealism is no longer a serious threat; no one today is making the argument that the Bible teaches that God has a body. To that extent, Maimonides' project had succeeded. Second and more important, because God is fundamentally mysterious, it is impossible to speak about him without the use of metaphors and anthropomorphisms. Here, Strauss's argument regarding the mysteries of the Bible, the *sithre torah*, should be mentioned again. Remember his cautionary reminder that we might not be able to speak about God and His interaction with man without contradicting ourselves. One of the things this means is that since we are finite beings, we cannot speak coherently of the infinite and omnipotent God except through analogy.

A related problem is the one of providence. Strauss points to it in his discussion of Aristotle to suggest that it cannot be understood philosophically. But Strauss knows that it is not sufficient to say that because Aristotle's god is incapable of providence, providence itself is impossible. As Strauss notes in "The Mutual Influence of Theology and Philosophy," philosophy "suffers a defeat as soon as it starts an offensive of its own, as soon as it tries to refute, not the necessarily inadequate proofs of revelation, but revelation itself."[12] In order to come to grips with this problem it might be best to turn away, at least momentarily, from Strauss so that we can see the problem from a different light. Ronald Knox illustrates that the problem of providence is not one for philosophy alone. Even if we believe that God is watching over us, it is still sometimes hard to trust and to obey, as difficult as it must have been for Abraham. Even Sarah laughed. Knox shows us the difficulty by reminding us of the account of the storm on the Lake of Galilee, in which the Apostles themselves, desperately afraid for their lives, woke up Christ to beg Him to calm the storm. As Knox points out, there is a tremendous lesson to be found both in the Apostles' panic and in the Lord's seeming disregard of their peril. It is a hard lesson for man. As Knox remarks:

> In his later parables, our Lord seems to change both the symbolism and the emphasis. Almighty God is represented not as a man who goes to sleep, but as a man who goes off on a journey to some far-off country, leaving his servants behind him on their good behaviour. The change of symbolism does not matter much; evidently the man who goes off on a journey, like the man who falls asleep, is in no position, here and now, to interfere; *it is God's apparent neglect of his creation that is thrown into relief* [emphasis mine]. But the change of emphasis is more important; our Lord is no longer concerned to arm us against despair, he is warning us against negligence. Because God seems to take no notice, man is tempted to take no notice either.[13]

The lesson is that God's providence is not always as obvious as we would like it to be; it might even appear as neglect. Again, it is a mystery, a *sithre torah*, one of which faith is well aware. As Strauss says in "Jerusalem and Athens":

> The apparent contradiction between the command to sacrifice Isaac and the divine promise to the descendants of Isaac is disposed of by the consideration that nothing is too wondrous for the Lord. Abraham's supreme trust in God, his simple, single-minded, child-like faith was rewarded, although or because it presupposed his entire unconcern with any reward, for Abraham was willing to forgo, to destroy, to kill the only reward with which he was concerned; God prevented the sacrifice of Isaac.[14]

The mystery of God's providence is somehow connected with the preservation of man's freedom to choose whether or not to serve Him. Remember that Strauss speaks of man's resemblance to his creator by stressing that man alone among creation can change his ways; this is also connected with his elevation above the heavens.

Another theme that Strauss avoids in "Jerusalem and Athens" is the possibility of a personal experience of God. He does point to this possibility in his discussion of Halevi through his reference to *Persecution and the Art of Writing*, the only time in which he refers to another of his own works. That in itself is important. When we look at the lengthy passage he references, we find that Strauss mentions personal experience of the divine twice. First, he speaks in terms of the philosophic stance of invincible ignorance because "a philosopher is untouched by, or has never tasted, that 'Divine thing' or 'Divine command' (*amr ilahi*) which is known from actual experience to the actual believer, the Jewish scholar, and the potential believer, the king."[15] His next reference to personal experience comes when he speaks of the natural limits of Halevi's arguments, which are "convincing to such naturally pious people only as have some foretaste of Divine revelation by having experienced a revelation by an angel or at least a rudimentary revelation of one kind or another."[16] Thus we are left with the impression that invincible ignorance of God is possible. But, when we turn to his "Introductory Essay," Strauss makes the following argument:

> God's revealing Himself to man, His addressing man, is not merely known through traditions going back to the remote past and therefore now "merely believed," but is genuinely known through present experience which every human being can have if he does not refuse himself to it. This experience is not a kind of self-experience, of the actualization of a human potentiality, of the human mind coming into its own, into what it desires or is naturally inclined to, but of something undesired, coming from the outside, going against man's grain. It is the only awareness of something absolute which cannot be relativized in any way as everything else, rational or non-rational can; it is the experience of God as the Thou, the father and king of all men; it is the experience of an unequivocal command addressed to me here and now as distinguished from general laws or ideas which are always disputable and permitting of exceptions. Only by surrendering to God's experienced call which calls for one's loving Him with all one's heart, with all one's soul and with all one's might can one come to see the other human being as one's brother and love him as oneself.[17]

This personal experience, Strauss is quick to admit, will not, in and of itself, lead to the biblical God who is essentially mysterious. Strauss's assertion that this experience is available to every man, not simply to the naturally pious, is a startling admission. Of course, we are also free to refuse this call. It is important not to underestimate this admission.

This call coincides with what Strauss says is the central teaching of the Bible: "God rightfully demands that He alone be loved unqualifiedly: God does not command that we love His chosen people with all our heart, with all our souls and with all our might."[18] Although Strauss's emphasis in "Jerusalem and Athens" is always on the obedience that this love requires, it is an obedience that also liberates. Fr. Schall summarizes the teaching of the Old Testament as follows:

> The Old Testament, in a sense, is an effort to prevent men and nations from settling for anything less than Yahweh. From this point of view, it is a much more graphic endeavor than that found in *The Ethics* of Aristotle with its relation to *The Metaphysics* or even in first questions of the Prima Secundae of Aquinas' *Summa Theologica* about the location of human beatitude. The net effect, consequently, is to prevent the nation from being an idol, an absolute, even though it is a good. Already in the Old Testament, we are aware that the most dangerous threat to human worth and dignity will probably be from a political system claiming the prerogatives of Yahweh. This is the power to set up a nation's own definition of right and wrong, its own idols, of which itself, the nation, the political power, is the most perilous and the most tempting.[19]

That Strauss would agree with this assessment is, I think, beyond question. As Strauss has shown, the biblical God is certainly more than a tribal god; this is certainly one of the lessons of the kingdom of Babel. Strauss reminds us of this fact at the end of the essay by pointing to Nathan's rebuke of David; the lesson is that even the king is not above God's law.

This very liberation, however, is not without its problems. As Strauss informs us in *Natural Right and History*: "The recognition of universal principles thus tends to prevent men from wholeheartedly identifying themselves with, or accepting, the social order that fate has allotted to them. It tends to alienate them from their place on earth. It tends to make them strangers, and even strangers on the earth."[20] It must be remembered that Strauss's discussion of the prophets concentrates on the Messianic promise in which men will beat their swords into plowshares. His critique of Cohen centers on Cohen's desire to achieve the Messianic promises through man's scientific achievement. Thus the very charge that is often lodged against Christianity is no less a problem for Judaism. Concern with a world outside our own making, a city of God, is not unique to Christianity. Hence we have another reason why Strauss chose to argue in terms that include both Christian and Jew. But this lack of rootedness, when properly channelled, is not a bad thing. Because modernity attempted to attain the city of God on earth, it is easy to overlook the fact that the ability to see universal principles can also have a good effect upon the body politic; for example, it allows men to see that they need not blindly serve tyranny. As Schall puts it, "Finally, since evil can occasion good—the patience of the sufferer, the humility of the proud—no social order or situation is hopeless. Nor is any well-governed society completely secure. . . . From the worst social orders can come the best men and women."[21] The very ability to transcend our present situation is liberating; we can use it for good or ill. Just what an important insight this is seems to have escaped some of Strauss's East Coast students, although it did not escape him.

Remember that according to Pangle's analysis of Strauss, the Bible is simply a subset of poetry. All of the essential elements of the quarrel between philosophy and revelation are already present in the quarrel between Plato and the poets.[22] For Pangle, Strauss's teaching is that philosophy, as represented by Socrates, is *the* guide for man. As he states most clearly and forcefully in his debate with Jaffa:

> If Jaffa believes that the "most essential" issue regarding prophecy or the Divine Law emerged only after the time of Plato, or in texts unknown to Plato; if he supposes that the most essential issue was not and could not have been addressed by Plato's philosophic spokesman in his dialogue with the poets and the statesmen and gentlemen who are the poets' followers—then it seems to me Jaffa has either broken with Strauss's teaching or failed to comprehend it.[23]

Pangle's collapse of the distinction between Yahweh and Zeus and his attribution of this teaching to Strauss do not seem to be warranted, however. Even though Strauss points to the similarities between Plato and the Bible, he still recognizes the profound differences, the unbridgeable gaps. As Strauss has shown throughout "Jerusalem and Athens," the understanding or possibility of a God who is holy forever changes how man views the world; it deepens his view. God's holiness, moreover, is not the same as His goodness, a tenet that Plato and the Bible hold in common. The god of the *Timaeus* and the God of Genesis are not alike. Pangle is wrong about Plato and Strauss's understanding in this respect. Plato did not envision a God who is holy. That does not make him any less of a philosopher. It just means that Plato is not a theologian: the God of the Bible has to be revealed to be known. Strauss, I think, understood that difference.

This essential difference also points to another misunderstanding or unjust accusation against Strauss. His critics, most notably Drury, charge that Strauss simply uses revelation for political ends. But the very fact that Strauss makes a compelling case for revelation in the manner that he does indicates that Jerusalem is not simply political. The reason that Jerusalem is compelling is not because it is such an agreeable story: Abraham did not know that Isaac would not be sacrificed; we are reminded that God at least asked for that sacrifice. It is compelling because it is an answer to philosophy.

It might be helpful at this point to reexamine the biblical account of the knowledge of good and evil. Remember that according to the creation account, man is forbidden autonomous knowledge of good and evil. Yet, at the same time, once man transgresses, the God of Abraham, Isaac, and Jacob does not immediately provide man with the law. There are several experiments first, which Strauss shows end in failure: Cain kills his brother; the Flood is necessary to return man to his original simplicity; God divides man into different nations so that universal tyranny does not prevail; even after the division into chosen and unchosen, the people of Sodom and Gomorra must be destroyed before they spread their pestilence. What is the lesson from these failed experiments? It seems to be that autonomous knowledge of good and evil is not sufficient to prevent man from doing evil. This lesson that Strauss shows us, however cryptically, looks amazingly similar to the Thomistic argument that, although the Ten Commandments are capable of being discerned by reason alone, i.e., they are drawn from natural law, they are needed because not all men can find them on their own. Strauss never allows Athens to triumph over Jerusalem.

That being said, the recovery of Jerusalem does not lessen the importance of the Socratic enterprise for Strauss. With the destruction of the understanding of the natural order wrought by modern science, the whole once again appears incomprehensible, and philosophy, impossible. Yet Strauss points to a way out. His insight from *What Is Political Philosophy?* bears repeating:

> Socrates was so far from being committed to a specific cosmology that his knowledge was knowledge of ignorance. Knowledge of ignorance is not ignorance. It is knowledge of the elusive character of the truth, of the whole. Socrates, then, viewed man in the light of the mysterious character of the whole. He held therefore that we are more familiar with the situation of man as man than with the ultimate causes of that situation. We may also say he viewed man in light of unchangeable ideas, i.e., of the fundamental and permanent problems.[24]

Strauss's insistence on the Socratic alternative to Jerusalem has another interesting effect: it allows Strauss to maintain his piety. For the Socratic enterprise is preeminently concerned with the human things. As he explains in *The City and Man*:

> A pious man will not investigate the divine things but only the human things, the things left to man's investigation. It is the greatest proof of Socrates' piety that he limited himself to the study of human things. His wisdom is knowledge of ignorance because it is pious and it is pious because it is knowledge of ignorance.[25]

Jaffa, too, sheds illumination on why Strauss focussed his attention on the Socratic enterprise:

> Socratic progress in wisdom—such progress as may be said to result from every Socratic conversation—always is accompanied by an increased awareness of what we do not know. How can a Socratic know that his "progress" is in "wisdom" if the goal of philosophy recedes with every supposed advance? Does not philosophy—confidence in the ultimate significance of reason—depend upon an act of faith as much a belief in the God of the Bible?[26]

In the end, there is a certain degree of mystery to both Jerusalem and Athens.

Thus we begin to understand why Strauss has such a peculiar and untraditional definition of philosophy: "Philosophy is essentially not possession of the truth, but quest for the truth. The distinctive trait of the philosopher is that 'he knows that he knows nothing' and that his insight into our ignorance concerning the most important things induces him to strive with all his power for knowledge."[27] Strauss realized that modernity, in attempting to answer all questions, destroyed itself. Strauss therefore keeps the philosopher as one who is searching in order to preserve the possibility of faith.

Again, Plato's "Second Letter" comes to mind. Plato gives us a hint as to why he wrote in the manner that he did. Plato's dialogues present philosophy, through Socrates, as something new and beautiful; Socrates on his own is not either of these things, but through the Platonic art he becomes compelling; the dialogues make Socrates, and through him philosophy, attractive.[28] It would not be going too far to say that Strauss imitates Plato by rarely writing in his own voice. Instead of writing in the form of a dialogue, however, he chose to write exegetical accounts of other texts. Strauss, too, was capable of making the search for wisdom beautiful; this is demonstrated most aptly by the opening paragraph of "Jerusalem and Athens." "Jerusalem and Athens" is a rare combination of personal reflection and dialogue: in this essay Strauss not only is more revealing of himself than usual, but he also allows reason and revelation to carry on a conversation that is not unlike a dialogue. And, as we have seen, Strauss employs his art to make both alternatives attractive. His unwillingness to come down on either side might also be a result of the caution he expresses in the following passage from "What is Liberal Education?":

> Philosophy, we have learned, must be on its guard against the wish to be edifying—philosophy can only be intrinsically edifying. We cannot

exert our understanding without from time to time understanding something important; and this understanding may be accompanied by the awareness of our understanding, by the understanding of understanding, by *noesis noeseus*, and this is so high, so pure, so noble an experience that Aristotle could ascribe it to his God. This experience is entirely independent of whether what we understand is primarily pleasing or displeasing, fair or ugly. It leads us to realize that all evils are in a sense necessary if there is to be understanding. It enables us to accept all evils which befall us and which may well break our hearts in the spirit of good citizens of the City of God. By becoming aware of the dignity of the mind, we realize the true ground of the dignity of man and therewith the goodness of the world, whether we understand it as created or as uncreated, which is the home of man because it is the home of the human mind.[29]

If, as Strauss has suggested elsewhere, the surface of things is the heart of things, then it behooves us to look at the surface of "Jerusalem and Athens." What we find there is that both reason and revelation are presented as powers to be reckoned with. By making it possible to consider Jerusalem and Athens again, Strauss has begun the recovery of man, a noble task. And if he tips the scales at all, it is toward Jerusalem. Just as Socrates' attempt to show that Apollo made a mistake in attributing wisdom to him ends with a vindication of the god, so too, does Strauss's exegetical defense come to the aid of the God of Abraham, Isaac, and Jacob. Such an endeavor may be considered a bit impious, but it is nonetheless undertaken with pious intentions and pious results.

Notes

Chapter One

1. Leo Strauss, *The City and Man* (Chicago: University of Chicago, 1964), p. 8; hereafter cited as *City*.
2. "An Epilogue," in Leo Strauss, *Liberalism: Ancient and Modern* (New York: Basic Books, 1968), p. 223; hereafter cited as *Liberalism*.
3. Leo Strauss, *Thoughts on Machiavelli* (Chicago: University of Chicago Press, 1958), p. 127; hereafter cited as *Thoughts*.
4. Leo Strauss, "What is Political Philosophy?," in *What Is Political Philosophy?* (Westport, Conn.: Greenwood Press, 1959), pp. 38–39; hereafter cited as *What?*.
5. *What?*, p. 68.
6. *What?*, pp. 10–11.
7. *City*, p. 1.
8. Leo Strauss, *Natural Right and History* (Chicago: University of Chicago Press, 1953), p. 32; hereafter cited as *Natural Right*.
9. See, for example, Strauss's comment in "Jerusalem and Athens: Some Preliminary Reflections" that "the quarrel between the ancients and moderns seems to us to be more fundamental than either the quarrel between Plato and Aristotle or that between Kant and Hegel" in the appendix of this volume, p. 202. The City University of New York has granted me permission to reprint the text of the lecture "Jerusalem and Athens: Some Preliminary Reflections" from *The City College Papers*, No. 6 (The City College of New York, 1967). The essay can be found in the appendix, pp. 179–207; hereafter cited as "J & A."
10. Shlomo Pines, "On Leo Strauss," *Independent Journal of Philosophy* 5/6 (1988): 169.
11. A testament to this fact is the number of books recently published on Strauss, such as Alan Udoff, ed., *Leo Strauss's Thought: Towards a Critical Engagement* (Boulder, Colo.: Lynne Rienner, 1991); Peter Emberley and Barry Cooper, eds., *Faith and Political Philosophy: The Correspondence Between*

Leo Strauss and Eric Voegelin, 1934–1964 (University Park, Penna.: Pennsylvania State University Press, 1993); Kenneth Hart Green, *Jew and Philosopher: The Return to Maimonides in the Jewish Thought of Leo Strauss* (Albany: State University of New York Press, 1993); and Kenneth L. Deutsch and Walter Nicgorski, eds., *Leo Strauss: Political Philosopher and Jewish Thinker* (Lanham, Md.: Rowman & Littlefield, 1994).

12. Strauss's most accessible analysis on writing is the title essay in *Persecution and the Art of Writing* (Westport, Conn.: Greenwood Press, 1952), pp. 22–37; hereafter cited as *Persecution*.
13. *Thoughts*, p. 30.
14. Title essay, *What?*, p. 36.
15. Strauss's work on Machiavelli and Xenophon come readily to mind.
16. *Thoughts*, p. 34.
17. *City*, p. 54.
18. *City*, p. 54.
19. "Introduction," by Thomas Pangle, in Leo Strauss, *Studies in Platonic Political Philosophy*, ed. Thomas Pangle (Chicago: University of Chicago Press, 1983), p. 20; hereafter cited as *Studies*.
20. *Studies*, p. 11.
21. Harry V. Jaffa, "The Legacy of Leo Strauss," *Claremont Review of Books*, Fall 1984, p. 19. I am indebted to Professor Jaffa for making Pangle's analysis of Strauss clear.
22. Harry V. Jaffa, "'The Legacy of Leo Strauss' Defended," *Claremont Review of Books*, Spring 1985, p. 20.
23. From Harry V. Jaffa's essay on "Political Philosophy and Honor: The Leo Strauss Dissertation Award," in *How To Think About the American Revolution* (Durham, N.C.: Carolina Academic Press, 1978), p. 171.
24. The East Coast contingent gets rather vicious when attempting to deal with Professor Jaffa. Rather than concentrate on the logic of Jaffa's arguments, they prefer to resort to character assassination. For a particularly nasty example, see Pangle's response to Jaffa's review of his introduction for *Studies in Platonic Political Philosophy* in *Claremont Review of Books*, "The Platonism of Leo Strauss: A Reply to Harry Jaffa," Spring 1985, pp. 18–20, in which he none too subtly calls Professor Jaffa a fool as well as himself a wise man (p. 18).
25. Allan Bloom, *Giants and Dwarfs: Essays 1960–1990* (New York: Simon and Schuster, 1990), p. 18.
26. Bloom, *Giants and Dwarfs*, p. 26. This remark is so inaccurate that its disdain is illuminating.
27. Bloom, *Giants and Dwarfs*, p. 28.
28. The dialogue is Plato's *Laws*. See Leo Strauss, *The Argument and the Action of Plato's Laws* (Chicago: University of Chicago Press, 1975), p. 2, as well as the title essay in *What?*, p. 32.
29. *Persecution*, pp. 104–5.
30. *What?*, p. 11.
31. Leo Strauss, "Progress or Return? The Contemporary Crisis in Western Civilization," *Modern Judaism*, Volume 1 (Baltimore, Md.: Johns Hopkins Uni-

versity Press, 1981), p. 45; hereafter cited as "Progress or Return."

32. Harry V. Jaffa, "The American Founding as the Best Regime: The Bonding of Civil and Religious Liberty," Bicentennial Address delivered in Claremont on September 17, 1987, p. 17.

33. Leo Strauss, "Introductory Essay" in *Spinoza's Critique of Religion* (New York: Schocken, 1982), p. 29; hereafter cited as "Introductory Essay."

34. *Thoughts*, p. 40.

35. See, for example, Robert Sokolowski, *The God of Faith and Reason: Foundations of Christian Theology* (Notre Dame: University of Notre Dame Press, 1982); Charles N. R. McCoy, "On the Revival of Classical Political Philosophy," *The Review of Politics* 35 (April 1975), pp. 161–79; Frederick Wilhelmsen, *Christianity and Political Philosophy* (Athens: University of Georgia Press, 1978).

36. Shadia Drury, *The Political Ideas of Leo Strauss* (New York: St. Martin's Press, 1988), p. ix.

37. Drury, *The Political Ideas of Leo Strauss*, p. 20.

38. Thomas Pangle, ed., *The Rebirth of Classical Political Rationalism: An Introduction to the Thought of Leo Strauss* (Chicago: University of Chicago Press, 1989), p. 132; hereafter cited as *Rebirth*.

39. *Thoughts*, p. 19.

40. Aristotle, *Nicomachean Ethics* 1177 b 26–1178 a 3, trans. by Martin Ostwald (Indianapolis: Bobbs-Merrill, 1962), pp. 290–91.

41. "What Is Liberal Education?," in *Liberalism*, p. 8.

42. *Persecution*, p. 21.

43. *Rebirth*, p. 214.

44. "An Epilogue," in *Liberalism*, p. 218.

45. *City*, p. 241.

46. *What?*, pp. 12–13.

47. "Progress or Return," p. 22.

48. *Persecution*, p. 20.

49. "Introductory Essay," p. 6.

50. Harry V. Jaffa, "The Legacy of Leo Strauss," *Claremont Review of Books*, Fall 1984, p. 17.

51. Seth Benardete, "Review of *The City and Man*," in *The Political Science Reviewer*, Fall 1978, p. 1.

52. It does appear *prima facie* that when Strauss writes on the Jewish question, he reveals more of himself than he normally does.

53. Jacob Klein, "A Giving of Accounts" in *St. John's Review* XXII, No. 1 (April, 1970), p. 1.

54. Bloom, *Giants and Dwarfs*, p. 255.

Chapter Two

1. *What?*, p. 9.
2. *What?*, p. 10.

3. *City*, p. 231.
4. *Natural Right*, p. 74.
5. *City*, p. 1.
6. See, for example, "Progress or Return," p. 33.
7. *Natural Right*, pp. 74–75; see also "Progress or Return," p. 33.
8. Leo Strauss, "The Mutual Influence of Theology and Philosophy," in *The Independent Journal of Philosophy* III (1979): p. 114; hereafter cited as "Mutual Influence."
9. *Thoughts*, p. 13.
10. "Progress or Return," p. 45.
11. "On the Interpretation of Genesis," *L'Homme: Revue Française d'anthropologie* XXI, no. 1 (1981), pp. 5–20; hereafter cited as "On Genesis." *L'Homme* has granted permission to reprint "On Genesis" in the appendix of this volume, pp. 209–25.
12. "On Genesis," p. 209.
13. "Introductory Essay," p. 1.
14. *Natural Right*, p. 98.
15. *Natural Right*, p. 81.
16. For example, "The Literary Character of the *Guide For the Perplexed*," pp. 38–94 and "How to Study Spinoza's *Theologico-Political Treatise*," pp. 142–202 in *Persecution*; and "How To Begin To Study *The Guide of the Perplexed*," pp. 140–84 in *Liberalism*, which is a reprint of the "Introductory Essay" to Shlomo Pines's translation of Maimonides' *The Guide of The Perplexed* (Chicago: University of Chicago Press, 1963). For an excellent analysis of Maimonides and Strauss, see Kenneth Hart Green's *Philosopher and Jew: The Return to Maimonides in the Jewish Thought of Leo Strauss* (Albany: State University of New York Press, 1993).
17. "J & A," p. 200.
18. Frederick Wilhelmsen, *Christianity and Political Philosophy* (Athens: University of Georgia Press, 1978), p. 209.
19. Wilhelmsen, *Christianity and Politics*, p. 8. See especially his chapter, "Jaffa, the School of Strauss, and the Christian Tradition," pp. 209–25.
20. *Natural Right*, p. 163.
21. As an example, see the quote from *Natural Right*, cited on p. 27 of this chapter, where Strauss makes it clear that the *Hebrew* Bible specifically has no understanding of nature.
22. "How To Begin To Study *The Guide of the Perplexed*," in *Liberalism*, pp. 142–43.
23. The subdivision that follows is my own.

Chapter Three

1. "J & A," p. 179.
2. "J & A", p. 179.
3. "J & A", p. 179.

4. "J & A," p. 179.
5. "Progress or Return," p. 37.
6. Benedict de Spinoza, *A Theologico-Political Treatise*, trans. by R. H. M. Elwes (New York: Dover Publications, 1951), p. 6.
7. See, for example, "What Is Political Philosophy?" and "Political Philosophy and History," in *What?*, pp. 9–77, and "Liberal Education and Responsibility," "The Liberalism of Classical Political Philosophy," and "An Epilogue," in *Liberalism*, pp. 3–4 and 203–23.
8. In "Progress or Return," Strauss calls the result an "incredible barbarization," p. 29.
9. Alan Udoff, ed., *Leo Strauss's Thought: Toward a Critical Engagement* (Boulder: Lynne Rienner, 1991), p. 3.
10. "Introductory Essay," p. 2.
11. "J & A," p. 180.
12. "J & A," p. 180.
13. *Rebirth*, p. 41.
14. Friedrich Nietzsche, *Beyond Good and Evil*, trans. Walter Kaufmann (New York: Vintage Books, 1966), pp. 10–11.
15. Friedrich Nietzsche, *Thus Spake Zarathustra*, in *The Portable Nietzsche*, ed. and trans. Walter Kaufmann (New York: Penguin Books, 1954), p. 284.
16. See, for example, "Some Remarks on the Political Science of Maimonides and Farabi" (originally published in 1936), trans. Robert Bartlett, *Interpretation* 18 (Fall 1990), pp. 3–30; the "Introduction" to *Persecution*, pp. 9-21; and "How Farabi Read Plato's *Laws*," in *What?*, pp. 134–54.
17. Nietzsche, *Thus Spake Zarathustra*, p. 170.
18. "J & A," p. 180.
19. Nietzsche, *Thus Spake Zarathustra*, pp. 170–71.
20. *Natural Right*, pp. 86–91.
21. "J & A," p. 180.
22. Nietzsche, *Beyond Good and Evil*, p. 15.
23. "J & A," p. 181.
24. "J & A," p. 181.
25. "J & A," p. 181.
26. "J & A," p. 181.
27. "J & A," p. 181.
28. "Progress or Return," p. 20.
29. "J & A," p. 181.
30. See, for example, *Natural Right*, pp. 74–75, and "Progress or Return," p. 33.
31. "J & A," p. 182.
32. Robert D. Sacks, *A Commentary on the Book of Genesis* (Lewiston, N.Y.: Edwin Mellen Press, 1990), p. i.
33. *Liberalism*, pp. 151–52.
34. All citations are from the New English Bible with the Apocrypha, Oxford Study Edition.
35. For an interesting discussion on Job, see "How To Begin To Study the

Guide of the Perplexed," in *Liberalism,* p. 164 and p. 182.

36. "J & A," p. 182.

37. Catholics, for example, understand this fear in a two-fold sense: first, the fear that a slave would have for a master, i.e., fear of punishment; and second, the fear that a son has for a father, i.e., the fear of disappointing him. I wish to thank Rev. Sherman Orr for this insight.

38. For two recent examples of this opinion, see John G. Gunnell's "Strauss Before Straussianism: Reason, Revelation, and Nature," in Kenneth L. Deutsch and Walter Nicgorski, eds., *Leo Strauss: Political Philosopher and Jewish Thinker* (Lanham, Md.: Rowman & Littlefield, 1994), pp. 107–28, and James L. Wiser's "Reason and Revelation as Search and Response: A Comparison of Eric Voegelin and Leo Strauss," in Peter Emberley and Barry Cooper, eds., *Faith and Political Philosophy: The Correspondence Between Leo Strauss and Eric Voegelin, 1934–1964* (University Park, Penna.: Pennsylvania State University Press, 1993), pp. 237–48.

39. Genesis 1:27.

40. Strauss does not mention this in his interpretation of the second creation account.

41. "J & A," p. 182.

42. "J & A," p. 182.

43. "J & A," p. 182.

44. "Mutual Influence," p. 112.

45. Niccolo Machiavelli, *The Discourses,* trans. Leslie J. Walker, S.J., and ed. Bernard Crick (New York: Penguin Books, 1970), p. 155.

46. Machiavelli, *Discourses,* pp. 288–90.

47. Machiavelli, *Discourses,* p. 290.

48. *Thoughts,* p. 133; note Strauss's use of the words "I believe."

49. *Thoughts,* p. 141.

50. *Thoughts,* pp. 148–49.

51. "J & A," p. 182.

52. "Introductory Essay," p. 15.

53. "J & A," p. 182.

54. "J & A," p. 183.

55. "J & A," p. 183.

56. This change from author to immediate addressees also means that later interpretations cannot be considered.

57. This does not apply to the New Testament, in which one of the Apostles is known for his doubt (John 20:27); Thomas doubts Jesus's resurrection until he touches His flesh and can feel the wounds.

58. Francis Bacon, *The Essays* (New York: Penguin Books, 1985), p. 109.

59. Bacon, *Essays,* p. 108.

60. Bacon, *Essays,* p. 111.

61. "Mutual Influence," p. 116.

62. "Mutual Influence," p. 116.

63. *Natural Right,* p. 98; see also p. 27 of the last chapter.

64. This is the middle sentence.

65. This is the only time he raises the question of the literal meaning versus the true meaning of a biblical text.
66. Once again Strauss reminds us of his argument in *Natural Right and History* in which he states that the notion that creatures have "ways" is prior to the discovery of nature, pp. 82–83.
67. "Mutual Influence," p. 116.
68. "J & A," p. 184. Note, too, that this changes his argument from "immediate addressees" to simply "addressees," thus allowing him the role of biblical guide.
69. "J & A," p. 184.

Chapter Four

1. The title of this section of the essay is my own device to make it easier to discuss the section.
2. "J & A," p. 182.
3. *Persecution*, pp. 9–10. It is also interesting to note that by using the term "loyal philosophers" he implies that there may be a middle ground between the enmity between philosophy and theology.
4. *Persecution*, p. 163.
5. "An Introduction to Heideggerian Existentialism," in *Rebirth*, p. 42.
6. "On Genesis," p. 211.
7. *Natural Right*, p. 82.
8. Umberto Cassuto, *A Commentary on the Book of Genesis: From Adam to Noah*, trans. Israel Abrahams (Jerusalem: Magnes Press, 1978), pp. 7–18; hereafter cited as *Commentary, Part I*.
9. Cassuto, *Commentary, Part I*, pp. 11–12.
10. Cassuto, *Commentary, Part I*, pp. 19–27.
11. Alan Udoff, in his introductory essay to *Strauss's Thought: Toward a Critical Engagement*, makes the interesting argument that Strauss himself always writes in this manner: "the texts are cited without identifying the sources; that is to say, the authoritativeness of the texts is to rest on their instruction, not their authorship. For Strauss, anonymity is the preserve of philosophy." *Leo Strauss's Thought: Toward a Critical Engagement*, ed. Alan Udoff (Boulder: Lynne Rienner, 1991), p. 6.
12. This is the middle sentence of this paragraph.
13. Again, Strauss gives no citation for this passage.
14. "On Genesis," p. 212.
15. "On Genesis," p. 212.
16. "Progress or Return," pp. 38–39. Compare this with "How to Study Spinoza's *Theologico-Political Treatise*," in *Persecution*, p. 199.
17. *Liberalism*, p. 145.
18. "The Literary Character of the *Guide for the Perplexed*," in *Persecution*, pp. 45–46.
19. *Persecution*, p. 60.

20. "J & A," p. 185.
21. Empedocles, fragment A 70. It is in this paragraph that he first mentions Cassuto in a footnote. See also the discussion of Empedocles in "J & A," p. 198, and Chapter 5, pp. 107–9.
22. "J & A," p. 185.
23. "J & A," p. 185.
24. Cassuto shows that there are further parallels connecting the first three days with the second three days: light corresponds to luminaries; sea and heaven with fish and fowl; the earth with the land creatures. See p. 17 and corresponding passages in his *Commentary, Part I*.
25. Compare this with Strauss's earlier retelling of Nietzsche's "Of 1,000 Goals and One." See pp. 42–43.
26. "J & A," p. 185–86.
27. Strauss chooses not to address the problem of corporeality, which Maimonides considered crucial to this passage. For Strauss's discussion of the problem, see "How To Begin To Study The *Guide of the Perplexed*," in *Liberalism*, p. 154.
28. See "J & A," p. 206.
29. Christians, of course, have no trouble with this passage.
30. "J & A," p. 186.
31. "J & A," p. 186.
32. "On Genesis," pp. 216–17.
33. "On Genesis," p. 220.
34. "J & A," p. 186.
35. Strauss does not mention, as Cassuto does, that the only creature specifically named in the creation account is the sea monster, which, according to Cassuto, is a mythical remnant of the Israelite tale of Rahab, the sea monster who rebelled against God but was slain. Cassuto suggests that the creature is mentioned in Genesis to show that it, too, is simply a beast with no supernatural capabilities. See *Commentary On Genesis, Part I*, p. 49.
36. "J & A," p. 186.
37. "J & A," p. 186. Laurence Berns makes this interesting remark, which may shed some light on Strauss's understanding of evil, in "The Relation Between Philosophy and Religion: Reflections on Leo Strauss's Suggestion Concerning the Source and Sources of Modernity," *Interpretation*, Fall 1991, pp. 43–60. Berns asks his readers to compare the Jewish prayer that waits longingly for an end to evil with "Socrates' reply in the *Theaetetus* to an enthusiastic Theodorus: 'But it is not possible for evils to be done away with, Theodorus, for it is necessary that there always be something contrary to the good'" (p. 49). If Strauss takes his cue from Socrates, it would mean that Strauss understands evil philosophically.
38. "J & A," p. 186–87.
39. Cassuto, *Commentary, Part I*, p. 26.
40. James V. Schall, *The Politics of Heaven and Hell* (Lanham, Md.: University Press of America, 1984), p. 54.
41. "J & A," p. 187.

42. "Mutual Influence," p. 116.
43. "The Literary Character of the *Guide for the Perplexed*," in *Persecution*, p. 61.
44. "Literary Character," *Persecution*, p. 61.
45. Strauss is more explicit regarding woman's lower nature in "On Genesis," p. 222, and "Progress or Return," p. 34.
46. Cassuto, *Commentary, Part I*, pp. 71–96.
47. Cassuto, *Commentary, Part I*, p. 90.
48. "Progress or Return," p. 43.
49. "J & A," p. 187. It is interesting that he singles out two virtues: a moral one, justice, and a theological one, charity.
50. At this juncture, Strauss refers to Cassuto in a footnote for the second and final time.
51. Plato, *Republic*, 369 d-372 d.
52. "J & A," p. 188.
53. "J & A," p. 188. The childlike simplicity of our original condition is reminiscent of the New Testament passage, "unless, you turn round and become like children, you will never enter the kingdom of heaven" (Matt. 18:3), although this passage is not consistent with Strauss's interpretation that to be childlike means to be less than human.
54. "Progress or Return," p. 43.
55. "On Genesis," p. 223.
56. "On Genesis," p. 223.
57. Sacks, *A Commentary on the Book of Genesis*, p. 29. This commentary on Genesis is, according to Sacks, based on many discussions he had with Strauss.
58. Sacks, *A Commentary on the Book of Genesis*, p. 29.
59. Cassuto, *Commentary, Part I*, p. 112.
60. Cassuto, *Commentary, Part I*, p. 142.
61. "J & A," p. 188.
62. Cassuto also considers this a later interpretation not inherent in the text; see *Commentary, Part I*, p. 139.
63. "J & A," p. 188. See the discussion in footnote 37.
64. Emil Fackenheim, "Leo Strauss and Modern Judaism," *Claremont Review of Books*, Winter 1985, p. 22.
65. James Schall, S.J., *Redeeming the Time* (New York: Sheed and Ward, 1968), pp. 19–20.
66. "J & A," p. 188.
67. Drury, *The Political Ideas of Leo Strauss*, p. 44.
68. "J & A," p. 189.
69. "J & A," p. 189.
70. See p. 71 of the present chapter.
71. "J & A," p. 190.
72. "J & A," p. 190.
73. "J & A," p. 187.
74. Cassuto, *Commentary, Part I*, p. 205.

75. After the Flood, God will require man to punish murder with death.
76. "J & A," p. 190.
77. The Catholic answer would be the same as that for the distinction between the sin confessed and the penance required, i.e., that no punishment that any sinner could receive from God would be an adequate recompense for disobeying His laws: the punishment we receive is for us, to aid our spiritual growth, and not for God's benefit. In other words, we do not deserve forgiveness, but out of God's love for us, we get it.
78. Cassuto, *Commentary, Part I*, p. 218.
79. Isaac M. Kikawada and Arthur Quinn, *Before Abraham Was* (San Francisco: Ignatius Press, 1985), p. 55.
80. "J & A," p. 190.
81. "Progress or Return," p. 44.
82. "J & A," p. 190.
83. "J & A," p. 191.
84. "J & A," p. 191.
85. Cassuto, *Commentary, Part I*, p. 291.
86. See Cassuto's *Commentary, Part I*, pp. 291–301.
87. Cassuto, *Commentary, Part I*, p. 300.
88. Cassuto, *Commentary, Part I*, p. 300.
89. Sacks, *A Commentary on the Book of Genesis*, p. 54.
90. Sacks, *A Commentary on the Book of Genesis*, p. 49.
91. Catholic tradition has this element within it as well. During the Easter vigil, the Exultet is sung; in it our original parent's fall is referred to as a "happy sin" and a "joyous fall" because it led to the Incarnation of Christ and His redemption of fallen man.
92. "J & A," p. 191.
93. "J & A," p. 191.
94. Compare the Genesis account to that of Gilgamesh, in which the gods send the flood because men have become too noisy and are bothering the gods; this is just one example among many pagan ones in which the gods send cataclysmic events to compensate for overpopulation. See Kikawada and Quinn, *Before Abraham Was*, pp. 38–51, and Cassuto, *Commentary on Genesis, From Noah to Abraham* (Jerusalem: Magnes Press, 1984), pp. 10–19; hereafter cited as *Commentary, Part II*.
95. Cassuto, *Commentary, Part II*, p. 20.
96. "J & A," p. 191. This is the middle sentence of this paragraph.
97. "J & A," p. 191.
98. "J & A," p. 192.
99. "J & A," p. 192.
100. Cassuto, *Commentary, Part II*, p. 125.
101. "J & A," p. 192.
102. See, for example, Kikawada and Quinn, *Before Abraham Was*, pp. 102–3. Cassuto, however, disagrees; see *Commentary, Part II*, pp. 151–55.
103. It could be that Strauss is implying that incest is a manmade law since Ham incurs Noah's, not God's, wrath and curse. However, Strauss does use

the word "sacred"—a word not to be taken lightly. Remember that Noah was chosen by God for his righteousness. Thus it may be that Noah is called to participate in the sacred by cursing behavior that God would want cursed. The curse does occur after the covenant.

104. "J & A," p. 192.
105. Aristotle, *Politics* 1256 a 30–1256 b 26.
106. "J & A," p. 193.
107. "J & A," p. 193.
108. "J & A," p. 193.
109. "J & A," p. 193.
110. "J & A," pp. 193–94.
111. "J & A," p. 194.
112. "J & A," p. 194.
113. "J & A," p. 195.
114. "J & A," p. 195.

115. As he states in *What?*, p. 36: "the good is of higher dignity than one's own, or that the best regime is a higher consideration than the fatherland. The Jewish equivalent of this relation might be said to be the relation between the Torah and Israel."

116. Compare this passage to the earlier difficult passage regarding the duality of God.

117. "J & A," p. 194.

118. Again, Strauss fails to note the traditional lesson of the binding of Isaac, i.e., that God is teaching man that, unlike idols such as Moloch, the true God, the God of Abraham, will not demand human sacrifices to sate his appetite.

119. "J & A," p. 195.
120. "J & A," p. 195.
121. "J & A," p. 195.

122. The last time he did was in his reference to Moses's authorship of the Torah.

123. "J & A," pp. 195–96.

124. Strauss also uses the first person singular in "On Socrates and the Prophets."

125. For example, there is also no word for either "eternity" or "family" in Hebrew, although few would argue that the Israelites did not believe their God to be eternal or that family was unimportant.

126. I am indebted to Kevin Hasson for helping me work through this passage, and for his insights into the Hebrew language.

127. G. K. Chesterton, *Orthodoxy*, in *Collected Works*, Vol. I (San Francisco: Ignatius Press, 1986), p. 243.

128. "Mutual Influence," p. 112.

129. "Progress or Return," pp. 42–43.

130. Cassuto, *A Commentary on the Book of Exodus* (Jerusalem: Magnes Press, 1983), p. 38.

131. Cassuto, *Commentary on Exodus*, pp. 36–37.

Chapter Five

132. Cassuto, *Commentary on Exodus*, p. 38.
133. *Liberalism*, p. 145.
134. "J & A," p. 196.
135. "J & A," p. 196.

Chapter Five

1. "J & A," p. 196.
2. "J & A," p. 196.
3. "Mutual Influence," p. 112.
4. Hesiod, *Theogony*, lines 26–28, Richard Lattimore, trans., *Hesiod* (Ann Arbor: University of Michigan Press, 1978), p. 124.
5. "J & A," p. 196.
6. "J & A," p. 196.
7. "Mutual Influence," pp. 114–15. Perhaps this is why the Hebrew nation is known primarily for the honoring of parents. See earlier discussion in Chapter 3, pp. 42–43.
8. "J & A," p. 184.
9. "J & A," p. 197.
10. "J & A," p. 197.
11. "J & A," p. 197.
12. Hesiod, *Works and Days*, 202–13.
13. Hesiod, *Works and Days*, lines 210–11, in *Hesiod*, p. 43.
14. Hesiod, *Theogony*, 886–900.
15. Of course, wisdom is not mentioned in either of the creation accounts. That is not necessarily a contradiction. Wisdom might be above the heavens and the earth, and hence not part of the creation account.
16. In "Jerusalem and Athens," Strauss never speaks of the biblical God as being jealous.
17. Aristotle, *Nicomachean Ethics* 1100 a 10–1101 b 9.
18. Shadia Drury, "The Esoteric Philosophy of Leo Strauss," *Political Theory*, August 1985, p. 330.
19. Hesiod, *Works and Days*, line 4 in *Hesiod*, p. 19.
20. "J & A," p. 198.
21. "J & A," p. 198.
22. Hesiod, *Works and Days*, lines 268–73, in *Hesiod*, p. 51.
23. "J & A," p. 198.
24. Hesiod, *Works and Days*, line 105.
25. Hesiod, *Works and Days*, lines 483–84, in *Hesiod*, p. 75.
26. "Progress or Return," p. 39.
27. For a fuller account of the difference between chaos in the Bible and chaos in the Greek world, see Sacks, *Commentary on Genesis*, especially p. 21.
28. Joseph Owens, C.Ss.R., *A History of Ancient Philosophy* (Englewood Cliffs, New Jersey: Prentice-Hall, 1959), p. 56.

29. See "J & A," p. 185, and discussion in Chapter 4, p. 68.
30. Parmenides, fragment 2 of "On Nature," in Owens, *A History of Ancient Philosophy*, pp. 60–61.
31. Parmenides, fragment 6.
32. Empedocles, fragment 6.
33. Empedocles, fragment 8, in *The Presocratics*, ed. Philip Wheelwright (Indianapolis: Odyssey Press, 1966), p. 127.
34. Empedocles, fragment 17.
35. Aristotle, *Metaphysics* 985 a 5–10, from Hippocrates G. Apostle, trans., *Metaphysics* (Grinnell, Iowa: Peripatetic Press, 1979), p. 19.
36. "J & A," p. 277.
37. "J & A," p. 277.
38. "J & A," p. 277.
39. This is the first time that Strauss admits this possibility. Remember that in his discussion of the Divine Name, the emphasis was on will and the mystery of that will.
40. "J & A," p. 278.
41. Aristotle, *Metaphysics* 1072 b 14–30 and 1074 b 15–1075 a 11.
42. Aristotle, *Metaphysics*, trans. Hippocrates G. Apostle (Grinnell, Iowa: Peripatetic Press, 1966), p. 205, 1072 b 30.
43. Aristotle, *Metaphysics*, 1074 b 25–28, p. 209.
44. Aristotle, *De Anima*, 429 a 19–20.
45. Aristotle, *Nicomachean Ethics*, 1141 a 33-b 2.
46. Aristotle, *Nicomachean Ethics* (Ostwald translation), 1178 b 9–15, pp. 292–93.
47. Aristotle, *Eudemian Ethics* 1249 a 14–15, trans. J. Solomon, in *The Complete Works of Aristotle*, ed. Jonathan Barnes (Princeton: Princeton University Press, 1984), p. 1980.
48. "On the *Euthyphron*," in *Rebirth*, p. 198.
49. *City*, p. 55.
50. *City*, p. 68.
51. Strauss, *The Argument and the Action of Plato's Laws*, p. 1.
52. "J & A," p. 199.
53. "J & A," p. 199.
54. "J & A," p. 199.
55. *City*, p. 119.
56. See p. 202 of "J & A."
57. "J & A," p. 200.
58. Plato, *Timaeus*, 40 d 6–41 a 5.
59. Plato, *Timaeus*, 40 d 3–40 e 5, trans. Benjamin Jowett, in *Plato: The Collected Dialogues*, eds. Edith Hamilton and Huntington Cairns (Princeton: Princeton University Press, 1961), pp. 1169–70.
60. Leo Strauss, *Socrates and Aristophanes* (New York: Basic Books, 1966), p. 140.
61. *Socrates and Aristophanes*, p. 312.
62. *Socrates and Aristophanes*, p. 136.

63. *Socrates and Aristophanes*, p. 139. Aristophanes, *Peace*, 67–80.
64. *Socrates and Aristophanes*, p. 138.
65. Aristophanes, *Peace*, 404–13.
66. *Socrates and Aristophanes*, p. 146.
67. *Liberalism*, p. 151.
68. "J & A," p. 200.
69. "J & A," p. 200.
70. "J & A," p. 196.
71. Jaffa, "The Legacy of Leo Strauss," p. 17.

Chapter Six

1. "J & A," p. 196.
2. *Liberalism*, p. 162.
3. "Mutual Influence," p. 114.
4. *Liberalism*, p. 162.
5. *Liberalism*, pp. 167–68.
6. "Mutual Influence," p. 18.
7. *Liberalism*, p. 142.
8. *What?*, p. 242.
9. Leo Strauss and Jacob Klein, "A Giving of Accounts," *St. John's Review*, XXII, No. 1, p. 2.
10. *What?*, p. 17.
11. Kenneth L. Deutsch and Walter Nicgorski, eds., *Leo Strauss: Political Philosopher and Jewish Thinker* (Lanham, Md.: Rowman & Littlefield, 1994), "Introduction," p. 4.
12. "Introductory Essay," p. 18.
13. "Introductory Essay," p. 21.
14. *Studies*, p. 234.
15. Hermann Cohen, in *Reason and Hope: Selections from the Jewish Writings of Hermann Cohen*, trans. Eva Jospe (New York: Norton, 1971), p. 48.
16. *Studies*, p. 242.
17. *Studies*, p. 237.
18. "J & A," p. 200.
19. "A Giving of Accounts," p. 2.
20. "J & A," p. 200.
21. "J & A," p. 201.
22. Cohen, "The Social Ideal in Plato and the Prophets," in *Reason and Hope*, p. 68.
23. Cohen, "The Social Ideal," p. 68.
24. Cohen, "The Social Ideal," p. 73.
25. Cohen, "The Social Ideal," p. 74.
26. Cohen, "The Social Ideal," p. 74.
27. Cohen, "The Social Ideal," p. 74.

28. "J & A," p. 200.
29. "J & A," p. 200.
30. For a good treatment of this topic, see Joseph K. Woodard's "Why We Cannot Forget the Jews," unpublished paper, Claremont Graduate School, 1984, p. 22.
31. Ernest Fortin, "Rational Theologians and Irrational Philosophers: A Straussian Perspective," *Interpretation* 12, nos. 2–3 (1984): p. 350.
32. James V. Schall, *Christianity and Politics* (Boston: Daughters of St. Paul, 1981), pp. 66–67.
33. James V. Schall, *Reason, Revelation, and the Foundations of Political Philosophy* (Baton Rouge: Louisiana State University Press, 1987), pp. 3–4.
34. Schall, *Christianity and Politics*, p. 23.
35. G. K. Chesterton, *Orthodoxy*, p. 233.
36. For further evidence of this fact, see the Strauss–Voegelin correspondence in Peter Emberley and Barry Cooper, eds., *Faith and Political Philosophy: The Correspondence Between Leo Strauss and Eric Voegelin, 1934–1964* (University Park, Penna.: Pennsylvania State University Press, 1993), especially the letter of June 4, 1951.
37. John P. East, "Leo Strauss and American Conservatism," *Modern Age* 21, no. 1, p. 9.
38. "J & A," p. 201.
39. Cohen, "The Social Ideal," p. 74.
40. Cohen, "The Social Ideal," p. 74.
41. Cohen, "The Social Ideal," p. 74.
42. Cohen, "The Social Ideal," p. 72.
43. Cohen, "The Social Ideal," p. 70.
44. Cohen, "The Social Ideal," p. 71. Interestingly, Strauss never discusses God's love for man in this essay.
45. Cohen, "The Social Ideal," p. 70.
46. Cohen, "The Social Ideal," p. 74.
47. "J & A," p. 201.
48. "J & A," p. 201.
49. "Introductory Essay," p. 21.
50. "J & A," p. 202.
51. "J & A," p. 202.
52. "J & A," p. 195.
53. "J & A," p. 179.
54. *Liberalism*, pp. 167–68.
55. *Liberalism*, p. 167.
56. "J & A," p. 203.
57. Nahum Sarna, *Understanding Genesis: The Biblical Heritage of Israel* (New York: Schocken, 1966), p. 52.
58. "J & A," p. 203.
59. "J & A," p. 203.
60. "J & A," p. 203.

61. "J & A," p. 204.
62. "J & A," p. 204.
63. "J & A," p. 203.
64. "J & A," p. 204.
65. "J & A," p. 204.
66. Remember the distinction made earlier, i.e., that miracles persuade only those who believe in the possibility of a god.
67. "J & A," p. 204.
68. Judah Halevi, *The Kuzari*, trans. Hartwig Hirschfeld (New York: Schocken, 1968), p. 35.
69. Halevi, *Kuzari*, IV 13.
70. Halevi, *Kuzari*, V 14.
71. Halevi, *Kuzari*, pp. 273–74.
72. *Persecution*, p. 105.
73. *Persecution*, p. 106.
74. "J & A," p. 205.
75. *City*, p. 20.
76. "Progress or Return," p. 38.
77. Plato, *Apology* 40 b 6.
78. Plato, "Second Letter," 314 c-d.
79. "J & A," p. 205.
80. Aristotle, *Nicomachean Ethics*, 1129 b 26–1130 a 13.
81. ". . . and they shall beat their swords into plowshares, and their spears into pruning hooks: nation shall not lift up sword against nation, neither shall they learn war any more." Isaiah 2:2–4, as quoted in "J & A," p. 206.
82. "Progress or Return," p. 37.
83. James V. Schall, *The Politics of Heaven and Hell* (Lanham, Md.: University Press of America, 1984), p. 114.
84. "J & A," p. 206. It should be mentioned that the version of "Jerusalem and Athens" published in *Commentary* ends in the middle of the tenth paragraph with the quote from Micah 6:8.
85. "J & A," p. 206.
86. Leo Strauss, *On Tyranny*, revised and expanded edition including the Strauss-Kojéve correspondence, eds. Victor Gourevitch and Michael S. Roth (New York: Free Press, 1991), p. 275.
87. Halevi, *Kuzari*, p. 273.
88. "J & A," p. 206.
89. Xenophon, *Memorabilia*, I.2.29–30.
90. Xenophon, *Memorabilia*, I.2.31–33.
91. "Progress or Return," p. 38.
92. "Progress or Return," p. 38.
93. This should be compared to Emil Fackenheim's complaint mentioned earlier (p. 106) that Strauss shows a reticence toward evil altogether. This reticence may simply be a reflection of the fact that philosophy cannot adequately address the problem of evil.

94. Plato, *Republic* 614 b 1–621 d 1.
95. "Progress or Return," p. 37.
96. Schall, *Reason, Revelation, and the Foundations of Political Philosophy*, p. 208.

Chapter Seven

1. "J & A," p. 179.
2. "J & A," p. 181.
3. "Progress or Return," pp. 44–45.
4. Udoff, *Leo Strauss's Thought*, p. 6.
5. For example, Glaucon comes to mind as someone who was tamed by philosophy.
6. "J & A," p. 182.
7. "J & A," p. 182.
8. James Steintrager, "Political Philosophy, Political Theology, and Morality," *The Thomist* 32 (July 1968): pp. 307–22.
9. This modern desire to transcend our traditional religion is perhaps best summed up by Chesterton's opening statement in *Orthodoxy*: "It recounts my elephantine adventures in pursuit of the obvious. No one can think my case more ludicrous than I think it myself; no reader can accuse me of trying to make a fool of him. I am the fool of this story, and no rebel shall hurl me from my throne. . . . I did, like all other solemn little boys, try to be in advance of the age. Like them I tried to be some ten minutes in advance of the truth. And I found that I was eighteen hundred years behind it" (p. 214).
10. Schall, "Revelation, Reason and Politics, I," *Gregorianum*, 1981, no. 2 and 3, p. 354.
11. "J & A," p. 182.
12. "Mutual Influence," p. 116.
13. Ronald Knox, *A Retreat For Lay People* (Harrison, N.Y.: Roman Catholic Books, 1954), p. 45.
14. "J & A," p. 195.
15. *Persecution*, p. 105.
16. *Persecution*, p. 106.
17. "Introductory Essay," pp. 8–9.
18. "J & A," p. 195.
19. Schall, *The Politics of Heaven and Hell*, p. 7.
20. *Natural Right*, pp. 13–14.
21. Schall, *The Politics of Heaven and Hell*, p. 123.
22. Introduction to *Studies*, p. 20.
23. Pangle, "The Platonism of Leo Strauss: A Reply to Harry Jaffa," *Claremont Review of Books*, Spring 1985, p. 19.
24. *What?*, pp. 38–39.
25. *City*, p. 20.

26. Harry V. Jaffa, "Leo Strauss, the Bible, and Political Philosophy," in Deutsch and Nicgorski, eds., *Leo Strauss: Political Philosopher and Jewish Thinker*, pp. 199–200.
27. *What?*, p. 11.
28. Plato, "Second Letter," 314 c-d.
29. *Liberalism*, p. 8.

Appendix:
Two Works by Leo Strauss

Jerusalem and Athens: Some Preliminary Reflections

I. The Beginning of the Bible and Its Greek Counterparts

All the hopes that we entertain in the midst of the confusions and dangers of the present are founded positively or negatively, directly or indirectly on the experiences of the past. Of these experiences the broadest and deepest, as far as we Western men are concerned, are indicated by the names of the two cities Jerusalem and Athens. Western man became what he is and is what he is through the coming together of biblical faith and Greek thought. In order to understand ourselves and to illuminate our trackless way into the future, we must understand Jerusalem and Athens. As goes without saying, this is a task whose proper performance goes much beyond my power, to say nothing at all of the still narrower limits set to two public lectures. But we cannot define our tasks by our powers, for our powers become known to us through performing our tasks; it is better to fail nobly than to succeed basely. Besides, having been chosen to inaugurate the Frank Cohen Memorial Lectureship at the City College of the City University of New York, I must think of the whole series of lectures to be given by other men—let us hope by better and greater men—in the coming years or decades.

The objects to which we refer by speaking of Jerusalem and Athens, are today understood by the science devoted to such objects as cultures; "culture" is meant to be a scientific concept. According to this concept there is an indefinitely large number of cultures: n cultures. The scientist who studies them beholds them as objects; as scientist he stands outside of all of them; he has no preference for any of them; in his eyes all of them are of equal rank; he is not only impartial but objective; he is anxious not to distort any of them; in speaking about them he avoids any "culture-bound" concepts, i.e., concepts bound to any particular culture or kind of culture. In many cases the objects studied by the scientist of culture do or did not know that they are or were cultures. This causes no difficulty for him: electrons also do not know that they are electrons; even dogs do not know that they are dogs. By the mere fact that he speaks of his objects as cultures, the scientific student takes it for granted that he understands the people whom he studies better than they understood or understand themselves.

This whole approach has been questioned for some time but this questioning does not seem to have had any effect on the scientists. The man who started the questioning was Nietzsche. We have said that according to the prevailing view there were or are n cultures. Let us say there were or are 1,001 cultures, thus reminding ourselves of the Arabian Nights, the 1,001 Nights; the account of the cultures, if it is well done will be a series of exciting stories, perhaps of tragedies. Accordingly Nietzsche speaks of our subject in a speech of his Zarathustra that is entitled "Of 1,000 Goals and One." The Hebrews and the Greeks appear in this speech as two among a number of nations, not superior to the two others that are mentioned or to the 996 that are not mentioned. The peculiarity of the Greeks is the full dedication of the individual to the contest for excellence, distinction, supremacy. The peculiarity of the Hebrews is the utmost honoring of father and mother. (Up to this day the Jews read on their highest holiday the section of the Torah that deals with the first presupposition of honoring father and mother: the unqualified prohibition against incest between children and parents.) Nietzsche has a deeper reverence than any other beholder for the sacred tables of the Hebrews as well as of the other nations in question. Yet since he is only a beholder of these tables, since what one table commends or commands is incompatible with what the others command, he is not subject to the commandments of any. This is true also and especially of the tables, or "values" of modern Western culture. But according to him, all scientific concepts, and hence in particular the concept of culture, are culture-bound; the concept of culture is an outgrowth of 19th century Western culture; its application to "cultures" of other ages and climates is an act stemming from the spiritual imperialism of that particular culture. There is then a glaring contradiction between the claimed objectivity of the science of cultures and the radical subjectivity of that science. Differently stated, one cannot behold, i.e., truly understand, any culture unless one is firmly rooted in one's own culture or unless one belongs in one's capacity as a beholder to some culture. But if the universality of the beholding of all cultures is to be preserved, the culture to which the beholder of all cultures belongs, must be the universal culture, the culture of mankind, the world culture; the universality of beholding presupposes, if only by anticipating it, the universal culture which is no longer one culture among many. The variety of cultures that have hitherto emerged contradicts the oneness of truth. Truth is not a woman so that each man can have his own truth as he can have his own wife. Nietzsche sought therefore for a culture that would no longer be particular and hence in the last analysis arbitrary. The single goal of mankind is conceived by him as in a sense super-human: he speaks of the super-man of the future. The super-man is meant to unite in himself Jerusalem and Athens on the highest level.

However much the science of all cultures may protest its innocence of all preferences or evaluations it fosters a specific moral posture. Since it requires openness to all cultures, it fosters universal tolerance and the exhilaration deriving from the beholding of diversity; it necessarily affects all cultures that it can still affect by contributing to their transformation in one and the same direction; it willy-nilly brings about a shift of emphasis from the particular to the universal: by asserting, if only implicitly, the rightness of pluralism, it asserts that pluralism is *the* right way; it asserts the monism of universal tolerance and respect for diversity; for by virtue of being an -ism, pluralism is a monism.

One remains somewhat closer to the science of culture as commonly practiced if one limits oneself to saying that every attempt to understand the phenomena in question remains dependent on a conceptual framework that is alien to most of these phenomena and therefore necessarily distorts them. "Objectivity" can be expected only if one attempts to understand the various cultures or peoples exactly as they understand or understood themselves. Men of ages and climates other than our own did not understand themselves in terms of cultures because they were not concerned with culture in the present-day meaning of the term. What we now call culture is the accidental result of concerns that were not concerns with culture but with other things and above all with the Truth.

Yet our intention to speak of Jerusalem and Athens seems to compel us to go beyond the self-understanding of either. Or is there a notion, a word that points to the highest that the Bible on the one hand and the greatest works of the Greeks claim to convey? There is such a word: wisdom. Not only the Greek philosophers but the Greek poets as well were considered to be wise men, and the Torah is said in the Torah to be "your wisdom in the eyes of the nations." We must then try to understand the difference between biblical wisdom and Greek wisdom. We see at once that each of the two claims to be the true wisdom, thus denying to the other its claim to be wisdom in the strict and highest sense. According to the Bible, the beginning of wisdom is fear of the Lord; according to the Greek philosophers, the beginning of wisdom is wonder. We are thus compelled from the very beginning to make a choice, to take a stand. Where then do we stand? We are confronted with the incompatible claims of Jerusalem and Athens to our allegiance. We are open to both and willing to listen to each. We ourselves are not wise but we wish to become wise. We are seekers for wisdom, "philo-sophoi." By saying that we wish to hear first and then to act to decide, we have already decided in favor of Athens against Jerusalem.

This seems to be necessary for all of us who cannot be orthodox and therefore must accept the principle of the historical-critical study of the Bible. The Bible was traditionally understood as the true and authentic account of the deeds of God and men from the beginning till the restoration after the Babylonian exile. The deeds of God include His legislation as well as His inspirations of the prophets, and the deeds of men include their praises of God and their prayers to Him as well as their God-inspired admonitions. Biblical criticism starts from the observation that the biblical account is in important respects not authentic but derivative or consists not of "histories" but of "memories of ancient histories," to borrow a Machiavellian expression.[1] Biblical criticism reached its first climax in Spinoza's *Theological-Political Treatise*, which is frankly anti-theological; Spinoza read the Bible as he read the Talmud and the Koran. The result of his criticism can be summarized as follows: the Bible consists to a considerable extent of self-contradictory assertions, of remnants of ancient prejudices or superstitions, and of the outpourings of an uncontrolled imagination; in addition it is poorly compiled and poorly preserved. He arrived at this result by presupposing the impossibility of miracles. The considerable differences between 19th and 20th century biblical criticism and that of Spinoza can be traced to their difference in regard to the evaluation of imagination: whereas for Spinoza imagination is simply subrational, it was assigned a much higher rank in later times; it was understood as the vehicle of religious or spiritual experience, which necessarily expresses itself in symbols and the like. The historical-critical study of the Bible is the attempt to understand the various layers of the Bible as they were understood by their immediate addressees, i.e., the contemporaries of the authors of the various layers. The Bible speaks of many things that for the biblical authors themselves belong to the remote past; it suffices to mention the creation of the world. But there is undoubtedly much of history in the Bible, i.e., accounts of events written by contemporaries or near-contemporaries. One is thus led to say that the Bible contains both "myth" and "history." Yet this distinction is alien to the Bible; it is a special form of the distinction between *mythos* and *logos*; *mythos* and *historie* are of Greek origin. From the point of view of the Bible the "myths" are as true as the "histories": what Israel "in fact" did or suffered cannot be understood except in the light of the "facts" of Creation and Election. What is now called "historical" is those deeds and speeches that are equally accessible to the believer and to the unbeliever. But from the point of view of the Bible the unbeliever is the fool who has said in his heart "there is no God"; the Bible narrates everything as it is credible to the wise in the biblical sense of wisdom. Let us never forget that there is no biblical word for doubt. The biblical signs and wonders convince men who have little faith or who believe in other gods; they are not addressed to "the fools who say in their hearts 'there is no God.'"[2]

It is true that we cannot ascribe to the Bible the theological concept of miracles, for that concept presupposes that of nature and the concept of nature is foreign to the Bible. One is tempted to ascribe to the Bible what one may call the poetic concept of miracles as illustrated by Psalm 114: "When Israel went out of Egypt, the house of Jacob from a people of a strange tongue, Judah became his sanctuary and Israel his dominion. The sea saw and it fled; the Jordan turned back. The mountains skipped like rams, the hills like lambs. What ails thee, sea, that thou fleest, thou Jordan that thou turnst back? Ye mountains that ye skip like rams, ye hills like lambs? From the presence of the Lord tremble thou earth, from the presence of the God of Jacob who turns rock into a pond of water, the flint into a fountain of waters." The presence of God or His call elicits a conduct of His creatures that differs strikingly from their ordinary conduct; it enlivens the lifeless; it makes fluid the fixed. It is not easy to say whether the author of the psalm did not mean his utterance to be simply or literally true. It is easy to say that the concept of poetry—as distinguished from that of song—is foreign to the Bible. It is perhaps more simple to say that owing to the victory of science over natural theology the impossibility of miracles can no longer be said to be simply true but has degenerated to the status of an indemonstrable hypothesis. One may trace to the hypothetical character of this fundamental premise the hypothetical character of many, not to say all, results of biblical criticism. Certain it is that biblical criticism in all its forms makes use of terms having no biblical equivalents and is to this extent unhistorical.

How then must we proceed? We shall not take issue with the findings and even the premises of biblical criticism. Let us grant that the Bible and in particular the Torah consists to a considerable extent of "memories of ancient histories," even of memories of memories; but memories of memories are not necessarily distorting or pale reflections of the original; they may be re-collections of re-collections, deepenings through meditation of the primary experiences. We shall therefore take the latest and uppermost layer as seriously as the earlier ones. We shall start from the uppermost layer—from what is first for us, even though it may not be the first simply. We shall start, that is, where both the traditional and the historical study of the Bible necessarily start. In thus proceeding we avoid the compulsion to make an advance decision in favor of Athens against Jerusalem. For the Bible does not require us to believe in the miraculous character of events that the Bible does not present as miraculous. God's speaking to men may be described as miraculous, but the Bible does not claim that the putting together of those speeches was done miraculously. We begin at the beginning, at the beginning of the beginning. The beginning of the beginning happens to deal with *the* beginning: the creation of heaven and earth. The Bible begins reasonably.

"In the beginning God created heaven and earth." Who says this? We are not told; hence we do not know. Does it make no difference who says it? This would be a philosopher's reason; is it also the biblical reason? We are not told; hence we do not know. We have no right to assume that God said it, for the Bible introduces God's saying by expressions like "God said." We shall then assume that the words were spoken by a nameless man. Yet no man can have been an eye-witness of God's creating heaven and earth;[3] the only eye-witness was God. Since "there did not arise in Israel a prophet like Moses whom the Lord saw face to face," it is understandable that tradition ascribed to Moses the sentence quoted and its whole sequel. But what is understandable or plausible is not as such certain. The narrator does not claim to have heard the account from God; perhaps he heard it from some man or men; perhaps he retells a tale. The Bible continues: "And the earth was unformed and void. . . ." It is not clear whether the earth thus described was created by God or antedated His creation. But it is quite clear that while speaking about how the earth looked at first, the Bible is silent about how heaven looked at first. The earth, i.e., that which is not heaven, seems to be more important than heaven. This impression is confirmed by the sequel.

God created everything in six days. On the first day He created light; on the second, heaven; on the third, the earth, the seas and vegetation; on the fourth, sun, moon and the stars; on the fifth, the water animals and the birds; and on the sixth, the land animals and man. The most striking difficulties are these: light and hence days (and nights) are presented as preceding the sun, and vegetation is presented as preceding the sun. The first difficulty is disposed of by the observation that creation-days are not sun-days. One must add however at once that there is a connection between the two kinds of days, for there is a connection, a correspondence between light and sun. The account of creation manifestly consists of two parts, the first part dealing with the first three creation-days and the second part dealing with the last three. The first part begins with the creation of light and the second with the creation of the heavenly light-givers. Correspondingly the first part ends with the creation of vegetation and the second with the creation of man. All creatures dealt with in the first part lack local motion; all creatures dealt with in the second part possess local motion.[4] Vegetation precedes the sun because vegetation lacks local motion and the sun possesses it. Vegetation belongs to the earth;[5] it is rooted in the earth; it is the fixed covering of the fixed earth. Vegetation was brought forth by the earth at God's command; the Bible does not speak of God's "making" vegetation; but as regards the living beings in question, God commanded the earth to bring them forth and yet God "made" them. Vegetation was created at the end of the first half of the creation-days; at the end of the last half the living beings that spend their whole lives on the firm earth were created. The living beings—beings that possess life in addition to local motion—were created on the fifth and sixth days, on the days following the day on which the heavenly light-givers were created. The Bible presents the creatures in an ascending order. Heaven is lower than earth. The heavenly light-givers lack life; they are lower than the lowliest living beast; they serve the living creatures, which are to be found only beneath heaven; they have been created in order to rule over day and night: they have not been made in order to rule over the earth, let alone over man. The most striking characteristic of the biblical account of creation is its demoting or degrading of heaven and the heavenly lights. Sun, moon and stars precede the living things because they are lifeless: they are not gods. What the heavenly lights lose, man gains; man is the peak of creation. The creatures of the first three days cannot change their places; the heavenly bodies change their places but not their courses; the living beings change their courses but not their "ways"; men alone can change their "ways." Man is the only being created in God's image. Only in the case of man's creation does the biblical account of creation repeatedly speak of God's "creating" him; in the case of the creation of heaven and the heavenly bodies that account speaks of God's "making" them. Only in the case of man's creation does the Bible intimate that there is a multiplicity in God: "Let us make man in our image, after our likeness. . . . So God created man in his image, in the image of God he created him; male and female he created them." Bisexuality is not a preserve of man; but only man's bisexuality could give rise to the view that there are gods and goddesses: there is no biblical word for "goddess." Hence creation is not begetting. The biblical account of creation teaches silently what the Bible teaches elsewhere explicitly but not therefore more emphatically: there is only one God, the God whose name is written as the Tetragrammaton, the living God Who lives from ever to ever, Who alone has created heaven and earth and all their hosts; He has not created any gods and hence there are no gods beside Him. The many gods whom men worship are either nothings that owe such being as they possess to man's making them, or if they are something (like sun, moon and stars), they surely are not gods.[6] All non-polemical references to "other gods" occurring in the Bible are fossils whose preservation indeed poses a question but only a rather unimportant one. Not only did the biblical God not create any gods; on the basis of the biblical account of creation one could doubt whether He created any beings one would be compelled to call "mythical": heaven and earth and all their hosts are always accessible to man as man. One would have to start from this fact in order to understand why the Bible contains so many sections that, on the basis of the distinction between mythical (or legendary) and historical, would have to be described as historical.

According to the Bible, creation was completed by the creation of man; creation culminated in the creation of man. Only after the creation of man did God "see all that he had made, and behold, it was very good." What then is the origin of the evil or the bad? The biblical answer seems to be that since everything of divine origin is good, evil is of human origin. Yet if God's creation as a whole is very good, it does not follow that all its parts are good or that creation as a whole contains no evil whatever: God did not find all parts of His creation to be good. Perhaps creation as a whole cannot be "very good" if it does not contain some evils. There cannot be light if there is not darkness, and the darkness is as much created as light: God creates evil as well as He makes peace.[7] However this may be, the evils whose origin the Bible lays bare after it has spoken of creation, are a particular kind of evils: the evils that beset man. Those evils are not due to creation or implicit in it, as the Bible shows by setting forth man's original condition. In order to set forth that condition, the Bible must retell man's creation by making man's creation as much as possible the sole theme. This second account answers the question, not of how heaven and earth and all their hosts have come into being but of how human life as we know it—beset with evils with which it was not beset originally—has come into being. This second account may only supplement the first account but it may also correct it and thus contradict it. After all, the Bible never teaches that one can speak about creation without contradicting oneself. In post-biblical parlance, the mysteries of the Torah (*sithre torah*) are the contradictions of the Torah; the mysteries of God are the contradictions regarding God.

The first account of creation ended with man; the second account begins with man. According to the first account God created man and only man in His image; according to the second account, God formed man from the dust of the earth and He blew into his nostrils the breath of life; the second account makes clear that man consists of two profoundly different ingredients, a high one and a low one. According to the first account it would seem that man and woman were created simultaneously; according to the second account man was created first. The life of man as we know it, the life of most men, is that of tillers of the soil; their life is needy and harsh; they need rain which is not always forthcoming when they need it and they must work hard. If human life had been needy and harsh from the very beginning, man would have been compelled or at least irresistibly tempted to be harsh, uncharitable, unjust; he would not have been fully responsible for his lack of charity or justice. But man is to be fully responsible. Hence the harshness of human life must be due to man's fault. His original condition must have been one of ease: he was not in need of rain nor of hard work; he was put by God into a well-watered garden that was rich in trees good for food. While man was created for a life of ease, he was not created for a life of luxury: there was no gold or precious stones in the garden of Eden.[8] Man was created for a simple life. Accordingly, God permitted him to eat of every tree[9] of the garden except of the tree of knowledge of good and evil (bad), "for in the day that you eat of it, you shall surely die." Man was not denied knowledge; without knowledge he could not have known the tree of knowledge nor the woman nor the brutes; nor could he have understood the prohibition. Man was denied knowledge of good and evil, i.e., the knowledge sufficient for guiding himself, his life. While not being a child he was to live in child-like simplicity and obedience to God. We are free to surmise that there is a connection between the demotion of heaven in the first account and the prohibition against eating of the tree of knowledge in the second. While man was forbidden to eat of the tree of knowledge, he was not forbidden to eat of the tree of life.

Man, lacking knowledge of good and evil, was content with his condition and in particular with his loneliness. But God, possessing knowledge of good and evil, found that "it is not good for man to be alone, so I will make him a helper as his counterpart." So God formed the brutes and brought them to man, but they proved not to be the desired helpers. There upon God formed the woman out of a rib of the man. The man welcomed her as bone of his bones and flesh of his flesh but, lacking knowledge of good and evil, he did not call her good. The narrator adds that "therefore [namely because the woman is bone of man's bone and flesh of his flesh] a man leaves his father and his mother, and cleaves to his wife, and they become one flesh." Both were naked but, lacking knowledge of good and evil, they were not ashamed.

Thus the stage was set for the fall of our first parents. The first move came from the serpent, the most cunning of all the beasts of the field; it seduced the woman into disobedience and then the woman seduced the man. The seduction moves from the lowest to the highest. The Bible does not tell what induced the serpent to seduce the woman into disobeying the divine prohibition against eating of the tree of knowledge of good and evil. It is reasonable to assume that the serpent acted as it did because it was cunning, i.e., possessed a low kind of wisdom, a congenital malice; everything that God has created would not be very good if it did not include something congenitally bent on mischief. The serpent begins its seduction by suggesting that God might have forbidden man and woman to eat of any tree in the garden, i.e., that God's prohibition might be malicious or impossible to comply with. The woman corrects the serpent and in so doing makes the prohibition more stringent than it was: "we may eat of the fruit of the other trees of the garden; it is only about the tree in the middle of the garden that God said: you shall not eat of it or touch it, lest you die." God did not forbid the man to touch the fruit of the knowledge of good and evil. Besides, the woman does not explicitly speak of the tree of knowledge; she may have had in mind the tree of life. Moreover, God had said to the man: "thou mayest eat . . . thou wilt die"; the woman claims that God had spoken to both her and the man. She surely knew the divine prohibition only through human tradition. The serpent assures her that they will not die, "for God knows that when you eat of it, your eyes will be opened and you will be like God, knowing good and evil." The serpent tacitly questions God's veracity. At the same time it glosses over the fact that eating of the tree involves disobedience to God. In this it is followed by the woman. According to the serpent's assertion, knowledge of good and evil makes man immune to death, but we cannot know whether the serpent believes this. But could immunity to death be a great good for beings that did not know good and evil, to men who were like children? But the woman, having forgotten the divine prohibition, having therefore in a manner tasted of the tree of knowledge, is no longer wholly unaware of good and evil: she "saw that the tree was good for eating and a delight to the eyes and that the tree was to be desired to make one wise"; therefore she took of its fruit and ate. She thus made the fall of the man almost inevitable, for he was cleaving to her: she gave some of the fruit of the tree to the man, and he ate. The man drifts into disobedience by following the woman. After they had eaten of the tree, their eyes were opened and they knew that they were naked, and they sewed fig leaves together and made themselves aprons: through the fall they became ashamed of their nakedness; eating of the tree of knowledge of good and evil made them realize that nakedness is evil (bad).

The Bible says nothing to the effect that our first parents fell because they were prompted by the desire to be like God; they did not rebel high-handedly against God; they rather forgot to obey God; they drifted into disobedience. Nevertheless God punished them severely. He also punished the serpent. But the punishment did not do away with the fact that, as God Himself said, as a consequence of his disobedience "man has become like one of us, knowing good and evil." As a consequence there was now the danger that man might eat of the tree of life and live forever. Therefore God expelled him from the garden and made it impossible for him to return to it. One may wonder why man, while he was still in the garden of Eden, had not eaten of the tree of life of which he had not been forbidden to eat. Perhaps he did not think of it because, lacking knowledge of good and evil, he did not fear to die and, besides, the divine prohibition drew his attention away from the tree of life to the tree of knowledge.

The Bible intends to teach that man was meant to live in simplicity, without knowledge of good and evil. But the narrator seems to be aware of the fact that a being that can be forbidden to strive for knowledge of good and evil, i.e., that can understand to some degree that knowledge of good and evil is evil for it, necessarily possesses such knowledge. Human suffering from evil presupposes human knowledge of good and evil and *vice versa*. Man wishes to live without evil. The Bible tells us that he was given the opportunity to live without evil and that he cannot blame God for the evils from which he suffers. By giving man that opportunity God convinces him that his deepest wish cannot be fulfilled. The story of the fall is the first part of the story of God's education of man. This story partakes of the unfathomable character of God.

Man has to live with knowledge of good and evil and with the sufferings inflicted on him because of that knowledge or its acquisition. Human goodness or badness presupposes that knowledge and its concomitants. The Bible gives us the first inkling of human goodness and badness in the story of the first brothers. The oldest brother, Cain, was a tiller of the soil; the youngest brother, Abel, a keeper of sheep. God preferred the offering of the keeper of sheep who brought the choicest of the firstlings of his flock, to that of the tiller of the soil. This preference has more than one reason, but one reason seems to be that the pastoral life is closer to original simplicity than the life of the tillers of the soil. Cain was vexed and despite his having been warned by God against sinning in general, killed his brother. After a futile attempt to deny his guilt—an attempt that increased his guilt ("Am I my brother's keeper?")—he was cursed by God as the serpent and the soil had been after the Fall, in contradistinction to Adam and Eve who were not cursed; he was punished by God, but not with death: anyone slaying Cain would be punished much more severely than Cain himself. The relatively mild punishment of Cain cannot be explained by the fact that murder had not been expressly forbidden, for Cain possessed some knowledge of good and evil, and he knew that Abel was his brother, even assuming that he did not know that man was created in the image of God. It is better to explain Cain's punishment by assuming that punishments were milder in the beginning than later on. Cain—like his fellow fratricide Romulus—founded a city, and some of his descendants were the ancestors of men practicing various arts: the city and the arts, so alien to man's original simplicity, owe their origin to Cain and his race rather than to Seth, the substitute for Abel, and his race. It goes without saying that this is not the last word of the Bible on the city and the arts but it is its first word, just as the prohibition against eating of the tree of knowledge is, as one may say, its first word simply and the revelation of the Torah, i.e, the highest kind of knowledge of good and evil that is vouchsafed to men, is its last word. One is also tempted to think of the difference between the first word of the first book of Samuel on human kingship and its last word. The account of the race of Cain culminates in the song of Lamech who boasted to his wives of his slaying of men, of his being superior to God as an avenger. The (antediluvian) race of Seth cannot boast of a single inventor; its only distinguished members were Enoch who walked with God and Noah who was a righteous man and walked with God: civilization and piety are two very different things.

By the time of Noah the wickedness of man had become so great that God repented of His creation of man and all other earthly creatures, Noah alone excepted; so He brought on the Flood. Generally speaking, prior to the Flood man's life-span was much longer than after it. Man's antediluvian longevity was a relic of his original condition. Man originally lived in the garden of Eden where he could have eaten of the tree of life and thus have become immortal. The longevity of antediluvian man reflects this lost chance. To this extent the transition from antediluvian to postdiluvian man is a decline. This impression is confirmed by the fact that before the Flood rather than after it the sons of God consorted with the daughters of man and thus generated the mighty men of old, the men of renown. On the other hand, the fall of our first parents made possible or necessary in due time God's revelation of his Torah, and this was decisively prepared, as we shall see, by the Flood. In this respect the transition from antediluvian to postdiluvian mankind is a progress. The ambiguity regarding the Fall—the fact that it was a sin and hence evitable and that it was inevitable—is reflected in the ambiguity regarding the status of antediluvian mankind.

The link between antediluvian mankind and the revelation of the Torah is supplied by the first Covenant between God and men, the Covenant following the Flood. The Flood was the proper punishment for the extreme and well-nigh universal wickedness of antediluvian men. Prior to the Flood mankind lived, so to speak, without restraint, without law. While our first parents were still in the garden of Eden, they were not forbidden anything except to eat of the tree of knowledge. The vegetarianism of antediluvian men was not due to an explicit prohibition (cf. 1:29); their abstention from meat belongs together with their abstention from wine (cf. 9:20); both were relics of man's original simplicity. After the expulsion from the garden of Eden, God did not punish men, apart from the relatively mild punishment which He inflicted on Cain. Nor did He establish human judges. God as it were experimented, for the instruction of mankind, with mankind living in freedom from law. This experiment just as the experiment with men remaining like innocent children, ended in failure. Fallen or awake man needs restraint, must live under law. But this law must not be simply imposed. It must form part of a Covenant in which God and man are equally, though not equal, partners. Such a partnership was established only after the Flood; it did not exist in antediluvian times either before or after the Fall. The inequality regarding the Covenant is shown especially by the fact that God's undertaking never again to destroy almost all life on earth as long as the earth lasts is not conditioned on all men or almost all men obeying the laws promulgated by God after the Flood: God's promise is made despite, or because of, His knowing that the devisings of man's heart are evil from his youth. Noah is the ancestor of all later men just as Adam was; the purgation of the earth through the Flood is to some extent a restoration of mankind to its original state; it is a kind of second creation. Within the limits indicated, the condition of postdiluvian men is superior to that of antediluvian men. One point requires special emphasis: in the legislation following the Flood, murder is expressly forbidden and made punishable with death on the ground that man was created in the image of God (9:6). The first Covenant brought an increase in hope and at the same time an increase in punishment. Man's rule over the beasts, ordained or established from the beginning, was only after the Flood to be accompanied by the beasts' fear and dread of man (cf. 9:2 with 1:26–30 and 2:15).

The Covenant following the Flood prepares the Covenant with Abraham. The Bible singles out three events that took place between the Covenant after the Flood and God's calling Abraham: Noah's curse of Canaan, a son of Ham; the excellence of Nimrod, a grandson of Ham; and men's attempt to prevent their being scattered over the earth through building a city and a tower with its top in the heavens. Canaan whose land came to be the promised land, was cursed because of Ham's seeing the nakedness of his father Noah, because of Ham's transgressing a most sacred, if unpromulgated, law; the curse of Canaan was accompanied by the blessing of Shem and Japheth who turned their eyes away from the nakedness of their father; here we have the first and the most fundamental division of mankind, at any rate of postdiluvian mankind, the division into a cursed and a blessed part. Nimrod was the first to be a mighty man on earth—a mighty hunter before the Lord; his kingdom included Babel; big kingdoms are attempts to overcome by force the division of mankind; conquest and hunting are akin to one another. The city that men built in order to remain together and thus to make a name for themselves was Babel; God scattered them by confounding their speech, by bringing about the division of mankind into groups speaking different languages, groups that cannot understand one another: into nations, i.e., groups united not only by descent but by language as well. The division of mankind into nations may be described as a milder alternative to the Flood.

The three events that took place between God's Covenant with mankind after the Flood and His calling Abraham point to God's way of dealing with men knowing good and evil and devising evil from their youth; well-nigh universal wickedness will no longer be punished with well-nigh universal destruction; well-nigh universal wickedness will be prevented by the division of mankind into nations in the sense indicated; mankind will be divided, not into the cursed and the blessed (the curses and blessings were Noah's, not God's), but into a chosen nation and the nations that are not chosen. The emergence of nations made it possible that Noah's Ark floating alone on the waters covering the whole earth be replaced by a whole, numerous nation living in the midst of the nations covering the whole earth. The election of the holy nation begins with the election of Abraham. Noah was distinguished from his contemporaries by his righteousness; Abraham separates himself from his contemporaries and in particular from his country and kindred at God's command—a command accompanied by God's promise to make him a great nation. The Bible does not say that this primary election of Abraham was preceded by Abraham's righteousness. However this may be, Abraham shows his righteousness by at once obeying God's command, by trusting in God's promise the fulfillment of which he could not possibly live to see, given the short life-spans of postdiluvian men: only after Abraham's offspring will have become a great nation, will the land of Canaan be given to them forever. The fulfillment of the promise required that Abraham not remain childless, and he was already quite old. Accordingly, God promised him that he would have issue. It was Abraham's trust in God's promise that, above everything else, made him righteous in the eyes of the Lord. It was God's intention that His promise be fulfilled through the offspring of Abraham and his wife Sarah. But this promise seemed to be laughable to Abraham, to say nothing of Sarah: Abraham was 100 years old and Sarah 90. Yet nothing is too wondrous for the Lord. The laughable announcement became a joyous announcement. The joyous announcement was followed immediately by God's announcement to Abraham of His concern with the wickedness of the people of Sodom and Gomorra. God did not yet know whether those people were as wicked as they were said to be. But they might be; they might deserve total destruction as much as the generation of the Flood. Noah had accepted the destruction of his generation without any questioning. Abraham, however, who had a deeper trust in God, in God's righteousness, and a deeper awareness of his being only dust and ashes than Noah, presumed in fear and trembling to appeal to God's righteousness lest He, the judge of the whole earth, destroy the righteous along with the wicked. In response to Abraham's insistent pleading, God as it were promised to Abraham that He would not destroy Sodom if ten righteous men were found in the city: He would save the city for the sake of the ten righteous men within it. Abraham acted as the moral partner in God's righteousness; he acted as if he had some share in the responsibility for God's acting righteously. No wonder that God's Covenant with Abraham was incomparably more incisive than His Covenant immediately following the Flood.

Abraham's trust in God thus appears to be the trust that God in His righteousness will not do anything incompatible with His righteousness and that while or because nothing is too wondrous for the Lord, there are firm boundaries set to Him by His righteousness, by Him. This awareness is deepened and therewith modified by the last and severest test of Abraham's trust: God's command to him to sacrifice Isaac, his only son from Sarah. Before speaking of Isaac's conception and birth, the Bible speaks of the attempt made by Abimelech, the king of Gerar, to lie with Sarah; given Sarah's old age Abimelech's action might have forestalled the last opportunity that Sarah bear a child to Abraham; therefore God intervened to prevent Abimelech from approaching Sarah. A similar danger had threatened Sarah many years earlier at the hands of the Pharaoh; at that time she was very beautiful. At the time of the Abimelech incident she was apparently no longer very beautiful, but despite her being almost 90 years old she must have been still quite attractive;[10] this could seem to detract from the wonder of Isaac's birth. On the other hand, God's special intervention against Abimelech enhances that wonder. Abraham's supreme test presupposes the wondrous character of Isaac's birth: the very son who was to be the sole link between Abraham and the chosen people and who was born against all reasonable expectations, was to be sacrificed by his father. This command contradicted, not only the divine promise, but also the divine prohibition against the shedding of innocent blood. Yet Abraham did not argue with God as he had done in the case of Sodom's destruction. In the case of Sodom, Abraham was not confronted with a divine command to do something and in particular not with a command to surrender to God, to render to God, what was dearest to him: Abraham did not argue with God for the preservation of Isaac because he loved God, and not himself or his most cherished hope, with all his heart, with all his soul and with all his might. The same concern with God's righteousness that had induced him to plead with

God for the preservation of Sodom if ten just men should be found in that city, induced him not to plead for the preservation of Isaac, for God rightfully demands that He alone be loved unqualifiedly: God does not command that we love His chosen people with all our heart, with all our soul and with all our might. The fact that the command to sacrifice Isaac contradicted the prohibition against the shedding of innocent blood, must be understood in the light of the difference between human justice and divine justice: God alone is unqualifiedly, if unfathomably, just. God promised to Abraham that He would spare Sodom if ten righteous men should be found in it, and Abraham was satisfied with this promise; He did not promise that He would spare it if nine righteous men were found in it; would those nine be destroyed together with the wicked? And even if all Sodomites were wicked and hence justly destroyed, did their infants who were destroyed with them deserve their destruction? The apparent contradiction between the command to sacrifice Isaac and the divine promise to the descendants of Isaac is disposed of by the consideration that nothing is too wondrous for the Lord. Abraham's supreme trust in God, his simple, single-minded, child-like faith was rewarded, although or because it presupposed his entire unconcern with any reward, for Abraham was willing to forgo, to destroy, to kill the only reward with which he was concerned; God prevented the sacrifice of Isaac. Abraham's intended action needed a reward although he was not concerned with a reward because his intended action cannot be said to have been intrinsically rewarding. The preservation of Isaac is as wondrous as his birth. These two wonders illustrate more clearly than anything else the origin of the holy nation.

The God Who created heaven and earth, Who is the only God, Whose only image is man, Who forbade man to eat of the tree of knowledge of good and evil, Who made a Covenant with mankind after the Flood and thereafter a Covenant with Abraham which became His Covenant with Abraham, Isaac and Jacob—what kind of God is He? Or, to speak more reverently and more adequately, what is His name? This question was addressed to God Himself by Moses when he was sent by Him to the sons of Israel. God replied: "*Ehyeh-Asher-Ehyeh.*" This is mostly translated: "I am That (Who) I am." One has called that reply "the metaphysics of Exodus" in order to indicate its fundamental character. It is indeed the fundamental biblical statement about the biblical God, but we hesitate to call it metaphysical, since the notion of *physis* is alien to the Bible. I believe that we ought to render this statement by "I shall be What I shall be," thus preserving the connection between God's name and the fact that He makes covenants with men, i.e., that He reveals himself to men above all by His commandments and by His promises and His fulfillment of the promises. "I shall be What I shall be" is as it were explained in the verse (Ex. 33:19), "I shall be gracious to whom I shall be gracious and I shall show mercy to whom I shall show mercy." God's actions cannot be predicted, unless He Himself predicted them, i.e., promised them. But as is shown precisely by the account of Abraham's binding of Isaac, the way in which He fulfills His promises cannot be known in advance. The biblical God is a mysterious God: He comes in a thick cloud (Ex. 19:9); He cannot be seen; His presence can be sensed but not always and everywhere; what is known of Him is only what He chose to communicate by His word through His chosen servants. The rest of the chosen people knows His word—apart from the Ten Commandments (Deut. 4:12 and 5:4–5)—only mediately and does not wish to know it immediately (Ex. 20:19 and 21, 24:1–2, Deut. 18:15–18, Amos 3:17). For almost all purposes the word of God as revealed to His prophets and especially to Moses became *the* source of knowledge of good and evil, the true tree of knowledge which is at the same time the tree of life.

This much about the beginning of the Bible and what it entails. Let us now cast a glance at some Greek counterparts to the beginning of the Bible and in the first place at Hesiod's *Theogony* as well as the remains of Parmenides' and Empedocles' works. They all are the works of known authors. This does not mean that they are, or present themselves as, merely human. Hesiod sings what the Muses, the daughters of Zeus who is the father of gods and men, taught him or commanded him to sing. One could say that the Muses vouch for the truth of Hesiod's song, were it not for the fact that they sometimes say lies resembling what is true. Parmenides transmits the teachings of a goddess, and so does Empedocles. Yet these men composed their books; their songs or speeches are books. The Bible on the other hand is not a book. The utmost one could say is that it is a collection of books. But are all parts of that collection books? Is in particular the Torah a book? Is not rather the work of an unknown compiler or of unknown compilers who wove together writings and oral traditions of unknown origin? Is this not the reason why the Bible can contain fossils that are at variance even with its fundamental teaching regarding God? The author of a book in the strict sense excludes everything that is not necessary, that does not fulfill a function necessary for the purpose that his book is meant to fulfill. The compilers of the Bible as a whole and of the Torah in particular seem to have followed an entirely different rule. Confronted with a variety of pre-existing holy speeches, which as such had to be treated with the utmost respect, they excluded only what could not by any stretch of the imagination be rendered compatible with the fundamental and authoritative teaching; their very piety, aroused and fostered by the pre-existing holy speeches, led them to make such changes in those holy speeches as they did make. Their work may then abound in contradictions and repetitions that no one ever intended as such, whereas in a book in the strict sense there is nothing that is not intended by the author. Yet by excluding what could not by any stretch of the imagination be rendered compatible with the fundamental and authoritative teaching, they prepared the traditional way of reading the Bible, i.e., the reading of the Bible as if it were a book in the strict sense. The tendency to read the Bible and in particular the Torah as a book in the strict sense was infinitely strengthened by the belief that it is the only holy writing or the holy writing par excellence.

Hesiod's *Theogony* sings of the generation or begetting of the gods; the gods were not "made" by anybody. So far from being created by a god, earth and heaven are the ancestors of the immortal gods. More precisely, according to Hesiod everything that is has come to be. First there arose Chaos, Gaia (Earth) and Eros. Gaia gave birth first to Ouranos (Heaven) and then, mating with Ouranos, she brought forth Kronos and his brothers and sisters. Ouranos hated his children and did not wish them to come to light. At the wish and advice of Gaia, Kronos deprived his father of his generative power and thus unintentionally brought about the emergence of Aphrodite; Kronos became the king of the gods. Kronos' evil deed was avenged by his son Zeus whom he had generated by mating with Rheia and whom he had planned to destroy; Zeus dethroned his father and thus became the king of the gods, the father of gods and men, the mightiest of all the gods. Given his ancestors it is not surprising that while being the father of men and belonging to the gods who are the givers of good things, he is far from being kind to men. Mating with Mnemosyne, the daughter of Gaia and Ouranos, Zeus generated the nine Muses. The Muses give sweet and gentle eloquence and understanding to the kings whom they wish to honor. Through the Muses there are singers on earth, just as through Zeus there are kings. While kingship and song may go together, there is a profound difference between the two—a difference that, guided by Hesiod, one may compare to that between the hawk and the nightingale. Surely Metis (Wisdom), while being Zeus's first spouse and having become inseparable from him, is not identical with him; the relation of Zeus and Metis may remind one of the relation of God and Wisdom in the Bible.[11] Hesiod speaks of the creation or making of men not in the *Theogony* but in his *Works and Days*, i.e., in the context of his teaching regarding how man should live, regarding man's right life, which includes the teaching regarding the right seasons (the "days"): the question of the right life does not arise regarding the gods. The right life for man is the just life, the life devoted to working, especially to tilling the soil. Work thus understood is a blessing ordained by Zeus who blesses the just and crushes the proud: often even a whole city is destroyed for the deeds of a single bad man. Yet Zeus takes cognizance of men's justice and injustice only if he so wills. (35–36, 225–85) Accordingly, work appears to be not a blessing but a curse: men must work because the gods keep hidden from them the means of life and they do this in order to punish them for Prometheus' theft, inspired by philanthropy, of fire. But was not Prometheus' action itself prompted by the fact that men were not properly provided for by the gods and in particular by Zeus? Be this as it may, Zeus did not deprive men of the fire that Prometheus had stolen for them; he punished them by sending Pandora to them with her box that was filled with countless evils such as hard toils. (42, 105) The evils with which human life is beset, cannot be traced to human sin. Hesiod conveys the same message by his story of the five races of men which came into being successively. The first race, the golden race, was made by the gods while Kronos was still ruling in heaven; these men lived without toil and grief; they had all good things in abundance because the earth by itself gave them abundant fruit. Yet the men made by father Zeus lack this bliss; Hesiod does not make clear whether this is due to Zeus's ill-will or to his lack of power; he gives us no reason to think that it is due to man's sin. He creates the impression that human life became ever more miserable as one race of men succeeds the other; there is no divine promise, supported by the fulfillment of earlier divine promises, that permits one to trust and to hope.

The most striking difference between the poet Hesiod and the philosophers Parmenides and Empedocles is that according to the philosophers not everything has come into being: that which truly is, has not come into being and does not perish. This does not necessarily mean that what is always is a god or gods. For if Empedocles, e.g., calls one of the eternal four elements Zeus, this Zeus has hardly anything in common with what Hesiod, or the people generally, understood by Zeus. At any rate according to both philosophers the gods as ordinarily understood have come into being, just as heaven and earth, and therefore will perish again.

At the time when the opposition between Jerusalem and Athens reached the level of what one may call its classical struggle, in the twelfth and thirteenth centuries, philosophy was represented by Aristotle. The Aristotelian god like the biblical God is a thinking being, but in opposition to the biblical God he is only a thinking being, pure thought: pure thought that thinks itself and only itself. Only by thinking himself and nothing but himself does he rule the world. He surely does not rule by giving orders and laws. Hence he is not a creator-god: the world is as eternal as god. Man is not his image: man is much lower in rank than other parts of the world. For Aristotle it is almost a blasphemy to ascribe justice to his god; he is above justice as well as injustice.[12]

It has often been said that the philosopher who comes closest to the Bible is Plato. This was said not the least during the classical struggle between Jerusalem and Athens in the Middle Ages. Both Platonic philosophy and biblical piety are animated by the concern with purity and purification: the "pure reason" in Plato's sense is closer to the Bible than the "pure reason" in Kant's sense or for that matter in Anaxagoras' and Aristotle's sense. Plato teaches, just as the Bible, that heaven and earth were created or made by an invisible God whom he calls the Father, who is always, who is good and hence whose creation is good. The coming-into-being and the preservation of the world that he has created depends on the will of its maker. What Plato himself calls the theology consists of two teachings: 1) God is good and hence is no way the cause of evil; 2) God is simple and hence unchangeable. On the divine concern with men's justice and injustice, the Platonic teaching is in fundamental agreement with the biblical teaching; it even culminates in a statement that agrees almost literally with biblical statements.[13] Yet the differences between the Platonic and the biblical teaching are no less striking than the agreements. The Platonic teaching on creation does not claim to be more than a likely tale. The Platonic God is a creator also of gods, of visible living beings, i.e., of the stars; the created gods rather than the creator God create the mortal living beings and in particular man; heaven is a blessed god. The Platonic God does not create the world by his word; he creates it after having looked to the eternal ideas which therefore are higher than he. In accordance with this, Plato's explicit theology is presented within the context of the first discussion of education in the *Republic*, within the context of what one may call the discussion of elementary education; in the second and final discussion of education—the discussion of the education of the philosophers—theology is replaced by the doctrine of ideas. As for the thematic discussion of providence in the *Laws*, it may suffice here to say that it occurs within the context of the discussion of penal law.

In his likely tale of how God created the visible whole, Plato makes a distinction between two kinds of gods, the visible cosmic gods and the traditional gods—between the gods who revolve manifestly, i.e., who manifest themselves regularly, and the gods who manifest themselves so far as they will. The least one would have to say is that according to Plato the cosmic gods are of much higher rank than the traditional gods, the Greek gods. Inasmuch as the cosmic gods are accessible to man as man—to his observations and calculations—, whereas the Greek gods are accessible only to the Greeks through Greek traditions, one may ascribe in comic exaggeration the worship of the cosmic gods to the barbarians. This ascription is made in an altogether noncomic manner and intent in the Bible: Israel is forbidden to worship the sun and the moon and the stars which the Lord has allotted to the other peoples everywhere under heaven.[14] This implies that the other peoples', the barbarians', worship of the cosmic gods is not due to a natural or rational cause, to the fact that those gods are accessible to man as man but to an act of God's will. It goes without saying that according to the Bible the God Who manifests Himself as far as He wills, Who is not universally worshipped as such, is the only true god. The Platonic statement taken in conjunction with the biblical statement brings out the fundamental opposition of Athens at its peak to Jerusalem: the opposition of the God or gods of the philosophers to the God of Abraham, Isaac and Jacob, the opposition of Reason and Revelation.

II. On Socrates and the Prophets

Fifty years ago, in the middle of World War I, Hermann Cohen, the greatest representative of German Jewry and spokesman for it, the most powerful figure among the German professors of philosophy of his time, stated his view on Jerusalem and Athens in a lecture entitled "The social ideal in Plato and the prophets."[15] He repeated that lecture shortly before his death. We may then regard it as stating his final view on Jerusalem and Athens and therewith on *the* truth. For, as Cohen says right at the beginning, "Plato and the prophets are the two most important sources of modern culture." Being concerned with "the social ideal," he does not say a single word on Christianity in the whole lecture. Crudely but not misleadingly one may restate Cohen's view as follows. *The* truth is the synthesis of the teaching of Plato and that of the prophets. What we owe to Plato is the insight that the truth is in the first place the truth of science but that science must be supplemented, overarched by the idea of the good which to Cohen means, not God, but rational, scientific ethics. The ethical truth must not only be compatible with the scientific truth; the ethical truth even needs the scientific truth. The prophets are very much concerned with knowledge: with the knowledge of God, but this knowledge as the prophets understood it, has no connection whatever with scientific knowledge; it is knowledge only in a metaphorical sense. It is perhaps with a view to this fact that Cohen speaks once of the divine Plato but never of the divine prophets. Why then can he not leave matters at Platonic philosophy? What is the fundamental defect of Platonic philosophy that is remedied by the prophets and only by the prophets? According to Plato, the cessation of evils requires the rule of the philosophers, of the men who possess the highest kind of human knowledge, i.e., of science in the broadest sense of the term. But this kind of knowledge, as to some extent all scientific knowledge, is according to Plato the preserve of a small minority: of the men who possess certain gifts that most men lack—of the few men who possess a certain nature. Plato presupposes that there is an unchangeable human nature. As a consequence, he presupposes that there is such a fundamental structure of the good human society as is unchangeable. This leads him to assert or to assume that there will be wars as long as there will be human beings, that there ought to be a class of warriors and that that class ought to be higher in rank and honor than the class of producers and exchangers. These defects are remedied by the prophets precisely because they lack the idea of science and hence the idea of nature, and hence they can believe that men's conduct toward one another can undergo a change much more radical than any change ever dreamt of by Plato.

Cohen has brought out very well the antagonism between Plato and the prophets. Nevertheless we cannot leave matters at his view of that antagonism. Cohen's thought belongs to the world preceding World War I. Accordingly he had a greater faith in the power of modern Western culture to mold the fate of mankind than seems to be warranted now. The worst things that he experienced were the Dreyfus scandal and the pogroms instigated by Czarist Russia: he did not experience Communist Russia and Hitler Germany. More disillusioned regarding modern culture than Cohen was, we wonder whether the two ingredients of modern culture, of the modern synthesis, are not more solid than that synthesis. Catastrophes and horrors of a magnitude hitherto unknown, which we have seen and through which we have lived, were better provided for, or made intelligible, by both Plato and the prophets than by the modern belief in progress. Since we are less certain than Cohen was that the modern synthesis is superior to its pre-modern ingredients, and since the two ingredients are in fundamental opposition to each other, we are ultimately confronted by a problem rather than by a solution.

More particularly, Cohen understood Plato in light of the opposition between Plato and Aristotle—an opposition that he understood in the light of the opposition between Kant and Hegel. We, however, are more impressed than Cohen was by the kinship between Plato and Aristotle on the one hand and the kinship between Kant and Hegel on the other. In other words, the quarrel between the ancients and the moderns seems to us to be more fundamental than either the quarrel between Plato and Aristotle or that between Kant and Hegel.

We prefer to speak of Socrates and the prophets rather than of Plato and the prophets, for the following reasons. We are no longer as sure as Cohen was that we can draw a clear line between Socrates and Plato. There is traditional support for drawing such a clear line, above all in Aristotle; but Aristotle's statements on this kind of subject no longer possess for us the authority that they formerly possessed, and this is due partly to Cohen himself. The clear distinction between Socrates and Plato is based, not only on tradition, but on the results of modern historical criticism; yet these results are in the decisive respect hypothetical. The decisive fact for us is that Plato as it were points away from himself to Socrates. If we wish to understand Plato, we must take him seriously; we must take seriously in particular his deference to Socrates. Plato points not only to Socrates' speeches but to his whole life, to his fate as well. Hence Plato's life and fate do not have the symbolic character of Socrates' life and fate. Socrates, as presented by Plato, had a mission; Plato did not claim to have a mission. It is in the first place this fact—the fact that Socrates had a mission—that induces us to consider, not Plato and the prophets, but Socrates and the prophets.

I cannot speak in my own words of the mission of the prophets. Surely here and now I cannot do more than remind you of three prophetic utterances of singular force and grandeur. Isaiah 6: "In the year that King Uzziah died I saw also the Lord sitting upon a throne, high and lifted up, and his train filled the temple. Above it stood the seraphim: each one had six wings; with twain he covered his face, and with twain he covered his feet, and with twain he did fly. And one cried unto another, and said, Holy, holy, holy is the Lord of hosts: the whole world is full of his glory. And the posts of the door moved at the voice of him that cried, and the house was filled with smoke. Then I said, Woe is me! for I am undone; because I am a man of unclean lips, and I dwell in the midst of a people of unclean lips: for mine eyes have seen the King, the Lord of hosts. Then flew one of the seraphim unto me, having a live coal in his hand, which he had taken with the tongs from off the altar: And he laid it upon my mouth, and said, Lo, this hath touched thy lips; and thine iniquity is taken away, and thy sin purged. Also I heard the voice of the Lord, saying, Whom shall I send, and who will go for us? Then said I, Here am I; send me." Isaiah, it seems, volunteered for his mission. Could he not have remained silent? Could he refuse to volunteer? When the word of the Lord came unto Jonah, "Arise, go to Nineveh, that great city, and cry against it; for their wickedness is come up before me," "Jonah rose up to flee unto Tarshish from the presence of the Lord"; Jonah ran away from his mission; but God did not allow him to run away; He compelled him to fulfill it. Of this compulsion we hear in different ways from Amos and Jeremiah. Amos 3:7-8: "Surely the Lord God will do nothing but he revealeth his secret unto his servants the prophets. The lion hath roared, who will not fear? the Lord God hath spoken; who will not prophesy?" The prophets overpowered by the majesty of the Lord, by His wrath and His mercy, bring the message of His wrath and His mercy. Jeremiah 1:4–10: "Then the word of the Lord came unto me, saying, Before I formed thee in the belly I knew thee and before thou camest out of the womb I sanctified thee, and I ordained thee a prophet unto the nations. Then said I, Ah, Lord God! behold, I cannot speak; for I am a child. But the Lord said unto me, Say not, I am a child; for thou shalt go to all that I shall send thee, and whatsoever I command thee thou shalt speak. Be not afraid of their faces; for I am with thee to deliver thee, saith the Lord. Then the Lord put forth his hand, and touched my mouth. And the Lord said unto me, Behold, I have put my words in thy mouth. See, I have this day set thee over the nations and over the kingdoms, to root out, and to pull down, and to destroy, and to throw down, to build, and to plant."

The claim to have been sent by God was raised also by men who were not truly prophets but prophets of falsehood, false prophets. Many or most hearers were therefore uncertain as to which kinds of claimants to prophecy were to be trusted or believed. According to the Bible, the false prophets simply lied in saying that they were sent by God: "they speak a vision of their own heart, and not out of the mouth of the Lord. They say . . . the Lord hath said, Ye shall have peace." (Jer. 23:16 17) The false prophets tell the people what the people like to hear; hence they are much more popular than the true prophets. The false prophets are "prophets of the deceit of their own heart" (ibid. 26); they tell the people what they themselves imagined (consciously or unconsciously) because they wished it or their hearers wished it. But: "Is not my word like as a fire? saith the Lord, and like a hammer that breaketh the rock in pieces?" (ibid. 29) Or, as Jeremiah put it when opposing the false prophet Hananiah: "The prophets that have been before me and before thee of old prophesied both against many countries, and against great kingdoms, of war, and of evil, and of pestilence." (28:8) This does not mean that a prophet is true only if he is a prophet of doom; the true prophets are also prophets of ultimate salvation. We understand the difference between the true and the false prophets if we listen to and meditate on these words of Jeremiah: "Thus saith the Lord; Cursed is the man, that trusteth in man, and makes flesh his arm, and whose heart departeth from the Lord. . . . Blessed is the man that trusteth in the Lord, and whose hope the Lord is." The false prophets trust in flesh, even if that flesh is the temple in Jerusalem, the promised land, nay, the chosen people itself, nay, God's promise to the chosen people if that promise is taken to be an unconditional promise and not as a part of a Covenant. The true prophets, regardless of whether they predict doom or salvation, predict the unexpected, the humanly unforeseeable—what would not occur to men, left to themselves, to fear or to hope. The true prophets speak and act by the spirit and in the spirit of *Ehyeh-asher-ehyeh*. For the false prophets on the other hand there cannot be the wholly unexpected, whether bad or good.

Of Socrates' mission we know only through Plato's *Apology of Socrates*, which presents itself as the speech delivered by Socrates when he defended himself against the charge that he did not believe in the existence of the gods worshipped by the city of Athens and that he corrupted the young. In that speech he denies possessing any more than human wisdom. This denial was understood by Yehudah Ha-levi among others as follows: "Socrates said to the people: 'I do not deny your divine wisdom, but I say that I do not understand it; I am wise only in human wisdom.'"[16] While this interpretation points in the right direction, it goes somewhat too far. At least Socrates refers immediately after having denied possessing any more than human wisdom, to the speech that originated his mission, and of this speech he says that it is not his but he seems to ascribe to it divine origin. He does trace what he says to a speaker who is worthy of credence to the Athenians. But it is probable that he means by that speaker his companion Chairephon who is worthy of credence to the Athenians, more worthy of credence to the Athenians than Socrates, because he was attached to the democratic regime. This Chairephon, having once come to Delphi, asked Apollo's oracle whether there was anyone wiser than Socrates. The Pythia replied that no one was wiser. This reply originated Socrates' mission. We see at once that Socrates' mission originated in human initiative, in the initiative of one of Socrates' companions. Socrates takes it for granted that the reply given by the Pythia was given by the god Apollo himself. Yet this does not induce him to take it for granted that the god's reply is true. He does take it for granted that it is not meet for the god to lie. Yet this does not make the god's reply convincing to him. In fact he tries to refute that reply by discovering men who are wiser than he. Engaging in this quest he finds out that the god said the truth: Socrates is wiser than other men because he knows that he knows nothing, i.e., nothing about the most important things, whereas the others believe that they know the truth about the most important things. Thus his attempt to refute the oracle turns into a vindication of the oracle. Without intending it, he comes to the assistance of the god; he serves the god; he obeys the god's command. Although no god had ever spoken to him, he is satisfied that the god had commanded him to examine himself and the others, i.e., to philosophize, or to exhort everyone he meets to the practice of virtue: he has been given by the god to the city of Athens as a gadfly.

While Socrates does not claim to have heard the speech of a god, he claims that a voice—something divine and demonic—occurs to him from time to time, his daimonion. This daimonion, however, has no connection with Socrates' mission, for it never urges him forward but only keeps him back. While the Delphic oracle urged him forward toward philosophizing, toward examining his fellow men, and thus made him generally hated and thus brought him into mortal danger, his daimonion kept him back from political activity and thus saved him from mortal danger.

The fact that both Socrates and the prophets have a divine mission means or at any rate implies that both Socrates and the prophets are concerned with justice or righteousness, with the perfectly just society which as such would be free from all evils. To this extent Socrates' figuring out of the best social order and the prophets' vision of the Messianic age are in agreement. Yet whereas the prophets predict the coming of the Messianic age, Socrates merely holds that the perfect society is possible: whether it will ever be actual, depends on an unlikely, although not impossible, coincidence, the coincidence of philosophy and political power. For, according to Socrates, the coming-into-being of the best political order is not due to divine intervention; human nature will remain as it always has been; the decisive difference between the best political order and all other societies is that in the former the philosophers will be kings or that the natural potentiality of the philosophers will reach its utmost perfection. In the most perfect social order as Socrates sees it, knowledge of the most important things will remain, as it always was, the preserve of the philosophers, i.e., of a very small part of the population. According to the prophets however, in the Messianic age "the earth shall be full of knowledge of the Lord, as the waters cover the earth" (Isaiah 11:9), and this will be brought about by God Himself. As a consequence, the Messianic age will be the age of universal peace: all nations shall come to the mountain of the Lord, to the house of the God of Jacob, "and they shall beat their swords into plowshares, and their spears into pruning hooks: nation shall not lift up sword against nation, neither shall they learn war any more." (Isaiah 2:2–4) The best regime, however, as Socrates envisages it, will animate a single city which as a matter of course will become embroiled in wars with other cities. The cessation of evils that Socrates expects from the establishment of the best regime will not include the cessation of war.

The perfectly just man, the man who is as just as is humanly possible, is according to Socrates the philosopher and according to the prophets the faithful servant of the Lord. The philosopher is the man who dedicates his life to the quest for knowledge of the good, of the idea of the good; what we would call moral virtue is only the condition or by-product of that quest. According to the prophets, however, there is no need for the quest for knowledge of the good: God "hath shewed thee, o man, what is good; and what doth the Lord require of thee, but to do justly, and to love mercy, and to walk humbly with thy God." (Micah 6:8) In accordance with this the prophets as a rule address the people and sometimes even all the peoples, whereas Socrates as a rule addresses only one man. In the language of Socrates the prophets are orators while Socrates engages in conversations with one man, which means he is addressing questions to him.

There is one striking example of a prophet talking in private to a single man, in a way addressing a question to him. 2 Sam. 12:1–7: "And the Lord sent Nathan unto David. And he came unto him, and said unto him, There were two men in one city; the one rich, and the other poor. The rich man had exceeding many flocks and herds: But the poor man had nothing, save one little ewe lamb, which he had brought and nourished up: and it grew up together with him, and with his children; it did eat of his own meat, and drank of his own cup, and lay in his bosom, and was unto him as a daughter. And there came a traveller unto the rich man and he spared to take of his own flock and of his own herd, to dress for the wayfaring man that was come unto him; but took the poor man's lamb, and dressed it for the man that was come unto him. And David's anger was greatly kindled against the man; and he said to Nathan, As the Lord liveth, the man that hath done this thing shall surely die; And he shall restore the lamb fourfold, because he did this thing, and because he had no pity. And Nathan said to David, Thou art the man." The nearest parallel to this event that occurs in the Socratic writings is Socrates' reproof of his former companion, the tyrant Critias. "When the thirty were putting to death many citizens and by no means the worst ones, and were encouraging many in crime, Socrates said *somewhere*, that it seemed strange that a herdsman who lets his cattle decrease and go to the bad should not admit that he is a poor cowherd; but stranger still that a statesman when he causes the citizens to decrease and go to the bad, should feel no shame nor think himself a poor statesman. This remark was *reported* to Critias. . . ." (Xenophon, *Memorabilia* I 2.32–33.)

Notes

1. *Discorsi* I 16.
2. Bacon, *Essays*, "Of Atheism."
3. Job 38:4.
4. Cf. U. Cassuto, *A Commentary on the Book of Genesis*, Part I, Jerusalem 1961, p. 42.
5. Cf. the characterization of the plants as engeia ("in or of the earth") in Plato's *Republic* 491 d 1. Cf. Empedocles A 70.
6. Cf. the distinction between the two kinds of "other gods" in Deut. 4:15–19, between the idols on the one hand and sun, moon and stars on the other.
7. Isaiah 45:7.
8. Cassuto, *loc. cit.*, pp. 77–79.
9. One does not have to stoop in order to pluck the fruit of trees.
10. The Bible records an apparently similar incident involving Abimelech and Rebekah (26:6–11). That incident took place after the birth of Jacob; this alone would explain why there was no divine intervention in this case.
11. *Theogony* 53–97 and 886–900; cf. Proverbs 8.
12. *Metaphysics* 1072 b 14–30, 1074 b 15–1075 a 11; *De Anima* 429 a 19–20; *Eth. Nic.* 1141 a 33-b 2, 1178 b 1–12; *Eth. Eud.* 1249 a 14–15.
13. Cf. *Laws* 905 a 4-b 2 with Amos 9:1–3 and Psalm 139:7–10.
14. *Timaeus* 40 d 6–41 a 5; Aristophanes, *Peace* 404–13; Deut. 4:19.
15. *Hermann Cohens Jüdische Schriften*, Berlin 1924, I, 306-330. Cf. the editor's note on p. 341.
16. *Cuzari* IV 13 and V 14. Cf. Strauss, *Persecution and the Art of Writing*, 105–106.

On the Interpretation of Genesis*

I want to begin with the remark that I am not a biblical scholar; I am a political scientist specializing in political theory. Political theory is frequently said to be concerned with the values of the Western world. These values, as is well-known, are partly of biblical and partly of Greek origin. The political theorist must, therefore, have an inkling of the agreement as well as the disagreement between the biblical and the Greek heritage. Everyone working in my field has to rely most of the time on what biblical scholars or classical scholars tell him about the Bible on the one hand and Greek thought on the other. Still I thought it would be defensible if I were to try to see whether I could not understand something of the Bible without relying entirely on what the authorities both contemporary and traditional tell me. I began with the beginning because this choice seems to me to be least arbitrary. I have been asked to speak here about Genesis—or rather about the beginning of Genesis. The context of a series of lectures on the "Works of the Mind" raises immediately a very grave question. Works of the mind are works of the human mind. Is the Bible a work of the human mind? Is it not the work of God? The work of God, of the divine mind? The latter view was generally accepted in former ages. We have to reflect on this alternative approach to the Bible because this alternative is decisive as to the way in which we will read the Bible. If the Bible is a work of the human mind, it has to be read like any other

---

* This is the text of a lecture given by Leo Strauss on January 25, 1957, at the University of Chicago for its series, "Works of the Mind." It was originally printed in the January–March 1981 edition of *L'Homme: Revue française d'anthropologie*. Permission was given by *L'Homme* to reprint the text as it originally appeared.

book—like Homer, like Plato, like Shakespeare—with respect but also with willingness to argue with the author, to disagree with him, to criticize him. If the Bible is the work of God, it has to be read in an entirely different spirit than the way in which we must read the human books. The Bible has to be read in a spirit of pious submission, of reverent hearing. According to this view only a believing and pious man can understand the Bible—the substance of the Bible. According to the view which prevails today, the unbeliever, provided he is a man of the necessary experience or sensitivity, can understand the Bible as well as the believer. This difference between the two approaches can be described as follows. In the past the Bible was universally read as the document of revelation. Today it is frequently read as one great document of the human mind among many such documents. Revelation is a miracle. This means, therefore, that before we even open the Bible we must have made up our minds as to whether we believe in the possibility of miracles. Obviously we read the account of the burning bush or the Red Sea deliverance in an entirely different way in correspondence with the way in which we have decided previously regarding the possibility of miracles. Either we regard miracles as impossible or we regard them as possible or else we do not know whether miracles are possible or not. The last view at first glance recommends itself as the one most agreeable to our ignorance or, which is the same thing, as most open-minded.

I must explain this briefly. The question as to whether miracles are possible or not depends on the previous question as to whether God as an omnipotent being exists. Many of our contemporaries assume tacitly or even explicitly that we know that God as an omnipotent being does not exist. I believe that they are wrong; for how could we know that God as an omnipotent being does not exist? Not from experience. Experience cannot show more than that the conclusion from the world, from its manifest order and from its manifest rhythm, to an omnipotent creator is not valid. Experience can show at most that the contention of biblical faith is improbable; but the improbable character of biblical belief is admitted and even proclaimed by the biblical faith itself. The faith could not be meritorious if it were not faith against heavy odds. The next step of a criticism of the biblical faith would be guided by the principle of contradiction alone. For example, people would say that divine omniscience—and there is no omnipotence without omniscience—is incompatible with human freedom. They contradict each other. But all criticism of this kind presupposes that it is at all possible to speak about God without making contradictory statements. If God is incomprehensible and yet not unknown, and this is implied in the idea of God's omnipotence, it is impossible to speak about God without making contradictory statements about him. The comprehensible God, the God about whom we can speak without making contradictions, we can say is the God of Aristotle and not the God of Abraham, Isaac, and Jacob. There is then only one way in which the belief in an omnipotent God can be refuted, by showing that there is no mystery whatever, that we have clear and distinct knowledge, or scientific knowledge, in principle of everything, that we can give an adequate and clear account of everything, that all fundamental questions have been answered in a perfectly satisfactory way, in other words that there exists what we may call the absolute and final philosophic system. According to that system (there was such a system; its author was Hegel) the previously hidden God, the previously incomprehensible God, has now become perfectly revealed, perfectly comprehensible. I regard the existence of such a system as at least as improbable as the truth of the Bible. But, obviously, the improbability of the truth of the Bible is a contention of the Bible whereas the improbability of the truth of the perfect philosophic system creates a serious difficulty for that system. If it is true then that human reason cannot prove the non-existence of God as an omnipotent being, it is, I believe, equally true that human reason cannot establish the existence of God as an omnipotent being. From this it follows that in our capacity as scholars or scientists we are reduced to a state of doubt in regard to the most important question. We have no choice but to approach the Bible in this state of doubt as long as we claim to be scholars or men of science. Yet that is possible only against a background of knowledge.

What then do we know? I disregard the innumerable facts which we know, for knowledge of mere facts is not knowledge, not true knowledge. I also disregard our knowledge of scientific laws for these laws are admittedly open to future revision. We might say, what we truly know are not any answers to comprehensive questions but only these questions, questions imposed upon us as human beings by our situation as human beings. This presupposes that there is a fundamental situation of man as man which is not affected by any change, any so-called historical change in particular. It is man's fundamental situation within the whole—within a whole that is so little subject to historical change that it is a condition of every possible historical change. But how do we know that there is this whole? If we know this, we can know it only by starting from what we may call the phenomenal world, the given whole, the whole which is permanently given, as permanently as are human beings, the whole which is held together and constituted by the vault of heaven and comprising heaven and earth and everything that is within heaven and on earth and between heaven and earth. All human thought, even all thought human or divine, which is meant to be understood by human beings willy nilly begins with this whole, the permanently given whole which we all know and which men always know. The Bible begins with an articulation of the permanently given whole; this is one articulation of the permanently given whole among many such articulations. Let us see whether we can understand that biblical articulation of the given whole.

The Bible begins at the beginning. It says something about the beginning. Who says that in the beginning God created heaven and earth? Who says it we are not told; hence we do not know. Is this silence about the speaker at the beginning of the Bible due to the fact that it does not make a difference who says it? This would be a philosopher's reason. Is it also the biblical reason? We are not told; hence we do not know. The traditional view is that God said it. Yet the Bible introduces God's speeches by "and God said" and this is not said at the beginning. We may, therefore, believe the first chapter of Genesis is said by a nameless man. Yet he cannot have been an eye-witness of what he tells. No man can have been an eye-witness of the creation; the only eye-witness was God. Must not, therefore, the account be ascribed to God as was traditionally done? But we have no right to assert this as definite. The beginning of the Bible is not readily intelligible. It is strange. But the same applies to the content of the account. "In the beginning God created heaven and earth; and the earth was without form and void; and darkness was upon the face of the deep and the spirit of God moved upon the face of the waters." It would appear, if we take this literally, that the earth in its primeval form, without form and void, was not created, the creation was formation rather than creation out of nothing. And what does it mean that the spirit was moving upon the face of the waters? And what does "the deep," which is perhaps a residue of certain Babylonian stories, mean? Furthermore, if in the beginning God created heaven and earth and all the other things in six days, the days cannot be days in the ordinary sense, for days in the ordinary sense are determined by the movements of the sun. Yet the sun was created only on the fourth creation day. In brief all these difficulties, and we could add to them, create the impression, which is shared by many people today, that this is a so-called mythical account. This means in fact, as most people understand it, that we abandon the attempt to understand.

I believe we must take a somewhat different approach. Fortunately, not everything is strange in this account. Some of the things mentioned in it are known to us. Perhaps we may begin with that part of the first chapter of Genesis which we can understand. The Hebrew word for creation used there is applied in the Bible only to God. Yet this term, *bara*, is used synonymously, at least apparently, with the Hebrew word for doing or making, *asah*. In one case, and twice in this special case, doing or making is used of something other than God: the fruit tree making the fruit, to translate literally. So here we have another case of creation. The word *bara* is applied only to God. What this means is not explained in the Bible. But there is a synonymous term (*asah*) for creating—making—which is applied also to other beings, to trees for example, to say nothing of human beings. Let us therefore see what this word *making* means in the cases in which it occurs within the first chapter of Genesis. The fruit tree making fruit, what kind of making is this? The fruit is originated almost entirely by the tree and, as it were, within the tree. Secondly, the fruit does not have the looks of a tree. Thirdly, the fruit is a complete and finished product. And last, the fruit can be separated from the tree. Perhaps creation has a certain kinship with this kind of making as distinguished from the following kinds of making: First, the making of something which does not originate almost entirely in the maker, artifacts, which require clay and so on in addition to the maker; secondly, the making of something which looks like the maker, the generation of animals; third, the making of something which is not complete but needs additional making or doing, the eggs; and finally, the making of something which cannot be separated from the maker: for example, deeds, human deeds, cannot be separated from the man who does them (deeds and makings would be the same word in Hebrew). We keep only one thing in mind: creation seems to be the making of separable things, just as fruits are separable from trees; creation seems to have something to do with separation. The first chapter of the Bible mentions separation quite often—I mean the term; five times it is explicitly mentioned and ten times implicitly in expressions like "after its kind" which means, of course, the distinction or separation of one kind from the other. Creation is the making of separated things, of species of plants, animals and so on; and creation means even the making of separating things—heaven separates water from water, the heavenly bodies separate day from night.

Let us consider now the most glaring difficulty, namely the difficulty created by the fact that the Bible speaks of days prior to the creation of the sun. The sun was created only on the fourth creation day. We have no difficulty in admitting that the sun came into being so late; every natural scientist would say this today; but the Bible tells us that the sun was created after the plants and trees, the vegetative world, was created. The vegetative world was created on the third day and the sun on the fourth day. That is the most massive difficulty of the account given in the first chapter of the Bible. From what point of view is it intelligible that the vegetative world should precede the sun? How are the vegetative world, on the one hand, and the sun, on the other, understood so that it makes sense to say the vegetative world precedes the sun? The creation of the vegetative world takes place on the third day, on the same day on which the earth and the sea were created first. The vegetative world is explicitly said to have been brought forth by the earth. The vegetative world belongs to the earth. Hence the Bible does not mention any divine making in the creation of the vegetative world. The earth is told by God to bring forth the plants, and the earth brings them forth, whereas God made the world of heaven and sun and moon and stars, and above all God commands the earth to bring forth the animals and God made the animals. The earth does not bring them forth. The vegetative world belongs to the earth. It is, we may say, the covering of the earth, as it were, the skin of the earth, if it could produce skin. It is not separable from the earth. The vegetative world is created on the same day on which the earth and the seas are created; the third day is the day of the double creation. In most of the six cases, one thing or a set of things is created. Only on the third day and the sixth day are there double creations. On the sixth day the terrestrial brutes and man are created. There seems to be here a kind of parallelism in the biblical account. There are two series of creation, each of three days. The first begins with the creation of light, the second with that of the sun. Both series end with a double creation. The first half ends with the vegetative world, the second half ends with man. The vegetative world is characterized by the fact that it is not separable from the earth. Could the distinction between the non-separable and the separable be the principle underlying the division? This is not sufficient. The kinds of plants are separable from each other, although they are not separable from the earth; and creation altogether is a kind of separation. Creation is the making of separated things, of things or groups of things which are separated from each other, which are distinguished from each other, which are distinguishable, which are discernible. But that which makes possible distinguishing and discerning is light. The first thing created is, therefore, light. Light is the beginning, the principle of distinction or separation. Light is the work of the first day. We know light primarily as the light of the sun. The sun is the most important source of light for us. The sun belongs to the work of the fourth day. There is a particularly close kinship between light and the sun. This kinship is expressed by the fact that the light is the beginning of the first half of the creation and the sun is the beginning of the second half of creation.

If this is so we are compelled to raise this question: could the second half of creation have a principle of its own, a principle different from light or separation or distinction? This must be rightly understood. Separations or distinction are obviously preserved in the second half. Men are distinguished from brutes, for example. Hence, a principle different from light or separation or distinction would have to be one which is based on, or which presupposes, separation or distinction but which is not reducible to separation or distinction. The sun presupposes light but is not light. Now let us look at the creations of the fourth to sixth days—on the fourth day, sun, moon and stars; on the fifth day, the water animals and birds; on the sixth day, land animals and man. Now what is common to all creations of the second half? I would say local motion. I shall therefore suggest that the principle of the first half is separation or distinction simply. The principle of the second half, the fourth to sixth day, is local motion. It is for this reason and for this very important reason that the vegetative world precedes the sun; the vegetative world lacks local motion. The sun is what it is by rising and setting, by coming and going, by local motion. The difficulty from which I started is solved or almost solved once one realizes that the account of creation consists of two main parts which are parallel. The first part begins with light, the second part begins with the sun. Similarly there is a parallelism of the end of the two parts. Only on the third and sixth days were there two acts of creation. To repeat, on the third day, earth and seas and the vegetative world; on the sixth day, the land animals and man. I have said that the principle of the first half of creation is separation or distinction and that of the second half of the creation is local motion, but in such a way that separation or distinction is preserved in the idea underlying the second part, namely local motion. Local motion must be understood, in other words, as a higher form of separation. Local motion is separation of a higher order, because local motion means not merely for a thing to be separated from other things; an oak tree is separated or distinguished from an apple tree. Local motion is separation of a higher order because it means not merely for a thing to be separated from other things but to be able to separate itself from its place, to be able to be set off against a background which appears as a background by virtue of the thing's moving. The creation of the heavenly bodies on the fourth day is immediately followed by the creation of the water animals and the birds. These animals are the first creatures which are blessed by God and he blesses them by addressing them:

"Be fruitful and multiply." They are the first creatures which are addressed, addressed in the second person—not like the earth: "the earth should bring forth"; whereas the earth and water are addressed, they are not addressed in the second person. Water animals and birds belong to the class, or the genus, of living beings. (I try to translate the Hebrew term.) What does it mean that on the fourth day we have the first beings capable of local motion, the heavenly bodies, and that on the fifth day we have animals? Local motion is followed by life. Life too must be understood as a form of separation. In the first place life is here characterized by the capacity of being addressed, of hearing, of sense-perception. It is of the greatest importance that the Bible singles out hearing and not seeing or touch as characteristic of the living being. But for our present purpose it is more important to note that animal life appears in the context of the whole chapter as representing a still higher degree of separation than do the heavenly bodies. Animals can change not only their place; but also their courses. The sun and moon and stars cannot change their courses, except miraculously; but, as you see from every dog for example when he's running along, he can change his course; as a matter of fact, he doesn't have such a course. Animals are not limited to changing their places. From this it follows that the being created last, namely man, is characterized by the fact that he is a creature which is separated in the highest degree; man is the only being created in the image of God. If we consider the parallelism of man and plants and that plants are the only creatures to which the term *making* is explicitly ascribed, we may also recognize that man is capable of doing, making deeds, to the highest degree of all creatures.

It seems then that the sequence of creation in the first chapter of the Bible can be stated as follows: from the principle of separation, light; via something which separates, heaven; to something which is separated, earth and sea; to things which are productive of separated things, trees, for example; then things which can separate themselves from their places, heavenly bodies; then things which can separate themselves from their courses, brutes; and finally a being which can separate itself from its way, the right way. I repeat, the clue to the first chapter seems to be the fact that the account of creation consists of two main parts. This implies that the created world is conceived to be characterized by a fundamental dualism: things which are different from each other without having the capacity of local motion and things which in addition to being different from each other do have the capacity of local motion. This means the first chapter seems to be based on the assumption that the fundamental dualism is that of distinctness, otherness, as Plato would say, and of local motion. To understand the character of this dualism, otherness, and local motion, let us confront it with the only other fundamental dualism referred to in the chapter. I quote the twenty-sixth verse: "and God created man in his image, in his image, in the image of God, did God create him, male and female did he create them." That is a very difficult sentence. The dualism of the male and female could well be used for the fundamental articulation of the world and it was used in this way in many cosmogonies—the male and female gender of nouns seems to correspond to the male and female gender of all things and this could lead to the assumption of two principles, a male and a female, a highest god and a highest goddess. The Bible disposes of this possibility by ascribing the dualism of male and female, as it were, to God himself by locating, as it were, the root of their dualism within God. God created man in his image and, therefore, he created him male and female. And also the Bible mentions the distinction of male and female only in the case of man, hence saying, as it were, that male and female are not universal characters. There are many things that are neither male nor female but all things are what they are by being distinguished from each other; and all things are either fixed to a place or capable of local motion. Therefore, the fundamental dualism, male and female, is replaced by the fundamental dualism, distinctness, or otherness, and local motion. This latter dualism, distinctness-local motion, does not lend itself to the assumption of two gods, a distinguishing god and a moving god, as it were. Furthermore, it excludes the possibility of conceiving of the coming into being of the world as an act of generation, the parents being two gods, a male and a female god; or, it disposes of the possibility of conceiving of the coming into being of the world itself, as a progeny of a male and of a female god. The dualism chosen by the Bible, the dualism as distinguished from the dualism of male and female, is not sensual but intellectual, noetic, and this may help to explain the paradox that plants precede the sun. Another point which I mentioned of which I will have to make use: all created beings mentioned in the Bible are non-mythical beings in the vulgar sense of the word; I mean they are all beings which we know from daily sense-perception. Having reached this point, we reconsider the order of creation: the first thing created is light, something which does not have a place. All later creatures have a place. The things which have a place either do not consist of heterogeneous parts—heaven, earth, seas; or they do consist of heterogeneous parts, namely, of species or individuals. Or as we might prefer to say, the things which have a place either do not have a definite place but rather fill a whole region, or something to be filled—heaven, earth, seas; or else they do consist of heterogeneous parts, of species and individuals or they do not fill a whole region but a place within a region, within the sea, within heaven, on earth. The things which fill a place within a region either lack local motion—the plants; or they possess local motion. Those which possess local motion either lack life, the heavenly bodies; or they possess life. The living beings are either non-terrestrial, water animals and birds; or they are terrestrial. The terrestrial living beings are either not created in the image of God, brutes; or in the image of God—man. In brief, the first chapter of Genesis is based on a division by two, or what Plato calls *diairesis* (division by two).

These considerations show, it seems to me, how unreasonable it is to speak of the mythical or pre-logical character of biblical thought as such. The account of the world given in the first chapter of the Bible is not fundamentally different from philosophic accounts; that account is based on evident distinctions which are as accessible to us as they were to the biblical author. Hence we can understand that account; these distinctions are accessible to man as man. We can readily understand why we should find something of this kind in the Bible. An account of the creation of the world, or more generally stated, a cosmogony, necessarily presupposes an articulation of the world, of the completed world, of the cosmos, that is to say, a cosmology. The biblical account of creation is based on a cosmology. All the created things mentioned in the Bible are accessible to man as man regardless of differences of climate, origin, religion, or anything else. Someone might say, that is very well, we all know what sun, moon, and stars, fruits and plants are, but what about the light as distinguished from the sun? Who knows it? But do we not all know a light which is not derivative from the sun, empirically, ordinarily? I say yes, lightning. And perhaps there is a connection between what the Bible says about the light and the biblical understanding of lightning. The Bible starts then from the world as we know it and as men always knew it and will know it, prior to any explanation, mythical or scientific. I make only this remark about the word "world". The word "world" does not occur in the Bible. The Hebrew Bible says "heaven and earth" where we would ordinarily say "world". The Hebrew word which is mostly translated by "world" means something different; it means, in the first place, the remote past, "once" in the sense of "then", the early time or since early time. It means secondly "once" or "then" in the future. And it means finally, "once and for all", for all times, never ceasing, permanent. It means, therefore, that which is permanent. The Hebrew word for world in other words means, therefore, primarily something connected with time, a

On the Interpretation of Genesis 219

character of time rather than something which we see. If there are other beings mentioned in other cosmogonies where all kinds of so-called mythical beings are mentioned, for example, in Babylonian stories, we must go back behind these dragons or what-not, at least, by wondering whether these beings exist. And we must go back to those things mentioned in the first chapter of the Bible and familiar to all of us now and familiar to all men at all times. The Bible really begins, in this sense also, with the beginning.

But you will say, and quite rightly, that what I have discussed is the least important part or aspect of the first chapter. The cosmology used by the biblical author is not the theme of the biblical author. That cosmology, that articulation of the visible universe is the unthematic presupposition of the biblical author. His theme is that the world has been created by God in these and these stages. We prepare our reflection on this theme by considering another feature of the account which we have disregarded hitherto. The Bible in this first chapter makes a distinction between things which are named by God and things which are not named by God and a distinction between things which are called good by God and things which are not called good by God. The things named by God are day, as the name of light, and night, as the name of darkness, and furthermore, heaven, earth, and seas. All other things are not named by God; only these general things, only the things which lack particularization, which do not have a place, properly speaking, are named by God. The rest is left to be named by man. Almost all things are called good by God; the only ones excepted are heaven and man. But one can say that it was not necessary to call man good, explicitly, because man is the only being created in the image of God and because man is blessed by God. However this may be, certainly the only thing which is not called good without being redeemed, as it were, by being blessed by God or by being said to be created in the image of God, is heaven. We may say that the concern of the author of this chapter is a depreciation or a demotion of heaven; in accordance with this, creation appears to be preceded by a kind of rudimentary earth, "in the beginning God created heaven and earth, and the earth. . .". There is no kind of rudimentary heaven, and the heavenly bodies, sun, moon, and stars are, according to the first chapter, nothing but tools, instruments for giving light to the earth; and, most important, these heavenly bodies are lifeless; they are not gods. Heaven is depreciated in favor of the earth, life on earth, man. What does this mean? For cosmology, strictly understood, Greek cosmology, heaven is a more important theme than earth, than life on earth. Heaven means for the Greek thinkers the same as the world, the cosmos. Heaven means a whole, the vault which comprises everything else. Life on earth needs heaven, rain, and not vice versa. And if the more sophisticated Greek cosmologists realized that one cannot leave it at the primacy of heaven, they went beyond heaven, as Plato says, to a super-heavenly place. The human thing is a word of depreciation in Greek philosophy.

There is then a deep opposition between the Bible and cosmology proper, and since all philosophy is cosmology ultimately, between the Bible and philosophy. The Bible proclaims cosmology is a non-thematic implication of the story of creation. It is necessary to articulate the visible universe and understand its character only for the sake of saying that the visible universe, the world, was created by God. The Bible is distinguished from all philosophy because it simply asserts that the world is created by God. There is not a trace of an argument in support of this assertion. How do we know that the world was created? The Bible declared it so. We know it by virtue of declaration, pure and simple, by divine utterance ultimately. Therefore, all knowledge of the createdness of the world has an entirely different character than our knowledge of the structure or articulation of the world. The articulation of the world, the essential distinction between the plants, brutes, and so on, is accessible to man as man; but our knowledge of the createdness of the world is not evident knowledge. I will read you a few verses from Deuteronomy, chapter 4, verses 15 to 19, "Take ye, therefore, good heed unto yourselves for ye saw no manner of similitude on the day that the Lord spake unto you in Horeb out of the midst of the fire, lest ye corrupt yourselves and make you a graven image, the similitude of any figure, the likeness of male or female, the likeness of any beast that is on the earth, the likeness of any winged fowl that flieth in the air, the likeness of any thing that creepeth on the ground, the likeness of any fish that is in the waters beneath the earth; and lest thou lift up thine eyes unto heaven, and when thou seest the sun, and the moon, and the stars, even all the host of heaven, shouldest be driven to worship them, and serve them, which the Lord thy God hath divided unto all nations under the whole heaven," which means which the Lord thy God has assigned, attributed to all nations under the whole heaven. All nations, all men as men cannot help but be led to this cosmic religion, if they do not go beyond the created things. "But the Lord has taken you and brought you forth out of the iron furnace out of Egypt, to be under Him a people of inheritance as you are this day." In other words, the fact that the world has a certain structure is known to man as man. That the world is created is known by the fact that God speaks to Israel on the Horeb; that is the reason why Israel knows that sun and moon and stars do not deserve worship, that heaven must be depreciated in favor of human life on earth, and ultimately, that the origin of the world is divine creation. There is no argument in favor of creation except God speaking to Israel. He who has not heard that speech either directly or by tradition will worship the heavenly bodies, will remain, in other words, within the horizon of cosmology.

I would like to say a very few words about the second chapter, because one great difficulty of the beginning of the Bible is that there is a two-fold account of creation, one in chapter one and another in chapters two to three. The first chapter of the Bible contains a cosmology which is overarched by an account of the creation of the world, a cosmology which is integrated into an account of the creation of the world. This integration of cosmology into an account of creation implies the depreciation of heaven. Heaven is not divine; heaven is subordinate in rank to earth, to life on earth. But this cosmology used by the Bible, as distinguished from the assertion regarding creation, I mean the articulation of the visible world, this cosmology is based on evidence accessible to man as man, whereas the assertion of the createdness of the world is not based on such evidence. Hence the question arises: with what right is the horizon of cosmology, of the things we see, describe and understand, transcended, or, in other words, what's wrong with cosmology? What is wrong with man's effort to find his bearing in the light of what is evident to man as man? What is the true character of human life? What is the right life of man? This question is the starting point of the second account of creation in the second chapter. The first account ends with man; the second account begins with man. It seems that an account which ends with man is not sufficient. Why? In the first account, man is created on the same day as the terrestrial animals, he is seen as part of the whole,—if as its most exalted part. In this perspective, the absolute difference between man and all other creatures is not adequately seen. It appears from the first account that man is separated to the highest degree, that he can move or change his place, in a very metaphorical sense even, to the highest degree. But this privilege, this liberty, freedom, is also a great danger. Man is the most ambiguous creature; hence man is not called good, just as heaven is not called good. There is a connection between the ambiguity of man, the danger to which man is essentially exposed, and heaven, with what heaven stands for, the attempt to find one's bearing in the light of what is evident to man as man, the attempt to possess knowledge of good and evil like the gods. Now if man is the most ambiguous creature, in fact the only ambiguous creature, we need a supplement to that account in which man appears also as part of the whole. We need an account which focuses on man alone; more precisely, since ambiguity means ambiguity in regard to good and evil, we need an additional account in which man's place is defined, not only as it was in the first account by a command "Be fruitful and multiply" in general, but by a negative command, a prohibition. For a prohibition sets forth explicitly the limitations of man—up to this point and not beyond!—the limit separating the good from the evil. The second chapter of the Bible answers the question not about how the world has come into being but how human life, human life as we know it, has come into being. Just as the answer to the question regarding the world as a whole, requires an articulation of the world, the answer to the question regarding human life requires an articulation of human life. Human life, the life of most men, is the life of tillers of the soil or is at least based on that life. If you do not believe the Bible, you may believe Aristotle's *Politics*. Human life is, therefore, characterized most obviously by need for rain and need for hard work. Now, this cannot have been the character of human life at the beginning; for if man was needy from the very beginning, and essentially, he is compelled or at least seriously tempted to be harsh, uncharitable, unjust; he is not fully responsible for his lack of charity or justice because of his neediness. But somehow we know that man is responsible for his lack of charity and justice; therefore, his original state must have been one in which he was not forced or seriously tempted to be uncharitable or unjust. Man's original condition was, therefore, a garden, surrounded by rivers; originally man did not need rain nor hard work; there was a state of affluence and of ease. The present state of man is due to man's fault, to his transgression of a prohibition with which he could easily have complied. But man was created in the image of God, in a way like God. Was he not, therefore, congenitally tempted to transgress any prohibitions, any limitations? Was this likeness to God not a constant temptation to be literally like Him? To dispose of this difficulty the second account of creation distributes accents differently than the first account had done. Man is now said to be, not created in the image of God, but dust from the earth. Furthermore, in the first account man is created as the ruler of the beasts. In the second account the beasts come to sight rather as helpers or companions of man. Man is created in lowliness; he was not tempted therefore to disobey either by need or by his high estate. Furthermore, in the first account man and woman were created in one act. In the second account, man is created first, thereafter the brutes and finally only the woman out of the rib of man. Woman, that is the presupposition, is lower than man. And this low creature, I apologize, woman, lower still than man, begins the transgression. Disobedience is shockingly ill founded. Note, furthermore, that in spite of these differences, the second account fundamentally continues the tendency of the first account in two points. First, there was no need for rain at the beginning, which again means a depreciation of heaven, the source of rain. And secondly, the derivative character of woman implies a further depreciation of the dualism male/female which plays such a role in the first part. Only one more word about this second chapter. Man's original sin, original transgression, consisted in eating of the fruit of the tree of knowledge of good and evil. We have no reason to suppose on the basis of the biblical account as distinguished from later explanations, that man was guided by desire for knowledge of good and evil for he would have had to have some knowledge of good and evil in order to have such desire. It is even hard to say that man desired to transgress the divine command. It comes out rather accidentally. Man's transgression is a mystery, but he did transgress and he knew that he did. Man certainly chose to disobey. He chose therewith the principle of disobedience. This principle is called knowledge of good and evil. We may say that disobedience means autonomous knowledge of good and evil, a knowledge which man possesses by himself, the implication being that the true knowledge is not autonomous; and, in the light of later theological developments, one could say the true knowledge of good and evil is supplied only by revelation.

What I am suggesting then is this: the crucial thesis of the first chapter, if we approach it from the point of view of Western thought in general, is the depreciation of heaven. Heaven is a primary theme of cosmology and of philosophy. The second chapter contains this explicit depreciation of the knowledge of good and evil, which is only another aspect of the thought expressed in the first chapter. For what does forbidden knowledge of good and evil mean? It means ultimately such knowledge of good and evil as is based on the understanding of the nature of things as philosophers would say; but that means, somewhat more simply expressed, knowledge of good and evil which is based on the contemplation of heaven. The first chapter, in other words, questions the primary theme of philosophy; and the second chapter questions the intention of philosophy. The biblical authors, as far as we know, did not know anything of philosophy, strictly so-called. But we must not forget that they were probably familiar, and certainly familiar with certain things, in Babylon for example, which are primitive forms of philosophy, contemplation of heaven and becoming wise in human conduct through the contemplation of heaven. The fundamental idea is the same as that of philosophy in the original sense.

Chapters two and three of Genesis are animated by the same spirit as the first chapter; what the Bible presents is the alternative to the temptation and this temptation we can call, in the light of certain things we happen to know, philosophy. The Bible, therefore, confronts us more clearly than any other book with this fundamental alternative: life in obedience to revelation, life in obedience, or life in human freedom, the latter being represented by the Greek philosophers. This alternative has never been disposed of, although there are many people who believe that there can be a happy synthesis which is superior to the isolated elements: Bible on the one hand and philosophy on the other. This is impossible. Syntheses always sacrifice the decisive claim of one of the two elements. And I shall be glad if we can take up this point in the discussion.

I would like to make only one concluding remark because I understand that in this group you are particularly interested in books. And therefore I would like to say something about the problem of books in so far as it affects the Bible on the one hand and philosophy on the other. The Greek philosophic view has as its primary basis the simple notion, that contemplation of heaven, an understanding of heaven, is the ground by which we are led to the right conduct. True knowledge, the Greek philosophers said, is knowledge of what is always. Knowledge of the things which are not always, and especially knowledge of what happened in the past, is knowledge of an entirely inferior character. As regards knowledge of the remote past, in particular, it comes to be regarded as particularly uncertain. When Herodotus speaks of the first inventor of the various arts he does not say, as the Bible does, that X was the fist inventor of this or that art. Herodotus says he was the first inventor as far as we know. Now this kind of thought, which underlies all Greek thought, creates as its vehicle the book, in the strict sense of the term, the book as a work of art. The book in this sense is a conscious imitation of living beings. There is no part of it, however small and seemingly insignificant, which is not necessary so that the whole can fulfill well its function. When the artisan or artist is absent or even dead, the book is living in a sense. Its function is to arouse to thinking, to independent thinking, those who are capable of it; the author of the book, in this highest sense, is sovereign. He determines what ought to be the beginning and the end and the center. He refuses admission to every thought, to every image, to every feeling which is not evidently necessary for the purpose or the function of the book. Aptness and graces are nothing except handmaids of wisdom. The perfect book is an image or an imitation of that all-comprehensiveness and perfect evidence of knowledge which is aspired to but not reached.

The perfect book acts, therefore, as a countercharm to the charm of despair which the never satisfied quest for perfect knowledge necessarily engenders. It is for this reason that Greek philosophy is inseparable from Greek poetry. Now let us look, on the other hand, at the Bible. The Bible rejects the principle of autonomous knowledge and everything that goes with it. The mysterious God is the last theme and highest theme of the Bible. Given the biblical premise, there cannot be a book in the Greek sense, for there cannot be human authors who decide in the sovereign fashion what is to be the beginning and the end and who refuse admission to everything that is not evidently necessary for the purpose of the book. In other words, the purpose of the Bible, as a book, partakes of the mysterious character of the divine purpose. Man is not master of how to begin; before he begins to write he is already confronted with writings, with the holy writings, which impose their law on him. He may modify these holy writings, compile these holy writings, so as to make out of them a single writing as the compilers of the Old Testament probably did, but he can do this only in a spirit of humility and reverence. His very piety may compel him to alter the texts of the holy writings which came down to him. He may do this for reasons of piety because certain passages in an older source may lend themselves to misunderstanding, which is grave. He may change, therefore, but his principle will always be to change as little as possible. He will exclude not everything that is not evidently necessary for an evident purpose but only what is evidently incompatible with a purpose whose ground is hidden. The sacred book, the Bible, may then abound in contradictions and in repetitions which are not intended, whereas a Greek book, the greatest example being the Platonic dialogue, reflects the perfect evidence to which the philosopher aspires; there is nothing which does not have a knowable ground because Plato had a ground. The Bible reflects in its literary form the inscrutable mystery of the ways of God which it would be impious even to attempt to comprehend.

Bibliography

Works by Leo Strauss

"A Giving of Accounts," with Jacob Klein. *St. John's Review* XXII, no. 1: 1–5.

The Argument and Action of Plato's Laws. Chicago: University of Chicago, 1975.

The City and Man. Chicago: University of Chicago Press, 1964.

"Correspondence Concerning Modernity," with Karl Löwith. *The Independent Journal of Philosophy* IV (1983): 105–19, and V/VI (1988): 177–92.

"Correspondence with Hans-Georg Gadamer Concerning *Wahrheit und Methode.*" *The Independent Journal of Philosophy* 2 (1978): 5–12.

Faith and Political Philosophy: The Correspondence Between Leo Strauss and Eric Voegelin. Edited and translated by Barry Cooper and Peter Emberley. University Park, Penna.: Pennsylvania State University Press, 1993.

History of Political Philosophy. Edited with Joseph Cropsey. 2nd ed. Chicago: Rand McNally College Publishing Company, 1963.

"Letter to Helmut Kuhn." *The Independent Journal of Philosophy* 2: 23–26.

Liberalism: Ancient and Modern. New York: Basic Books, Inc., 1968.

"The Mutual Influence of Theology and Philosophy." *The Independent Journal of Philosophy* III (1979): 111–18.

Natural Right and History. Chicago: University of Chicago Press, 1953.

"On the Interpretation of Genesis." *L'Homme: Revue Française d'anthropologie* XXI, no. 1 (1981): 5–20.

On Tyranny, the revised and expanded edition including the Strauss-Kojéve correspondence. Edited by Victor Gourevitch and Michael S. Roth. New York: Free Press, 1991.

Persecution and the Art of Writing. Westport, Conn.: Greenwood Press, 1952.

Philosophy and Law. Translated by Fred Baumann. Philadelphia: Jewish Publication Society, 1987.

Political Philosophy: Six Essays. Edited by Hilail Gildin. Indianapolis: Bobbs-Merrill Company, Inc., 1975.

"Progress or Return: The Contemporary Crisis in Western Civilization." *Modern Judaism* I (1981): 17–45.

The Rebirth of Classical Political Philosophy. Chicago: University of Chicago Press, 1989.

Socrates and Aristophanes. New York: Basic Books, Inc., 1966.

"Some Remarks on the Political Science of Maimonides and Farabi." Translated by Robert Bartlett. *Interpretation* 18 (Fall 1990): 3–30.

Spinoza's Critique of Religion. New York: Schocken Books, 1965.

Studies in Platonic Political Philosophy. Chicago: University of Chicago Press, 1983.

Thoughts on Machiavelli. Chicago: University of Chicago Press, 1958.

What Is Political Philosophy? Westport, Conn.: Greenwood Press, 1973.

"Why We Remain Jews." Lecture delivered at Hillel House, University of Chicago. Reprinted in Kenneth L. Deutsch and Walter Nicgorski, editors, *Leo Strauss: Political Philosopher and Jewish Thinker*. Lanham, Md.: Rowman & Littlefield, 1994.

Xenophon's Socrates. Ithaca: Cornell University Press, 1972.

Xenophon's Socratic Discourse: An Interpretation of the Oeconomicus. Translated by Carnes Lord. Ithaca: Cornell University Press, 1970.

Other References

Anastaplo, George. *The Artist as Thinker: From Shakespeare to Joyce.* Chicago: Swallow Press, 1983.

Aristophanes. *Peace.* Translated by Benjamin Bickley Rogers. Loeb edition. Cambridge: Harvard University Press, 1961.

Aristotle. *Eudemian Ethics.* Translated by J. Solomon. In *The Complete Works of Aristotle*, edited by Jonathan Barnes. Princeton: Princeton University Press, 1984.

———. *Metaphysics.* Translated by Hippocrates G. Apostle. Grinnell, Iowa: Peripatetic Press, 1966.

———. *Nicomachean Ethics.* Translated by Martin Ostwald. Indianapolis: Bobbs-Merrill, 1962.

———. *Selected Works.* Translated by Hippocrates G. Apostle and Lloyd P. Gerson. Grinnell, Iowa: Peripatetic Press, 1982.

Bacon, Francis. *The Essays.* New York: Penguin Classics, 1985.

Benardete, Seth. "Review of *The City and Man*." *The Political Science Reviewer* (Fall 1978): 1–20.

Berns, Laurence. "Leo Strauss: 1899–1973." *The Independent Journal of Philosophy* 2 (1978): 1–5.

———. "The Relation Between Philosophy and Religion: Reflections on Leo Strauss's Suggestion Concerning the Source and Sources of Modernity." *Interpretation* 19 (Fall 1991): 43–60.

Berns, Walter, Herbert Storing, Harry V. Jaffa, and Werner Dannhauser. "The Achievement of Leo Strauss." *National Review* 25, no. 49: 1347–57.

Bloom, Allan. *The Closing of the American Mind.* New York: Simon and Schuster, 1987.

———. *Giants and Dwarfs.* New York: Simon and Schuster, 1990.

Brown, Harold O. J. "Ancient Gods and Cardboard Heroes." *National Review* 37, no. 7: 26–28.

Burnyeat, M. B. "Sphinx Without a Secret." *New York Review of Books* 32 (30 May 1985): 30–36.

Carpino, Joseph J. "Review of Wilhelmsen's *Christianity and Political Philosophy*." *Interpretation* 8 (May, 1980): 204–22.

Cassuto, U. *A Commentary on the Book of Exodus*. Translated by Israel Abrahams. Jerusalem: Magnes Press, 1983.

———. *A Commentary on the Book of Genesis: Part One, From Adam to Noah*. Translated by Israel Abrahams. Jerusalem: Magnes Press, 1978.

———. *A Commentary on the Book of Genesis: Part Two, From Noah to Abraham*. Translated by Israel Abrahams. Jerusalem: Magnes Press, 1984.

Chesterton, G. K. *The Everlasting Man*. In G. K. Chesterton's *Collected Works*, vol. II. San Francisco: Ignatius Press, 1986.

———. *Orthodoxy*. In G. K. Chesterton's *Collected Works*, vol. II. San Francisco: Ignatius Press, 1986.

Cohen, Hermann. *Reason and Hope: Selections from the Jewish Writings of Hermann Cohen*. Translated by Eva Jospe. New York: W. W. Norton & Company, 1971.

———. *Religion of Reason Out of the Sources of Judaism*. Translated by Simon Kaplan, with an introduction by Leo Strauss. New York: Frederick Ungar Publishing Company, 1972.

Colmo, Christopher. "Reason and Revelation in the Thought of Leo Strauss." *Interpretation* 18 (Fall 1990): 145–60.

Cropsey, Joseph, ed. *Ancients and Moderns: Essays on the Tradition of Political Philosophy in Honor of Leo Strauss*. New York: Basic Books, 1964.

———. "Leo Strauss: A Bibliography and Memorial, 1899–1973." *Interpretation* 5, no. 2 (1975): 133–47.

Dannhauser, Werner. "Leo Strauss: Becoming Naive Again." *The American Scholar* 44 (Autumn 1975): 636–42.

Deutsch, Kenneth L., and Walter Nicgorski, eds. *Leo Strauss: Political Philosopher and Jewish Thinker*. Lanham, Md.: Rowman & Littlefield, 1994.

Deutsch, Kenneth L., and Walter Soffer. *The Crisis of Liberal Democracy*. Albany: State University of New York Press, 1988.

Drury, Shadia B. "The Esoteric Philosophy of Leo Strauss." *Political Theory* (August 1985): 315–37.

———. "Leo Strauss on the Jewish Question." Paper read at the Annual Meeting of the American Political Science Association, September 1, 1991, Washington, D.C. Photocopy.

———. *The Political Ideas of Leo Strauss*. New York: St. Martin's Press, 1988.

———. "Review of *The Rebirth of Classical Political Rationalism*." *Political Theory* (November 1991): 671–75.

East, John P. "Leo Strauss and American Conservatism." *Modern Age* 21 (Winter 1977): 2–19.

Emberley, Peter, and Barry Cooper, eds. and trans. *Faith and Political Philosophy: The Correspondence Between Leo Strauss and Eric Voegelin*. University Park, Penna.: Pennsylvania State University Press, 1993.

Empedocles. *The Poem of Empedocles*. Translated by Brad Inwood. Toronto: University of Toronto Press, 1992.

Fackenheim, Emil L. "Leo Strauss and Modern Judaism." *Claremont Review of Books* (Winter 1985): 21–23.

———. *What is Judaism? An Interpretation for the Present Age*. New York: Collier Books, 1987.

Fortin, Ernest. "Between the Lines: Was Leo Strauss a Secret Enemy of Morality?" *Crisis* 7 (December 1989): 19–26.

———. "Rational Theologians and Irrational Philosophers: A Straussian Perspective." *Interpretation* 12, nos. 2 and 3: 349–56.

Gadamer, Hans-Georg. *Truth and Method*. New York: Crosswood Publishing Co., 1982, pp. 482–90.

———. "Gadamer on Strauss: An Interview," conducted by Ernest Fortin. *Interpretation* 12, no. 1: 1–13.

Germino, Dante. "The Revival of Political Theory." *Journal of Politics* 25 (August 1963): 437–60.

Gourevitch, Victor. "Philosophy and Politics, I and II." *Review of Metaphysics* 22 (September and December 1968): 58–84 and 281–328.

Green, Kenneth Hart. *Jew and Philosopher: The Return to Maimonides in the Jewish Thought of Leo Strauss.* Albany: State University of New York Press, 1993.

Gunnell, John G. "Political Theory and Politics." *Political Theory* 13 (August 1985): 339–61.

———. "Strauss Before Straussianism: Reason, Revelation, and Nature." In Kenneth L. Deutsch and Walter Nicgorski, eds., *Leo Strauss: Political Philosopher and Jewish Thinker.* Lanham, Md.: Rowman & Littlefield, 1994.

Halevi, Judah. *The Kuzari.* Translated by Hartwig Hirschfeld. New York: Schocken Books, Inc., 1968.

Hamilton, Edith, and Huntington Cairns, eds. *The Collected Works of Plato.* Princeton: Princeton University Press, 1961.

Jackson, Michael P. "Leo Strauss's Teaching: A Study of *Thoughts on Machiavelli.*" Ph.D. dissertation, Georgetown University, 1985.

Jaffa, Harry V. *How To Think About The American Revolution.* Durham: North Carolina Academic Press, 1978.

———. "The Legacy of Leo Strauss." *Claremont Review of Books* (Fall 1984): 14–21.

———. "'The Legacy of Leo Strauss' Defended." *Claremont Review of Books* (Spring 1985): 20–24.

———. "Leo Strauss, the Bible, and Political Philosophy." In Kenneth L. Deutsch and Walter Nicgorski, eds., *Leo Strauss: Political Philosopher and Jewish Thinker.* Lanham, Md.: Rowman & Littlefield, 1994.

———. "The Primacy of the Good: Leo Strauss Remembered." *Modern Age* 26 (Summer/Fall 1982) nos. 3 and 4: 266–69.

———. *Thomism and Aristotelianism.* Westport, Conn.: Greenwood Press, 1952.

Jaki, Stanley. *The Absolute Beneath the Relative and Other Essays.* Boston: University Press of America, 1988.

Jung, Hwa Yol. "Two Critics of Scientism: Leo Strauss and Edmund Husserl." *The Independent Journal of Philosophy* 2 (1978): 81–88.

Kass, Leon R. "Man and Woman: An Old Story." *First Things* (November 1991): 14–26.

Kikawada, Isaac M., and Arthur Quinn. *Before Abraham Was*. San Francisco: Ignatius Press, 1985.

Kirk, G. S., J. E. Raven, and M. Schofield. *The Presocratic Philosophers: A Critical History with a Selection of Texts*. 2nd ed. Cambridge: Cambridge University Press, 1957.

Klein, Jacob, and Leo Strauss. "A Giving of Accounts." *St. John's Review* XXII, no. 1: 1–5.

Knox, Ronald. *A Retreat For Lay People*. Harrison, N.Y.: Roman Catholic Books, 1954.

Lattimore, Richard, trans. *Hesiod*. Ann Arbor: University of Michigan Press, 1978.

Lewis, C. S. *Miracles: A Preliminary Study*. New York: MacMillan, 1947.

Lewis, Marlo, Jr. "Piety and Justice in Plato's *Euthyphro*." Ph.D. dissertation, Harvard University, 1980.

Machiavelli, Niccolo. *The Discourses*. Translated by Leslie J. Walker, S.J. New York: Penguin Books, 1970.

Maimonides. *Guide for the Perplexed*. Translated by M. Friedlander. London: George Routledge & Sons, Ltd., 1947.

———. *Guide for the Perplexed, Volumes I and II*. Translated by Shlomo Pines, with an introduction by Leo Strauss. Chicago: University of Chicago Press, 1963.

Maritain, Jacques. *Peasant of the Garonne*. New York: Holt, Rinehart & Winston, Inc., 1968.

McCoy, Charles N. R. "On the Revival of Classical Political Philosophy." *Review of Politics* 35 (April 1975): 161–79.

Mead, Walter B. "Christian Ambiguity and Social Disorder." *Interpretation* 3 (Winter 1973): 221–42.

Miller, Eugene F. "On Rules of Philosophic Interpretation: A Critique of Ryn's 'Knowledge and History.'" *Journal of Politics* 44 (May 1982): 409–19.

Owens, Joseph. *A History of Ancient Western Philosophy.* Englewood Cliffs, New Jersey: Prentice-Hall, Inc., 1959.

Neumann, Harry. "What is Philosophy? An Interpretation of the Theological-Political Problem." *The Independent Journal of Philosophy* I (1977): 31–38.

———. "Civic Piety and Socratic Atheism: An Interpretation of Strauss' *Socrates and Aristophanes*." *The Independent Journal of Philosophy* 2 (1978): 33–37.

Nicgorski, Walter. "Reason, Politics, and Christian Belief, A Review of Sokolowski's *The God of Faith and Reason: Foundations of Christian Theology*." *Claremont Review of Books* (Summer 1985): 18–21.

———. "Leo Strauss." *Modern Age* 26 (Summer/Fall 1982) nos. 3 and 4: 270–73.

Nietzsche, Friedrich. *Thus Spoke Zarathustra*. In *The Portable Nietzsche*, edited and translated by Walter Kaufmann. New York: Penguin Books, 1954.

Pangle, Thomas L. "The Platonism of Leo Strauss: A Reply to Harry Jaffa." *Claremont Review of Books* (Spring 1985): 18–20.

Pippin, Robert B. "The Modern World of Leo Strauss." *Political Theory* 20, no. 3 (August 1992): 448–72.

Pines, Shlomo. "On Leo Strauss." *Independent Journal of Philosophy* 5/6 (1988): 169–71.

Plato. *The Laws of Plato.* Edited and translated by Thomas L. Pangle. New York: Basic Books, 1980.

Plato. *Republic.* Translated with commentary by Allan Bloom. New York: Basic Books, 1968.

Plato. *The Collected Dialogues.* Edited by Edith Hamilton and Huntington Cairns. Princeton: Princeton University Press, 1961.

Rommen, Heinrich A. *The Natural Law: A Study in Legal and Social History and Philosophy.* St Louis: Herder Book, 1955.

Ryn, Claes G. "Knowledge and History." *Journal of Politics* 44 (May 1982): 394–408.

———. "Strauss and Knowledge: A Rejoinder." *Journal of Politics* 44 (May 1982): 420–25.

Sacks, Robert. *A Commentary on the Book of Genesis*. Lewiston, N.Y.: Edwin Mellen Press, 1990.

Sarna, Nahum. *Understanding Genesis: The Biblical Heritage of Israel*. New York: Schocken Books, 1966.

Schaefer, David L. "The Legacy of Leo Strauss: A Bibliographic Introduction." *The Intercollegiate Review* 9 (Summer 1974): 139–48.

Schall, James V. *Christianity and Politics*. Boston: Daughters of St. Paul, 1981.

———. *The Distinctiveness of Christianity*. San Francisco: Ignatius Press, 1982.

———. *The Politics of Heaven and Hell: Christian Themes from Classical, Medieval and Modern Political Philosophy*. Boston: University Press of America, 1984.

———. *Reason, Revelation, and the Foundations of Political Philosophy*. Baton Rouge: Louisiana State University Press, 1987.

———. *Redeeming the Time*. New York: Sheed and Ward, 1968.

———. "Revelation, Reason and Politics: Catholic Reflections on Strauss." *Gregorianum* nos. 2 and 3 (1981): 349–66 and 467–97.

Scholem, Gershom G. *Major Trends in Jewish Mysticism*. New York: Schocken Books, 1961.

Schram, Glenn N. "The Place of Leo Strauss in a Liberal Education." *Interpretation* 19 (Winter 1991–92): 201–216.

Sokolowski, Robert. *The God of Faith and Reason: Foundations of Christian Theology*. Notre Dame: University of Notre Dame Press, 1982.

Spinoza, Benedict. *A Theologico-Political Treatise*. Translated by R. H. M. Elwes. New York: Dover Publications, 1951.

Steintrager, James. "Political Philosophy, Political Theology, and Morality." *The Thomist* 32 (July 1968): 307–32.

Tarcov, Nathan, and Thomas Pangle. "Epilogue: Leo Strauss and the History of Political Philosophy." In Leo Strauss and Joseph Cropsey, eds., *History of Political Philosophy*. 3rd ed. Chicago: University of Chicago Press, 1987.

Udoff, Alan, ed. *Leo Strauss's Thought: Toward a Critical Engagement*. Boulder: Lynne Rienner Publishers, 1991.

West, Thomas G., and Grace S. West. *Four Texts on Socrates*. Ithaca: Cornell University Press, 1984.

Wheelwright, Philip, ed. *The Presocratics*. Indianapolis: Odyssey Press, 1966.

Wilhelmsen, Frederick D. *Christianity and Political Philosophy*. Athens, Georgia: University of Georgia Press, 1978.

———. "Faith and Reason." *Modern Age* (Winter 1979): 25–32.

Wiser, James L. "Reason and Revelation as Search and Response: A Comparison of Eric Voegelin and Leo Strauss." In Peter Emberley and Barry Cooper, eds., *Faith and Political Philosophy: The Correspondence Between Leo Strauss and Eric Voegelin, 1934–1964*. University Park, Penna.: Pennsylvania State University Press, 1993.

Woodard, Joseph K. "Why We Cannot Forget The Jews." Unpublished paper, Claremont Graduate School, 1984.

Wouk, Hermann. *This is My God: The Jewish Way of Life*. New York: Pocket Books, 1970.

Xenophon. *Memorabilia*. In *Conversations of Socrates*. Translated by Hugh Tredennick and Robin Waterfield. New York: Penguin Books, 1990.

Index

Abel, 60, 81–85
Abraham, 59, 60, 88, 89, 90–92, 93, 94, 97, 104, 126, 140, 151, 152, 155
Account of the Beginning, 30, 67, 122, 125, 134, 135
Account of the Chariot, 30, 67, 96, 122, 134, 135
Achilles, 86
Adam, 43, 76, 79–81, 85, 86, 94
Aeschylus, 21
Amos, 122, 134, 135; 3:7, 96; 9:1–3, 113
angel(s), 67, 85, 134, 137, 138–39, 153
anthropomorphism, 104, 151
Apollo, 139–41, 158
Apostles, 151–52, 164n57
Aquinas, Thomas, 28–29, 154, 156
Arabian Nights, 39, 42
Aristophanes, 116–17; *Clouds*, 137; *Peace*, 115, 116–17, 172
Aristotle, 4, 5, 7, 15, 30, 66–67, 75, 83, 98, 103, 108, 109–12, 113, 118, 133, 141, 151, 154, 158; *De Anima*, 110, 171n44; *Eudemian Ethics*, 111, 171n47; god, 15, 94, 109–12, 114, 118, 151–52, 158; *Metaphysics*, 108, 110, 154, 171n35, 41–42; *Nicomachean Ethics*, 15, 103, 110, 112, 154, 161n40, 170n17, 171n45–46, 174n80; *Politics*, 169n105
atheism, 49, 54–55, 150
Athena, 102
Athenian gods, 137–40. *See also* gods
Athens, city of, 21–22, 35–36, 46, 137, 140
Augustine, 72
Averroes, 28
awe, 49, 106

Baal, 55
Babel, 32, 60, 88–90, 104, 151, 154
Babylon, 127, 135
Babylonian exile, 50
Bacon, Francis, 54–55, 164n58–60
bad, badness, 44, 64, 76, 83, 84, 101, 104, 108, 110. *See also* evil
Bathsheba, 27, 142
"Beginning of the Bible and Its Greek Counterparts, The" 30, 31, 32, 33, 35–119, 122, 123
belief, 4, 10, 19, 29, 40, 41, 43–45, 53–55, 93, 100, 105, 131, 132, 133, 142. *See also* faith
Benardete, Seth, 18, 161n51
Berns, Laurence, 166n37
Beyond Good and Evil, 41, 43, 163n14, n22
Bible, 10, 11, 15, 24, 26, 27, 29,

30, 41, 45, 46–53, 59, 63, 90, 97, 98–100, 101, 102, 106, 108, 109, 111, 112, 113, 118–19, 122, 126, 128, 133, 134, 145, 148–49, 150, 151, 153, 155, 157. *See also* particular books of the Bible, Old Testament, New Testament; accessibility, 54, 142, 150; account of the beginning, 35–92, 98, 101, 122, 132, 150–1, 155–56; antagonism to philosophy, 27, 47–49, 61, 66–71, 75–76, 84, 93–96, 132, 151; biblical author, 31, 53, 62–64, 64–66, 77, 81, 87, 95, 98–100, 149; biblical criticism, 26, 31, 32, 45–57, 63, 67, 87, 100; biblical exegesis, 29–30, 90; biblical God, 45, 52, 59, 69, 72, 83, 92–93, 96, 101, 103–4, 106–7, 109, 110, 111, 112, 113–15, 117–19, 153, 154, 157; biblical teaching, 153–54; book, as a, 98–100; civilization, as understood by Bible, 60, 83–84; esoteric teaching, 66–67, 73, 117–18; Hebrew Bible, 27, 29, 55, 93, 126, 162n21; as myth, 52–55, 63
blessing, 19, 88–90, 105, 110
Bloom, Allan, 7, 9, 11—12, 19, 160n26–27, 161n54
Brutus, 50–51
Burnyeat, M. B., 7

Cain, 60, 81–85, 86, 87, 88, 89, 156
Canaan, 32, 60, 88–89
Carmel, 55
Cassuto, U., 26, 31, 63–64, 72, 73–74, 76–77, 78, 82, 85–86, 88, 95–96, 100, 150, 165n8–10, 166n21, n24, n35, n39, 166n21, n24, n35, 167n36–37, n50, n59–60, n62, n74, 168n78, n85–88, n94–95, n100, n102, 169n130–31, 170n32
Chairephon, 139
chaos, 66, 107, 128, 170n27

charity, 74, 167n49
Chesterton, G. K., 74, 130, 169n127, 173n35, 175n9
Christ, 14, 21, 151–52, 164n57, 168n91
Christian, Christianity, 11, 13, 21, 28–29, 60–62, 125, 126, 128–30, 150, 154, 166n29; Catholicism, 11, 28, 164n, 168n77, 91; God, 13; Protestantism, 45
Churchill, Winston, 10
Cicero, 54
Clearchus, 50–51, 52
Clouds. See Aristophanes
Cohen, Hermann, 28, 31, 32, 38, 115, 121, 123–33, 149, 154; *Religion of Reason*, 125; "The Social Ideal in Plato and the Prophets," 126–27, 130; Strauss's critique of, 132–33, 149; understanding of Plato, 128, 130–32; understanding of the prophets, 127–28
commandments, 43, 82, 83, 93, 153
Commentary, 18, 174n84
convention, 6, 116
Cooper, Barry, 159n11, 173n36
corporealism, 125, 151, 166n27
cosmology, 4, 70, 76, 156
cosmos, 66, 68, 97, 101, 105, 108, 142
covenant: Abraham, 84, 90–92, 93, 94; with Israel, 31, 93, 94, 96, 136; Noah, 85, 86, 88, 89, 104
creation, 51, 53, 65, 66–77, 85, 86, 88, 94, 100, 101, 102, 103, 106, 108, 109, 128, 138, 141, 152, 170n15; first creation account, 59, 64–71, 77; Platonic account, 112–14; second creation account, 59, 71–77, 164n40; vegetation, 67–68, 107, 109
Creator. *See* God
Critias, 143–44
critique of culture, 38–45
culture, 11, 32, 38, 123, 128

Index

curse, 32, 82, 84, 88–89, 105, 168–69n103

daimonion, 140
Darwin, 3
David, 27, 84, 143–44, 154
Democritus, 54
Deuteronomy, 47, 54, 65, 70; 4:12, 5:4–5, 18:15–18, 96; 4:19, 115, 117–18
Deutsch, Kenneth, 124, 160n11, 172n11
Discourses. See Machiavelli
disobedience, 74, 79–81, 104, 105
divine name, 92–96, 134, 171n39. *See also* God
divine science, 67, 96, 122, 134. *See also* theology
doubt, 22, 54, 138, 139, 164n57
Drury, Shadia, 7, 13–14, 16, 79, 103, 155, 161n36–37, 167n67, 170n18

earth, 22, 27, 65, 66–68, 70, 82, 89, 101, 102, 106, 107, 108, 113, 137, 141, 151, 154. *See also* heaven and earth
East, John, 130
Ecclesiasticus, 47–48
Eden, 74, 80, 81, 151; expulsion from, 80
Egypt, 70
Ehyeh–Asher–Ehyeh, 95
Einstein, 4
elements, 108
Elijah, 55
Emberley, Peter, 159n11, 173n36
Empedocles, 30, 68, 97, 98, 107–9, 166n21, 171n31–34
Enlightenment, 4, 16, 45, 132
Enoch, 84
envy of the gods, 103
epicureanism, 10
Epicurus, 74
Er, myth of, 144

esotericism, 7–9, 13, 150
eternity of world, 66, 109
Eve, 43, 76, 77, 78–81, 82, 85, 86, 94
evil, 16, 71–72, 77–81, 85, 88, 101, 108, 113, 130, 132, 136, 141, 142, 144, 154, 156, 158, 166n37, 174n93
ex nihilo, 64, 66–67
Exodus, 30, 50, 63, 92–96; 3:14, 93; 33:19, 19:19, 20:19 and 21, 24:1–2, 96; ch. 24, 122
Ezekiel, 30, 96, 122, 134

Fackenheim, Emil, 78, 167n64, 174n93
faith, 4, 7, 16, 17, 18–19, 21–24, 36, 38, 39, 41, 48, 49, 55, 61, 92, 93, 123, 125, 126, 129, 132, 137, 145, 151–52, 157
falasifa, 61
fall, 59, 73, 74, 77–81, 86–88, 168n91
fate, 97, 106
fear, 47–49, 54, 60, 72, 90, 93, 96, 106, 111, 136, 143, 144, 151, 164n37; animal's fear of man, 88, 90
Flood, 51, 60, 81, 84, 85–88, 90, 91, 104, 135, 156, 168n94
Fortin, Ernest, 129
freedom, 8, 13, 15, 24, 37–38, 50, 52, 78, 136, 142, 149, 152

Galilee, 151
gender, 69–70
Genesis, 16, 26, 31, 32, 38, 43, 47, 50, 51, 53, 59, 62, 63, 64–92, 98, 100, 122, 149, 151, 155, 166n35, 168n94; 1:4, 72; 3:23, 79; 3:6, 3.22, 3:23, 80; 4:7, 82; 4:23–4, 84; 6:1–4, 85; 11:5–7, 90; 1:27, 164n39
giants, race of, 85–86, 87
Giants and Dwarfs, 11, 160n, 161n

Gilgamesh, 168n
God, 4, 11, 12, 16, 18, 22, 25, 31, 32, 33, 37, 41, 43, 45, 49, 50, 52–57, 59, 60, 61, 65, 66–96, 97, 99, 101, 102–3, 109, 110, 115, 118, 122, 125–26, 127, 130, 131, 134–37, 138, 139, 141, 142, 143, 145, 150–56, 157, 158; compared to Greek gods, 101–7; Creator, 65–77, 83, 96, 137, 152; God of Abraham, Isaac, and Jacob 31, 59, 69, 93, 94–96, 97, 106, 117, 118, 126, 131, 136, 156, 158, 169n118; God's Name 59, 60, 92–96, 119, 122, 134, 136; of Israel, 55, 96, 125, 131, 135, 141, 144; Judeo–Christian God, 13, 14, 16, 41, 49; Lord, 47, 49, 54, 65, 89, 90, 91, 96, 103, 111, 126, 134, 135, 137; oneness, 43, 69–70, 71, 80, 119, 126
goddesses, 69–70, 98, 107–8, 109
gods, 10, 13–14, 68, 69–70, 71, 80, 97, 109, 110, 114, 128, 131, 139, 168n94; cosmic or visible gods, 68, 70, 114, 115, 117–19, 139, 141–42 *(see also* heavens); Greek gods, 14, 16, 97, 100–107, 110–11, 115–16, 128 (generation of, 101; concern for man, 101, 104–, 109–10, 139–40); heathen *(see* cosmic gods); of philosophy, 107–19; of poetry, 96–107, 114; traditional, 111, 115–19, 139–144
Gomorra, 91–92, 135, 156
good, 6, 8, 42, 44, 72, 77, 83, 84, 101, 103, 104, 105, 108, 111, 113, 130, 132, 141, 142, 143, 154, 169n115
good and evil. *See* knowledge
goodness: of creation, 77, 78, 83; of man, 145; of world, 158
Gorgias, 143
Greek Counterparts, 30–33, 35, 40, 83, 95, 97–119, 123

Greeks, 7, 14, 15, 16, 32, 36, 42–43, 66, 101; account of beginning, 30, 97, 101–2; philosophy, 30, 46, 66–67, 107–19, 140, 144–45; poets, 9–10, 30, 46, 67, 97, 100–107, 119; religion, 115–17, 128, 144; thought, 36, 37, 48, 66–67, 68, 95, 106
Green, Kenneth Hart, 160n11, 162n16
Gunnell, John, 38, 164n38

Hades, 113
Halevi, Judah, 11, 137–39, 143, 152–53
Ham, 89, 168n103
Hananiah, 136
heathens, 23, 70, 85, 118
heaven and earth, 93, 102, 113, 129, 140, 170n15
heavens, 27, 64, 65, 67–68, 67–69, 70, 90, 101, 110, 113, 115, 117, 118, 119, 140, 152, 167n53. *See also* cosmic gods
Hebrew language, 74, 93, 95, 136, 169n126, 170n7
Hebrews, 42–43. *See also* Israel, Jews
Hegel, 133, 159n9
Heidegger, 124
Hermes, 117
Hesiod, 16, 30, 32, 41, 62, 97, 98, 100–107, 109, 112, 113, 114–15, 118; account of the gods, 101–3; account of man, 103–7
Hiero, 144
historical–critical method, 49–57
historicism, 3–5, 127
Hitler, 17
Hobbes, 4, 74
holiness, holy, 41, 84, 99, 100, 155
Holy Land, 21
Homer, 97, 115
Horeb, 70
human nature, 125, 128, 131, 141. *See also* nature

Index

"I shall be what I shall be," 93–96, 119, 133, 136
ideas, 114, 119, 130, 156
image of God, 49, 68–70, 73, 78, 82, 88, 110, 118, 152
immortality, 15, 79, 80, 85
incest, 43, 89, 168n103
incorporeality, 47, 67
inspiration, 31, 50, 64, 73, 99–100, 137
Isaac, 59, 63, 70, 91–92, 96, 97, 126, 140, 152, 155
Isaiah, 72, 122, 134; ch. 6, 134–35; 11:9, 141; 2:24, 142; 2:24, 174n
Islamic thinkers, 14–15, 42, 61, 137
Israel, 55, 63, 68, 70, 83–84, 92, 96, 115, 118, 125, 126, 131, 135, 136, 137, 144, 166n35, 169n115, n125, 170n7 (*see also* God, Hebrews, Jews); chosen nation, 90, 92, 116, 136, 141, 153, 156; election, 53, 90–92, 126; people, 31, 55, 83, 85, 86, 117–18

Jacob, 97
Jaffa, Harry V., 7, 10–11, 12, 119, 155, 157, 160n21–24, 161n32, 162n19, 172n71, 175n26
jealousy, 42, 102, 103, 170n16
Jeremiah, 122, 134; 6:4–10, 135; 28:8, 136; ch. 26, 136–37; 1:6, 137
Jerusalem, city of, 21–22, 35, 46, 84
Jew(s)/Jewish, 17, 28–29, 42–43, 47, 49, 99, 122, 124, 127, 130, 150, 154, 166n37, 169n115 (*see also* Hebrews, Israel, Judaism); antagonism to philosophy, 61, 127, 137–38; law, 30, 47, 50, 60–61, 83, 87–88, 89, 90, 122, 128, 129, 132, 154 (*see also* law, revelation); nation, 90, 125 (*see also* Israel); philosophers, 14, 15 (*see also* Maimonides, Spinoza);

problem, 17–19, 25, 26, 45–46, 125–26, 130, 161n52; religion (*see* Judaism)
Job, 47–48, 65, 163–64n35
John the Baptist, 42
Jonah, 122, 134, 135
Judaism, 17, 21, 25, 29, 45, 60–62, 74, 89, 99, 124–28, 129, 130, 138, 154
justice, 6, 10, 22, 26–27, 35–36, 74, 92, 104–5, 110, 112, 113, 114, 116, 128, 129, 141, 142, 143, 144–45, 167n49

Kant, 124, 125, 133, 159n9
Khazars. See *Kuzari*
Kikawada, Isaac, 83, 168n94, n102
Kings, Book of, 55, 76
Klein, Jacob, 161n53
knowledge, 4–7, 8, 11–12, 23, 25, 26–27, 37, 39–40, 54, 71, 75, 84, 107–8, 111, 119, 122, 127, 128, 131, 139, 142, 153, 156; of God, 122, 127, 131, 141–42; moral, 76, 77, 82, 87, 89; philosophic, 26–27, 137–40, 142, 152–53, 156–58; prophetic, 122, 127–28, 131, 133–34; scientific, 127, 131
knowledge of good and evil, 23, 75–77, 82–83, 89, 96, 108, 122, 155–56
Knox, Ronald, 151
Kojéve, Alexander, 142
Koran, 52
Kronos, 101, 105
Kuzari, 11, 137–38, 143

Lamech, 83, 84, 85, 87
law, 17, 60–61, 82–83, 87–88, 88–89, 109, 116, 135, 144–45, 168n77; divine, 22, 30, 47, 50, 61, 83, 95, 118, 122, 129, 132, 154–56; Mosaic, 122, 125, 136; natural, 10, 29, 38, 156
Lincoln, Abraham, 10
logos, 129

McCoy, Charles, 161n35
Machiavelli, 3, 28, 49, 50–52, 55, 87, 160n15; *Discourses*, 50–52, 54, 87
Maimonides, 7, 23, 27, 29–30, 47, 66, 71, 73, 96, 117, 118, 122–23, 151, 162n16, 163n16, 166n27; *Guide for the Perplexed*, 7, 29–30, 47, 67, 117–18, 122–23, 162n16
Matthew, 5:17–18, 129; 18:3, 167n53
medieval thinkers, 4, 14–15, 71, 109, 113, 118, 124, 137
Memorabilia, 137, 143, 174n89–90
mercy, 43, 69, 135, 142, 145
Messiah, 122, 126, 154
Messianic age, 125, 141–42, 154
metaphysics, 67, 93–95, 107–112, 119, 128, 129–30
Metis, 102–3
Micah, 122; 6:8, 142, 174n84
Middle Ages. *See* medieval thinkers
Minos, 113
miracles, 49, 52, 54, 55–57, 136, 139, 174n66
modernity, 3–10, 14, 15–16, 23, 36–57, 61, 123–28, 130–33, 148–49, 154, 156–57
morality, 5–6, 10, 13, 25, 30–31, 38, 42, 44, 52, 82, 89, 109, 125, 130, 132, 144–45. *See also* knowledge of good and evil, moral knowledge
Moses, 32, 42, 59, 65, 73, 93–94, 96, 99, 118, 121, 122–23, 125, 134, 169n122
Mount Sinai, 63, 99, 122
Muses, 98, 102, 108
mystery, 73, 77, 78, 81, 94, 96, 100, 119, 151–52, 153, 157
myth, 13, 41, 53, 71, 78, 87, 95, 97–107, 118, 132, 144

Nathan, 27, 143–44, 154
natural right, 26–27, 28

nature, 6, 9, 22, 27, 43, 51, 55, 56, 67–68, 74, 76, 89, 93, 107, 108, 110, 116, 117, 125, 131, 141, 165n66
Nero, 3
New Atlantis, 54. *See also* Francis Bacon
New Testament, 129, 164n57, 167n53
Nicgorski, Walter, 124, 160n11, 172n11
Nietzsche, Friedrich, 40–45, 47, 55, 148, 166n25
nihilism, 13, 19, 79
Nimrod, 32, 60, 88–90
Nineveh, 135
Noah, 51, 60, 81, 84, 85–88, 89, 90, 91, 92, 94, 104, 168–69n103
nomos, 116

obedience, 17, 24, 25, 55, 60, 64, 75, 84, 108, 126, 140, 149, 151, 153
Old Testament, 27, 29, 30, 48, 63, 76, 126, 129, 153–54
"On Socrates and the Prophets," 27, 30–32, 56, 59, 121–45, 169n124
oracle, 138–39, 140
orthodoxy, 12, 25, 50, 53, 54, 56, 111, 149
overpopulation, 87, 168n94
Owens, Joseph, 170n28, 171n29

pagan, 41, 86, 135, 136. *See also* heathen
Pandora, 105–6
Pangle, Thomas, 7, 9–11, 16, 155, 160n24
Parmenides, 30, 97, 98, 107–9
Peace. See Aristophanes
Pentateuch, 85
Pericles, 21
Perses, 104–5
philosopher king, 131, 141
philosopher(s), 5, 8, 11, 13, 14, 36, 40, 41, 46, 48, 61, 68, 106, 113,

114, 124, 127, 131, 134, 137–38, 142, 144, 150, 165n3
philosophic ignorance, 4, 6–7, 11–12, 138–39, 152–53, 156–57
philosophy, 3–19, 21–25, 31, 39, 41–43, 49, 53, 54, 61–67, 69, 76, 84, 87, 94, 96, 98, 103, 107–15, 118–19, 123–28, 132, 135, 137, 138, 143, 144–45, 148–51, 155, 156, 157–58, 165n3, n11; defined, 6–7, 23, 62–63, 157; ineffectiveness, 143–45; modern, 3–4, 7, 9; tension with theology, 12, 16, 24, 25, 29, 31, 84, 148, 151, 155
physics, 67
physis, 93, 116
piety, pious, 13, 14, 37, 54, 84, 99, 111, 138–39, 140, 153, 156, 158
Pines, Shlomo, 7, 159n10, 162n16
Plato, 5, 7, 9–10, 11, 12, 13, 15, 28, 30, 31, 36, 41, 68, 98, 107, 111, 112–19, 123, 130, 131, 132, 133, 134, 137, 140–41, 142, 144, 145, 148, 155, 157; account of creation, 112–14; *Apology*, 19, 137; Cohen's analysis, 128–32; *Euthyphron*, 111, 119; evil, 72; god, 113–16, 118–19, 155; *Laws*, 112, 113, 114, 160n28; *Phaedrus*, 114; Platonism, 128, 132, 155; *Republic*, 35–36, 68, 74, 112, 114, 115, 134; "Second Letter to Dionysius," 140, 157; *Theaetetus*, 166n37; theology, 112–15; *Timaeus*, 112, 115–16, 155; writing, 9, 140–41, 157
pluralism, 44–45
poetry, 9–10, 13, 16, 30, 31, 42, 55, 63–64, 67–68, 97, 98, 100–107, 108, 118, 155; quarrel between philosophy and, 9–10, 31, 155
Polemarchus, 35
political philosophy, 3, 5–7, 13–16, 22, 28, 123, 129–30; classical, 4–6, 7, 10, 38, 112–19, 137–45, 147, 157–58; modern, 3–5, 37–38
polytheism, 43, 69–70, 71
positivism, 3–5
Presocratics, 97–98, 107–9, 110, 118
progress, 4, 25, 36, 38, 45, 94, 123, 125, 128, 132, 148, 157
Prometheus, 105–6
prophet(s), 16, 28, 30, 31, 32, 41, 49, 50, 61, 63, 65, 118, 121, 122, 123, 125, 126–28, 129, 131–37, 139, 140, 141–45, 154, 155; call, 122, 139; false, 33, 121, 136; knowledge, 122, 127, 131; mission, 133–36, 141–45
Proverbs, 47–48, 102–3
providence, 45, 54, 110, 111, 114, 119, 151–52
Psalms: Ps. 14, 53; Ps. 114, 55–56; Ps. 139, 113
punishment, 80, 82, 86, 104–5, 106, 131–32, 143
Pythia, 139

Quinn, Arthur, 83, 168n94, 102

Rahab, 166n35
reason, 7, 11, 12, 16–18, 21, 22–28, 30, 38, 40, 46, 49, 103, 118, 125–26, 131, 138, 147, 151, 156, 157; reasonableness of Bible, 56–57, 65–66, 77
Red Sea, 56
relativism, 44–45, 123
religion, 11, 13, 15–17, 21, 41, 43, 51, 52–54, 60, 61, 70, 125, 126, 129–30, 132, 138, 150
return, 25, 36, 38, 116, 122, 127, 148
revelation, 7, 9–11, 12, 13, 15–18, 21, 22–30, 38, 40, 46, 49, 56, 60, 61, 84, 87, 88, 89, 93, 96, 97, 99, 116, 118, 122, 126, 129, 130, 136, 138, 139, 142, 147, 150, 151, 155–57; Christian v.

Jewish and Islamic revelation, 60–62, 129, 137; divine, 23, 55, 139, 153; Greek, 109; law, 46, 61, 83, 128, 129; Mosaic, 122, 134; personal, 128–39, 152–53
righteousness, 22, 92, 104, 105; Abraham's, 90–91; God's, 91; Noah's 87, 89
Roman people, 51
Rome, 3, 29
Romulus, 83

Sacks, Robert, 47, 76, 86, 163n32, 167n57, 170n27
sacred, 7, 22, 43, 89, 116, 169n103
sacrifice, 55, 59, 126, 135, 152, 155
salvation, 129, 131
Samuel, 27, 76, 83–84, 143
Sarah, 91, 151
Sarna, Nahum, 135
Schall, James, 72, 129, 142, 145, 150, 153–54
Scheol, 113
science, 3–4, 11, 15–16, 38, 39, 40, 54, 56, 67, 117, 119, 127, 130–31, 134, 156
serpent, 76, 77–80, 82
Seth, 84
Simonides, 144
sin, 60, 81–83, 86, 87, 89, 105, 106, 131, 135, 168n77, n91
Sirach, 48
sithre torah. *See* mystery
social science, 5, 38–45, 52, 55, 123, 128, 149
Socrates, 4, 6, 11, 13, 14, 15, 16, 21, 30, 35–36, 37, 98, 107, 112, 114, 115, 121, 127, 137–41; mission, 133, 141–45, 147, 155, 156–57, 158, 166n37
Sodom, 91–92, 135, 156
Sokolowski, Robert, 161n35
Solomon, 27, 48, 76
Sparta, 43
Spinoza, 7, 12, 27, 30, 37–38, 45–46, 49–50, 52–53, 55, 60, 62, 73, 100, 125, 150; *Theological–Political Treatise*, 37, 52
Steintrager, James, 150
Strauss, Leo: *Argument and the Action of Plato's* Laws, 160n, 171n; *City and Man*, 16, 22, 23, 112, 139, 156, 159n, 160n, 161n, 162n, 171n, 174n, 175n; "A Giving of Accounts," 124, 161n, 172n; "Jerusalem and Athens," 179–207; *Liberalism: Ancient and Modern*, 157, 159n, 161n, 162n, 163n, 165n, 166n, 170n, 171n, 172n, 173n, 176n; "Mutual Influence," 25, 50, 55, 56, 73, 99, 151, 162n, 164n, 165n, 167n, 169n, 170n, 172n, 175n; *Natural Right and History*, 6, 23, 26–27, 30, 43, 143, 154, 159n, 162n, 163n, 164n, 165n, 175n; "On Genesis," 26, 66, 69–70, 75–76, 149, 162n, 165n, 166n, 167n, 209–25; *Persecution and the Art of Writing*, 15, 17, 60–61, 138, 152–53, 160n, 161n, 162n, 163n, 165n, 167n, 174n, 175n; *Philosophy and Law*, 7; "Progress or Return," 17, 25, 30, 37, 43, 66, 74, 75, 84, 94–95, 106, 140, 142, 144, 148, 149, 160n, 161n, 162n, 163n, 165n, 167n, 168n, 169n, 170n, 174n, 175n; *Rebirth of Classical Political Rationalism*, 161n, 163n, 165n, 171n; *Socrates and Aristophanes*, 116, 117, 171n, 172n; *Spinoza's Critique of Religion*, 7, 12, 17, 26, 39, 53, 125, 132, 153, 161n, 162n, 163n, 164n, 172n, 173n, 174n; *Studies in Platonic Political Philosophy*, 125, 172n; *Thoughts on Machiavelli*, 9, 24, 52, 159n, 160n, 161n, 162n, 164n; *What is Political Philosophy?*, 4, 5, 22, 124, 156, 159n, 160n, 161n, 163n, 169, 172n, 175n, 176n

Straussians: East Coast, 9, 12, 13, 16, 44, 155, 160n24; West Coast, 9, 12
superstition, 4, 16, 52–53, 54, 60, 63, 85, 100, 150–51
synthesis, 24, 28, 127, 132, 145, 148, 149, 165n3

Talmud, 52
teleology, 43, 45
Temple, 21, 37, 84, 135, 136
Ten Commandments, 75, 156
Tetragrammaton, 71
Theogony, 30, 62, 100, 101–3
theological–political predicament, 18, 26
theology, 7, 12, 14–19, 24, 25, 37, 55, 56, 94, 112–13, 148, 165n3
Thracymachus, 115
Thucydides, 22
Thus Spake Zarathustra, 41
Torah, 32, 45–47, 48, 54, 56, 63, 65, 73, 78, 84, 85–86, 96, 99, 100, 111, 119, 122, 125, 126, 132, 151, 169n115
tradition, 25, 27, 49, 56, 62, 63, 65, 70, 74, 77, 78–79, 86, 93, 99–100, 115–16, 122, 124, 126, 133, 138, 143, 153
tree of knowledge, 74–77, 78–81, 84, 87, 93, 96, 122
tree of life, 74, 80, 96, 122, 123
truth, 8, 11, 13, 28, 40, 43–44, 45, 98, 107, 116, 126, 130–31, 139, 149, 156

Trygaios, 116–17

Udoff, Alan, 39, 148, 159n11, 165n11
Uriah, 143

Voegelin, Eric, 173n36

Wilhelmsen, Frederick, 7
will, 93–95, 103, 106, 113, 117, 118, 125, 142, 171n39; Zeus's 104–6
wisdom, 43, 45, 46, 76, 77, 84, 109, 137, 148, 157, 158; biblical, 22, 46–49, 60, (8:35–36) 102–3, 150–51, 170n15; divine, 11–12, 137–39, 150; Greek, 43, 46–49; human, 137–39; philosophic, 6–7, 11–12, 22, 108, 109, 115, 137–38, 140, 157
Wiser, James, 164n38
woman, 40, 44, 73, 75–77, 78–79, 103, 104, 167n
work, 74–75, 81, 104–6
Woodard, Joseph, 173n30
Works and Days, 100, 102, 103–6

Xenophon, 137, 143, 144, 160n15

Yahweh, 14, 154, 155

Zarathustra, 40, 41–42
Zeus, 14, 41, 86, 101, 102–7, 108, 113, 115, 116–17, 155
Zionism, 17

About the Author

Susan Orr received her B.A. in politics from the University of Dallas and her M.A. and Ph.D. from Claremont Graduate School, where she studied political philosophy and American government. She contributed a chapter on women and equality to *The American Experiment*, edited by Peter Augustine Lawler and Robert Martin Schaefer (Rowman & Littlefield). She currently works on child and family issues for the National Center on Child Abuse and Neglect, U.S. Department of Health and Human Services.

DATE DUE

ILL# 2635395 FTO 03/06/05		